Oasis of stillness

Oasis *of* stillness

The Life and Wisdom
of Aghoreshwar Bhagwan Ramji,
a Modern-Day Saint

BABA HARIHAR RAM

Sonoma Ashram Foundation

Fullness
overflowing

BOOKS FROM AGHOR PUBLICATIONS
Aghor Guru Samhita: Daily Prayers
Aghor Yoga: A Practical Guide to Ancient Wisdom
At The Ashram: Discovering a Meaningful Life
The Book of Aghor Wisdom (from Indica Books)
Oasis of Stillness: The Life and Wisdom of Aghoreshwar Bhagwan Ramji,
   a Modern-Day Saint
Pearls of Shiksha

Published by
Aghor Publications, an imprint of
Sonoma Ashram Foundation
P.O. Box 950
Sonoma, California 95476
sonomaashram.org

Library of Congress Cataloging-in-Publication Data is available.
ISBN 978-0-9670701-6-2
First edition, 1997
Second edition, 2013
Printed in the United States of America on recycled paper.

Book design: traversosantana.com

TATSAT

O' Aghoreshwar, the limitless,
I ask your forgiveness
for trying to express the inexpressible
by speaking about you.

I chose to limit you by my words
only to allow my brothers and sisters
to learn about you and
your boundless compassion
that permeates your surroundings.

I want only to encourage everyone
to receive the gift of grace
that I have received from you.

I feel it is my duty to share with others
the great gift of yourself,
recognizing that my efforts are like
trying to touch the sky.

Contents

The Teachings of Aghoreshwar Bhagwan Ramji

The *Satsangs* of Aghoreshwar Bhagwan Ramji

O' traveler gone astray,
don't get lost trying to find God.
Don't you know that you are
the temple of God
and that God resides within you?
If your heart is pure,
God is with you.

Introduction

Everyone had left Baba's room after midnight. Sitting on the floor, I was caressing the soles of his feet while leaning my head against the bed. He was resting quietly with his eyes closed. "Baba never sleeps," words of my brother when describing him to me six years back, echoed in my mind.

The happiness that I experienced while living in the company of Baba was beyond description. He was a shining example of living a meaningful life. His joy was contagious. His compassion was immense. His wisdom was pure, and the simplicity of his words would resolve many complicated issues with ease.

How lucky I felt to be so close to Baba as a personal assistant during his time in the United States. Here I was in a suburb of New Jersey, spending 24 hours a day serving an *Aghoreshwar*, an enlightened being of our time. Baba had transformed the lives of millions of people in India. His mere glance or touch was enough to bring Divine intervention into a person's life. In the eyes of his followers, he was Shiva incarnate.

Who would have thought that after I had left India behind for the land of opportunity and material success, I would be sitting at the feet of a holy Master?

Having more was a natural attraction for a boy like me growing up in a rural Indian village with few amenities and a simple lifestyle. That desire had brought me to California, where I had become steeped in the race of acquiring more and more. In a short time I had completed my education, started a thriving business and acquired all the outward trappings of success. However, the idea of happiness based on wealth and recognition, which I had held since childhood and which society—be it in the East or the West—constantly reinforced, was proving wrong. Although by usual standards I had achieved a dream life for an Indian or an American, I was empty and unhappy.

My thoughts flowed back to my childhood outside Varanasi in north India. Our house was always open to visiting holy men and women. Rarely a day passed without my parents hosting overnight guests. Not having electricity or TV, at night we would listen to stories narrated by our guests. These stories were always very colorful and inspirational, filled with life lessons. Even in the U.S. I retained my childhood curiosity about living saints and their mysterious way of being. I had always wondered what it must feel like to be in the energy field of an enlightened being all the time.

When I heard that Baba was coming to the U.S. for medical treatment, my mind was made up. I knew this was the time to fulfill my hunger for being in the company of a saint. That first visit of one week turned into frequent visits that ended up giving a whole new purpose to my life.

Baba was the head of the ancient mystical lineage of *Aghor Siddhas*, yet his teachings on how to live a meaningful life were practical for modern times. Although an enlightened being, Baba was so in tune with the struggles of ordinary people. What an inspiring combination of wisdom, mystery and simplicity!

In his quest for God, Baba left his family home at age seven. He spent several years as a wanderer, visiting many holy shrines and spiritual teachers and following various methods of spiritual practice. At age 14, he arrived at the *Aghor* ashram in Varanasi. From there, his real spiritual journey began as he embraced *Aghor* and in a short time reached enlightenment.

Seeing the Divine in everything and everyone, followers of *Aghor* transcend the proscriptions of a "normal" social structure that classify people as high and low, pure and impure, male and female. They try to cultivate a state of mind and social practice of total nondiscrimination. To achieve this, early *Aghor* asthetics stretched their boundaries of fear, disgust, judgment and discrimination by embracing the forbidden in cremation grounds and places of seclusion.

Baba established his first ashram in Varanasi by inviting all the lepers living in the street to be its residents. This was a clear shift in the practice of *Aghor* while still retaining its principles. Baba's welcoming the forsaken in the form of lepers, but doing so while living in the midst of society, set the foundation for a new direction. From then on, *Aghor* ascetics lived in the community to be of service to all, especially the downtrodden.

Baba emphasized that each individual is a Divine being, whole and complete. Anything you undertake to come closer to your Divinity, whether meditation or practice with a mantra given by a guru, is called *sadhana*. The overflow of that internal wholeness into the world is *seva*, true selfless service. Baba said living with awareness of these two bookends brings purpose and stability to life. Because the practice is so simple, without dogma, lengthy rituals or intellectual concepts, *Aghor* offers unlimited personal freedom so appropriate for the present day.

It was during that night in New Jersey in Baba's room that the thought entered my mind to write about those cherished days with him. My heart was overflowing with this new experience, and I wished to share it with others who were in the same boat I had been in.

Tracing the path of a sage is like marking the course of a bird on the wing. Usually sages do not tell much of their lives to others, revealing only hints, even then in veiled language. Because they leave no detailed map of their journey, we lovingly remember and carefully preserve any traces that come to light by some good fortune. We pass along their sayings, teachings and stories.

Countless people who came in contact with Baba had the experience of being with a true sage. Those who knew him saw a saint without the least touch of worldliness, a living incarnation of matchless purity, clarity and compassion. Each story about Baba reveals the extraordinary phenomena that kept happening around him from the time he was born until his last days. But for me, the biggest miracle was that everyone who came to visit him left with a sense that Baba loved him or her the most.

Many books written in Hindi contain Baba's teachings and stories collected from his early years, but none of these accounts describe the details of his last few years of life. I was fortunate to be one of only a handful of people with Baba during his time in the U.S. Why he chose to take his last breath in the U.S. remains a mystery.

This book is an intimate portrait of Aghoreshwar Bhagwan Ramji. Although unable to keep pace with him, everyone felt uplifted in his presence and had a foretaste of the bliss that makes worldly pleasures seem trifling. It is rare that a spiritual being of Baba's magnitude visits this earth, and when such an event occurs, all humanity takes heart as a new era of hope opens.

Baba took *samadhi* in 1992, but great beings do not disappear with the end of the body. They are still available on a subtle level, continuing to give compassionate help to those who turn to them.

Today, in ashrams that Baba and his disciples established in India and around the world, *Aghor* monks carry on his way of living. They keep Baba's vision alive through service, conjoining spiritual ideals with social action. Such work comes at a time when seekers both in the East and in the West are searching for a purposeful path. As he did in life, Baba shows us the way.

BABA HARIHAR RAM
Sonoma Ashram
Sonoma, California
November 28, 2012
Mahasamadhi Day

The Life of
Aghoreshwar Bhagwan Ramji

You will have to look for the self
in the woods of the mind.

Chapter I  Darshan

On the road to Varanasi from my village, you can see an ashram on the banks of the Ganges. Just before the bridge that spans the mighty river, the left side of the road runs parallel to the ashram boundary. Every time I passed that way, I would read the name painted in large letters on the wall.

As a teenager, the thought of visiting this ashram never entered my mind. The very name, Avadhut Bhagwan Ram Leprosy Seva Ashram, was enough to keep me going straight ahead to Varanasi. There were so many more attractive things for a young man to do in the city than visit a leprosy center. Much later, in 1980, I would finally meet the baba of this ashram, which was also called Sri Sarveshwari Samooh.

To attend high school, I moved to the city from my village. I had to walk a couple of miles each way and passed many other ashrams and temples on this route. One of them was very close to where I was living. From the outside the ashram looked dilapidated. Shrouded in mystery, it had the appearance of antiquity. This was Baba Kinaram Ashram, also called Krim Kund.

Out of curiosity while returning home one day, I walked inside the compound. Within the boundaries were a number of elaborate tombs. In the center, a verandah surrounded a small courtyard on three sides. A pond filled with clear water enhanced the serenity of the place. In the middle of the hustle and bustle of the city, it was an Oasis of Stillness. A half-naked baba reclined on the verandah near a *dhuni*. Little did I know that this sacred fire had been burning for three centuries and that I was in the presence of a great being who was the head of the lineage of *Aghor Siddhas*. His eyes were half closed. He was different from any other baba I had come across. I bowed to him.

Looking at me sternly, he said, "What are you doing here? Go to school!" This was Baba Rajeshwar Ram, the initiating guru of Avadhut Bhagwan Ram, who much later in my life would become my guru.

The Avadhut Bhagwan Ram Leprosy Seva Ashram that I had seen on the way to the city from my village was across the river from Krim Kund. Its name was enough to keep away not only me but many others. I thought to myself, there are enough lepers sitting all around the city asking for money or food. If you go to an ashram, you don't want to encounter lepers. My reasoning was that it was not a place I wanted to visit and it was too far from my house to make it easy. I didn't know that the leprosy hospital was only part of the ashram founded as Sri Sarveshwari Samooh.

Many years passed without my ever thinking of either ashram.

In 1976 at the age of 19, I left for the United States and did not return to India for four years. Life in Berkeley, California, was very different from that in Varanasi, not to mention in my village. When I did visit India, my brother was shocked to see the change in me and suggested I go with him to see his guru. I had lost all interest in such things, but nonetheless, I went. To my surprise, he took me to the same ashram I used to see alongside the road to Varanasi—the Avadhut Bhagwan Ram Leprosy Seva Ashram.

Hesitatingly, yet carrying my pride of having just returned from the U.S., I followed my brother inside the compound, expecting to see lepers crowding around. There was no sign of lepers. My brother told me that although the leprosy hospital was inside the compound, it was separate from the other ashram buildings. A feeling of stillness permeated the atmosphere.

I followed my brother to the inner courtyard where his guru was giving *darshan* to visitors. Some people were sitting in front of him silently; others were coming and going. My brother and I stood there for a time, and at an appropriate moment, he introduced me to his guru. Baba's half-opened eyes turned toward me, and automatically I bowed. He nodded and asked one of his attendants to bring us some sweetmeats and water. After a while, with a nod, he gestured for us to leave. For me it was a very uneventful meeting, but my brother was convinced it would bring a big change in my life.

The next year I visited India again. Remembering the stillness and peace that permeated the ashram on my last trip, I asked my brother if I could visit Baba. He was delighted. This time Baba seemed much more cheerful. He had me sit next to him and asked many questions about the U.S. and my business there. When we parted, he gave me a coconut and filled my hands with hibiscus flowers. With a very sweet smile, he sent us away.

My brother was in awe at this meeting. He said it was very rare for Baba to give a coconut and red flowers to anyone with his own hands. "He filled your palms; from now on you will never lack anything in your life."

On my return to the U.S., as my brother had predicted, I landed some very good contracts for my travel company, and profits were much more than projected for the year. Often during that time I would remember Baba's sweet smile. Whenever I thought of him I would feel much lighter, inspired within. I felt Baba's grace was with me, and nothing was difficult to obtain. I was filled with a sense of security.

❊ By repeating the mantra imparted by the guru, the lines of fate begin to disappear, formidable karmas dissolve.

I visited my family in Varanasi in 1982 and went to see Baba on my own. He recognized me from a distance and smiling said, "You came from a far place."

I said, "Yes, Baba."

He asked, "Is there anything I can do for you?"

I felt encouraged. "Baba, with your grace I have enough, but my mind is very restless."

With a mysterious smile, he said, "You are young; go earn more money and play."

I kept sitting there, imbibing his presence. After a period of silence, except for saying a few things to others, he turned to me and said, "All right, come back Thursday morning and meet me in the temple right after my *puja*. I will give you a mantra."

When my brother heard about this, he found it hard to contain his excitement. Immediately he went to the market and returned with a bronze tray, a mug, a glass, a set of handkerchiefs, a *lungi* and a *dhoti*. He said to me, "You will need these things to show your appreciation to the guru at your initiation."

I arrived Thursday morning with all these items, plus fresh cut flowers and several pounds of sweetmeats. I stood near the temple with my gifts in my arms waiting for Baba to finish his daily prayers. After half an hour, he opened his eyes and turned to me. Motioning with his hands, he called me inside the temple. I put down my gifts. He placed a straw mat in front of him and motioned me to sit on it. Very slowly and patiently he explained various things relating to the mantra and then whispered the mantra to me. He had me repeat it until he was sure I remembered it. Then he reached over and applied red sandalwood paste to the center of my forehead, pressing down as he did so. The mere touch of Baba emptied my mind, and I entered a state of bliss, lost awareness of my surroundings and even lost awareness of Baba's presence next to me. I sat in that state for some time. When I opened my eyes, Baba was gone, and my brother was already distributing the sweet-meats to the ashramites.

Receiving my mantra was like finding a new friend. The more I thought of my mantra and of Baba, the more peaceful and secure I felt. It was a discovery for me. For the first few days, no matter where I went or whom I met, the sound of the mantra kept echoing within me, and the image of Baba kept appearing in my forehead. When this happened, immense joy welled up within me. I needed nothing more to be in a state of happiness. I was whole, I was complete. It was like falling in love with my deep self with utmost trust. I was overjoyed with this new experience. My entire life took on new meaning. Many addictions I used to have withered away. Nothing seemed more joyful than being with my mantra, and to be with my mantra in solitude was icing on the cake.

I returned to California with this newfound joy and applied myself wholeheartedly to my business. There would be ups and downs, and at times my joy would seem to fade. There were even moments when the mantra and the image of my guru would not hold the same sweetness or intensity as in the beginning. But every year I returned to India and delighted in the presence of Baba. He would always send me back with the same words, "Go make more money and play." That's what I did, but often I wondered what it would be like to be in his presence all the time.

In September 1986, I received a message from India that Baba was not well. He was arriving on the East Coast in a few days for medical treatment. My mind was made up immediately; this was my chance to be near him. I arranged my business affairs so I could leave. I ended up spending a whole year with him. I escorted Baba to India after he had recuperated, only to have him send me back to California to take care of my business. Over the next five years, Baba kept returning to the U.S. for several months annually. Whenever he did, I found a way to be near him.

Although he is not present among us in body form now, Baba's spirit is more alive and vibrant than ever. Great beings of his magnitude become more accessible after leaving their bodies. They become available to many people at the same time in different places and situations wherever they are remembered.

Few individuals know the details of Baba's life because he spoke very little about his past. Being in Baba's presence was enough; no history was necessary. Besides, the facts of his life cannot reveal his essence, but stories about how he lived and interacted with people offer a glimpse into his state of being.

Eternal peace is had
    in the solitary cave of the heart,
living in seclusion.
    You can never find it by dwelling
on the pleasures of the senses.

Chapter 2 Early Days

BHAGWAN

Bhagwan was born in a village called Gundi in the state of Bihar in northeast India. Known for its natural beauty, Gundi is near the confluence of the Ganges and Sone Rivers. Lush groves of fruit trees and thick flowering vegetation cover the land. Gundi is larger than a typical Indian village because it is very old, and all different castes have been living there for generations. For the same reason, there are many temples. Over the centuries, this village has produced many great beings.

On September 12, 1937, the baby born to the Baij Nath Singh family was named Bhagwan, meaning God. The father and mother had prayed for a child for years without results. They had given up hope. Now the proud father said, "God has blessed us, so we will call the child Bhagwan."

▣ Home in Gundi where Bhagwan was born ▣

Bhagwan Singh was descended from a line of wealthy landowners. His great-grandfather was Sri Hridaya Prasad Singh, well known for his generosity. His doors were always open to wandering holy men. Then came Sri Baij Nath Singh, the baby's father, who not only maintained the family tradition but also earned recognition in other areas. He had traveled widely to neighboring countries and started trading goods with Burma, becoming very successful in business. He loved sports and was a profi-

※ May my detractors be blessed.
Through their grace
I attain knowledge.

cient wrestler. At the same time, he loved music and was a fine singer. He sponsored both wrestling and musical events for the entertainment of the villagers.

Lakharaji Devi, his wife, had come to live with her husband's family when she was just a child, as was the custom in India. She and her husband had similar backgrounds. Being very devout, she spent several hours each day in prayer and meditation.

Besides the devoted parents and grandparents, there were aunts, uncles and cousins living in the household. But it was Bhagwan's grandmother who was most important in molding the mind of the child.

Bhagwan was only five years old when his father died. When he entered grade school, Bhagwan found he had no liking for study, preferring to spend his time on either sports or devotional activities. He liked the sports his father had been so fond of, but gradually his devotional activities became his primary interest. In the morning and again in the evening, he went to the local temple, where all the children his age would gather around him to chant and hear the legends his grandmother had told him of India's heroes.

By the time he was seven years old, Bhagwan was feeling a compulsion to find a place to be quiet, away from his family. The first time he left home, he went to ancestral land nearby and lived alone in the Shiva temple on the property. He would spend most of his time in a cavelike room near the temple. His grandmother soon sent for him, and he was obliged to stay at home for a while.

But he was restless at once. He again moved out, despite his grandmother's fear for his safety. This time he built a hut near the junior high school, where his friends and playmates would join him before and after classes. Most evenings his place was a major attraction for sports, singing and storytelling. The children called him Bhagwan Das, servant of God. He was happy there, but once again his grandmother convinced him to return home.

After another try at hiding in the temple, he chose a place people shunned even in the light of day, a gloomy part of the forest believed to be haunted. Even at noon it was dark, with thickets of giant trees and overgrown bushes cutting out sunlight. Bhagwan loved it there because people rarely interrupted his solitude. When his grandmother prevailed on him at least to go to a more habitable place if he wouldn't return home, he couldn't resist her pleas. He built a hut under a pipal tree in a grove of guavas belonging to his grandfather.

By this time, the women of the village had begun calling him Bhagwan Das, a sign of respect for a renunciate. They had noticed unusual happenings in his vicinity. Someone's cow was having difficulty giving birth. When Bhagwan Das touched the cow, pronouncing God's name, the cow calved without much pain. When the family maid asked for his blessings to have a favorable hearing in court, he said, "Truth will be victorious," and the maid had a positive outcome. Such stories pervaded the village.

Bhagwan had a mentor named Paramahansji, who encouraged him in his spiritual endeavors. The child had confided to Paramahansji that he had a vision of a magnificent shaft of light that appeared to come from the direction of the stable, crossing his body as he lay in bed, then descending to the street. His mentor was not surprised. He had noticed that Bhagwan had grown sensitive to certain sounds like ringing bells, the wind and rattling pots and pans. Paramahansji told him that all these experiences were indications of spiritual growth. He understood the boy's search for a simple quiet life but was unable to help because a serious problem arose in Bhagwan's family.

Bhagwan's extended family had been hostile to him in small ways from the beginning, but now these relatives grew openly greedy for the family fortune Bhagwan was supposed to inherit. The grandparents were growing old and were unable to defend him. The mother, still in her widow's veil, was no threat to anyone. The aunts, uncles and cousins made life unbearable for young Bhagwan. They found ways to embezzle money from the family fortune. At last they saw his interest in the religious life as a way to get rid of him altogether. They reasoned that if they could not starve him, at least his pursuit of the path of renunciation would take him away from the village. When Bhagwan became an adult, he would remember that he had seen with his own eyes the essence of human love as conditional, self-centered, greedy and egotistical.

The relatives had become so unkind to him that by the time Bhagwan was nine years old, he knew he had to leave home again, this time forever.

THE YOUNG RENUNCIATE

Hardships awaited Bhagwan. It was winter. He had left the house without any belongings or idea where he was going. Although he had been at the mercy of his relatives, he always felt protected by a maternal presence he did not fully understand. His mentor Paramahansji had tried to explain to him the various manifestations of spiritual life, but Bhagwan felt that he simply had been blessed from the beginning by the caress of the Divine Mother. This became all important to him. His love for the Divine Mother and faith in her unconditional love sustained him.

Bhagwan walked toward the city of Aara, begging for alms when hungry, like other *sadhus*. He approached a temple to seek food and shelter. The priest looked him over carefully and said, "The temple is closed at this late hour." Disconsolate, Bhagwan turned away. With a sudden change of heart, the priest took pity on the child and offered him a place to sleep on the floor in the back of the temple and a piece of burlap as a cover.

Many more days of wandering brought Bhagwan to Bodh Gaya, where Buddha had attained enlightenment. He spent several days visiting its holy places until the urge to keep going took him on the road to Puri.

In Puri he decided to get his head shaved as a monk. He took a refreshing bath and went to the famous temple of Jagganath. He sat in the inner temple and lost himself in contemplation. A priest appeared. Scowling at the boy, he scolded, "You have not made an offering, have you? I thought not!" Bhagwan didn't answer, but promptly gave him all the coins he had saved for his next simple meal. He was learning that all priests were not the same.

☀ What you think today, you will reap tomorrow.

In those days, Bhagwan adopted the austere lifestyle and practices of a Jain monk, reaching a stage where he experienced deep compassion for every creature. He felt uncomfortable walking in the night for fear of crushing ants or other insects under his feet. He ate only once a day, before dark.

After Bhagwan spent time in Puri, performing *puja* in all the temples, his restless spirit drew him to other unknown destinations. Several years passed in this way.

In July 1951, he took a train to Varanasi, the City of Shiva. He was now 14 years old, and his arrival was to mark a turning point in his life. Varanasi, which used to be called Kashi and then Benares, was considered the Eternal City of the East, an ancient cultural and religious capital for all Asia. Many great beings from different traditions, including Hindu, Jain and Buddhist, came from Varanasi.

Leaving the railway station, Bhagwan asked for directions to the city's famous Shiva temple. He set out on foot to find it. It was soon very dark. Rain fell in torrents. Stray dogs roamed the empty streets, barking and howling. Bhagwan became so tired he sat down to rest on a cart. The next thing he knew, dawn was breaking.

He awakened to the sound of bells and heard bathers calling to each other as they walked toward the river. He didn't know where he was, so he started to walk toward the river, too. At one point he stopped and looked around, trying to figure out if he was walking in the right direction. He was bewildered.

As he stood there, an elderly woman looking very beautiful in a white silk sari with red borders stopped in front of him and graciously said, "Tell me, where are you going, son?"

Her demeanor was so sweet and her voice so warm that he was encouraged to answer. He said, "I am looking for the way to the temple of Lord Shiva, Mataji."

The lady asked, "Have you bathed yet this morning?" When he said that he had not, she pointed to the river and said, "You should bathe in the holy Ganges."

Obeying her instructions, Bhagwan immersed himself in the river's blue-green water. Moved by some unknown inspiration, he took off his *lungi* and watched it float off in the river. This was the traditional gesture of a monk taking vows of *sannyasa*, renunciation. As he came back into the street, he was dressed only in his loincloth.

❀ While traveling on an auspicious path, don't stop; it makes the path lengthy. Keep walking.

The elderly woman was standing in the same spot with a tray of flowers and offerings. She smiled and beckoned him to follow her. With ardor and reverence, she showed him how to worship Shiva. Bhagwan was overwhelmed with joy, offering flowers and incense. After worshipping there, he followed the woman to another temple. Thinking it was her house, he did not enter, but stood outside. After some time when she didn't appear, he decided to go on without her. He learned later that the building was Annapurna Mandir, the primary temple of Shakti in Varanasi.

Returning on the same street he had come, Bhagwan was startled to find the mysterious woman again, standing in the same spot where he had met her. Seeing his surprise, she asked in a very loving voice, "Where are you from? Why did you come to this city?"

He told her a little of his story. It was then that she sent him to Baba Kinaram Ashram, one of the many ashrams in Varanasi.

She pointed out the direction to him carefully, saying, "It is not far."

When he looked back to ask her more questions, she had disappeared. Bhagwan knew intuitively that it would be favorable to follow her guidance. Perhaps it was Annapurna herself! He marveled at the luminous milestones the Great Mother had placed on his path to guide him.

INITIATION

When Bhagwan entered Baba Kinaram Ashram—also called Krim Kund—the Mahant Baba Rajeshwar Ram was in his room, so the young *sadhu*, clad in his loincloth, was told to wait in a corner of the verandah.

Baba Rajeshwar Ram took an unusually long time to emerge. When he did, he exchanged a few words with the child, with the only result being that Bhagwan was allowed to stay in his corner.

The following day, a devotee of the Mahant arrived with a gift for the ashram of some fish and rice, a dish customarily offered on special occasions. Baba Rajeshwar Ram's attendant gave Bhagwan some of the food. Having come from a Vaishnava background where only vegetarian food is eaten, Bhagwan did not want to consume it. Even though he was hungry, he ate just a little rice and, when no one was looking, dumped the rest of the meal into the nearby pond. At the moment the food fell into the water, he knew instinctively that if he were to stay in this ashram and progress on the path of *Aghor*, he would have to give up discriminating between what is considered pure and impure.

Although he soon felt no preference for one food or another, Bhagwan expected more tests, and there were. In addition to cleaning the grounds of the ashram, he was given the job of bringing leftover wood from the cremation grounds to the sacred fire at the ashram. Baba Kinaram had started this fire centuries ago when he established the ashram, and it had been kept burning ever since. Carrying heavy loads of scavenged half-charred wood was an arduous job. Bhagwan was

▣ Baba Rajeshwar Ram, Bhagwan's initiating guru ▣

not used to rigorous manual labor and was so exhausted and confused that he thought several times of leaving the ashram. If only he could see his old mentor Paramahansji!

One day Bhagwan had an opportunity to slip away. He walked to the village of his birth to seek guidance from Paramahansji. The advice his mentor gave him was to walk on the *Aghor* path with patience and confidence. Renewed in purpose, Bhagwan returned to the ashram.

Baba Rajeshwar Ram, having tested the boy in many ways, decided to initiate him as a monk. Bhagwan's head was shaved and a few hairs offered to the sacred fire. Baba then gave him a mantra. It was the beginning of Bhagwan's journey on the path of *Aghor* in the lineage of Baba Kinaram. To signify this, Bhagwan Singh became Bhagwan Ram.

With new enthusiasm, Bhagwan Ram applied himself fully to his practices. He began to repeat his mantra with total devotion. He would get up very early and go to the river, where he would submerge his whole body, with only his face sticking out, and repeat his mantra for hours.

One day after working very hard, he was lying near the sacred fire, half asleep. Suddenly he saw beside him a Divine being wearing wooden sandals. The being placed a foot on Bhagwan Ram's chest and murmured something in a clear voice. Bhagwan Ram repeated it. It resounded in his whole being as a mantra. When he awoke, he remembered everything.

A few days later, another event occurred that reinforced his faith in this new mantra. He was sweeping the verandah near Baba Kinaram's *samadhi* shrine when he heard the same words, louder this time. He took these events to be his new initiation and would repeat this mantra throughout his life.

At certain times, ashrams and monasteries provide what is needed for spiritual growth, and Bhagwan Ram continued his *sadhana* at Krim Kund with devotion. But sometimes it is necessary for a seeker to reenter the world, and sometimes the guru himself has to push the disciple to leave for his own good. The disciple may not know what is happening at the time, but eventually he understands.

And so it happened that one day when Baba Rajeshwar Ram went into the city, he left a bunch of keys with Bhagwan Ram. Finding the keys of the whole ashram in his hands, the new monk felt a momentary sense of awe and gratification. Not knowing what had overtaken him, he flung the keys into a deep well nearby. Someone in the ashram was watching and promptly ran after Baba Rajeshwar Ram to report the incident.

Baba returned to the ashram and asked for the keys. Seeing the look in his guru's eyes, Bhagwan Ram crouched in a corner, waiting for the beating that was sure to come.

As his guru moved toward him, Bhagwan Ram pointed

God's eyes, the sky
and the directions
are the eternal witness.
You cannot hide
your good or wicked actions.

with a trembling finger to the well. Threatening to beat him, the guru moved closer. When Baba Rajeshwar Ram raised his hand, the boy exclaimed, "The locks are open!"

The guru paused. He lowered his arm and asked an ashramite standing nearby to open the door. He could not budge it. Baba became really angry and reached to take hold of Bhagwan Ram. The boy pleaded with him to check the locks for himself. His guru went to the door. He put his hand on the lock. It opened! Not believing his eyes, he went to the other doors. All the locks, one after the other, opened. Amazed, he returned to question his neophyte monk, but he was nowhere to be seen. Bhagwan Ram had left the ashram.

Dissolve the mantra
into your mouth
and experience the bliss of it.
Life becomes fulfilled,
the self appears.

Chapter 3   The Search

THE WANDERER

Bhagwan Ram wandered around Varanasi for a while with no fixed place to sleep or eat. The loincloth he wore and his begging bowl were all he had. In the daytime he begged for alms and sat in contemplation, repeating his mantra, in one of the many temples in the city. He could be found on the banks of either the Ganges or Varuna river, or lying in a corner of a temple in a trancelike state.

A holy man named Chedi Baba took a liking to the young monk. He took care of the boy's necessities and introduced him to other holy men. The young renunciate cherished this period of his life when he did not have to bother about food and other practicalities and could apply himself more intensely to his meditations.

In early 1954, Bhagwan Ram heard that the Kumbha Mela was about to take place in Allahabad. This famous festival is a gathering of *sadhus* from all over India. They come by the thousands, even millions, and camp out for a month where the sacred rivers Ganges and Yamuna meet. Bhagwan Ram decided to go.

He set out on foot to cover the 150 miles between Varanasi and Allahabad. He walked all day and spent nights under trees or in temples where he could be protected from the winter cold. During this journey, he went many days without food. All he had with him was his bowl and a length of fine cotton sheeting he found discarded near the river.

Bhagwan Ram found Allahabad to be an old city with strange faces and stranger ways. The din of the crowds and the swirl of life around him at the Kumbha Mela were a novel and disconcerting experience. In the day he would wander around witnessing exhibitions by various religious orders. Ascetics practiced their austerities and defied anyone to come near. In the night he would join other *sadhus* sitting by their fires. If they offered him food, he accepted; otherwise he lived on water from the Ganges.

One day, in the midst of the extravagant scene of the Kumbha Mela, an elderly woman appeared at his side. In a kind voice, she invited him to go with her. He thought of the woman who had helped him in Varanasi, so he followed this woman without hesitation. She showed him a small hut and motioned for him to go in. After so many experiences with the Divine Mother, he felt no fear. Inside the hut, she fed him, gave him a new piece of cloth to wear and blessed him. For the next few years, every morning when he woke up, he would find a 10 rupee bill tucked under his pillow.

"Ten rupees," he would say later, "was a substantial amount in those days. Part of it went for my meals, the rest for refreshments for those who came to visit me. Ever since that time, I've never lacked food or the essentials to keep the body and spirit together."

To this day, Baba's ashrams on the 14th day of the dark side of the moon during the month of Magha, between January and February, commemorate that auspicious intervention of the Divine Mother, which blessed Bhagwan Ram forever with the necessities of existence.

After a month in Allahabad, Bhagwan Ram returned to Varanasi. He went to Baba Kinaram Ashram to pay respect to his guru, Baba Rajeshwar Ram. He didn't know what penance would be waiting for him, but he went regardless.

Despite Bhagwan Ram's attempt to resume his practices at the ashram, only a few weeks passed until his guru found another destiny for him. He was expelled on a trumped-up charge of stealing food. He suffered deeply and headed away from the ashram, Varanasi and everything he knew, toward the deep forests. He wanted to be far from humans, who seemed so skillful at inflicting pain.

THE SOLITARY WAY

In the deep forests, Bhagwan Ram thought that trees promised to be much kinder than people; ferocious animals, more companionable. In other parts of the world, wars were being fought, rockets were about to carry men to the moon, and soon the information revolution would diminish the size of the world, but Bhagwan Ram was not aware of any of this. His direction was inward. Sometimes a cheetah or other animal leapt suddenly out of nowhere. He was alarmed, but he was never attacked.

Walking along the banks of the Ganges, through lush woods and vegetation, he came to a formidable cremation ground in the heart of the wilderness. The stillness was unbroken, the seclusion complete. Here and there, funeral pyres were burning. Wild animals, dogs and jackals roamed the fearful place, keeping a watch on their favorite haunts, finishing off any partially cremated bodies. It was an awe-inspiring, forbidding place for most people, yet Bhagwan Ram saw it as merely the final resting place of the physical body.

Cremation grounds are not for the faint of heart. The tradition of many yogic systems in India included dwelling in a place like this to come face-to-face with one's fear of death, as well as many other taboos.

Bhagwan Ram sat with a bamboo stick in his hands, writing his mantra on the ashes of the dead. He erased it with the same stick, then wrote it again. Days passed. At night the dark was so intense that he had to put his hand close to his eyes to see it. The silence was so complete, he could hear his own breathing with great clarity. When the loneliness inside gushed forth to merge with the loneliness outside, the desperate monk would cry, "Where are you, Mother of mine?"

He summoned her repeatedly in this way. His absorption in deep thought of the Mother led him to wander like a derelict, forgetting food, sleep or even life itself. He would tell an intimate group of disciples one day:

> I used to dwell in the hillocks of Vindhyachal and on the banks of the Ganga between Mahraura and Kanwar. I lived without clothing.
> I usually ate only once a day. Sometimes I got by with one small serving of food, once a week. I was a vegetarian, also a non-vegetarian. I used to eat leftover grains on the farms, dry straw and wild berries. I wrapped myself with burlap. I also used material left in the cemeteries. I wore robes of the dead or clothes others threw away. I put on a deerskin and the bark of a banana tree.
> I treasured my seclusion while I wandered in the wilderness. When I saw a cowherd or a grass cutter or anyone at all, I would withdraw and go still deeper into the jungle. I did not want to be seen. Just as a fawn plunges farther into the woods when he sees a man, I, too, would retreat.

I had grown extremely compassionate toward all creatures. I had
feelings even for drops of water. I was constantly aware of not hurting the
space by sudden moves or crushing any unseen creatures under my feet.
Layers of dead skin covered my body, but I would not rub them off for
fear of hurting them.

In the snowy nights of winter, I wandered on the open ground.
During the day, I walked in the jungle. In summer, I roamed outside the
forest by day and inside the forest by night.

A seeker filled with the Divine is never lonely for other people, even in solitude. His pains become his companions, and conversing with these newly found friends, the seeker spends his time in peace. The external states begin to appear as fearsome and deadly snakes, so the seeker turns to the inner state, experiencing immense joy just being with himself in the darkness of night. This was Bhagwan Ram's intense *sadhana*, day after hungry day, week after cold week, month after silent month.

When he moved on, a cave by the banks of the Ganges became his new residence. In the middle of the day, he went to a nearby village for alms and returned to the cave. At other times he wandered in the cremation grounds, applying ashes all over his body. Wearing nothing but a small loincloth and a garland of flowers around his neck, he would carry his bowl in one hand and bamboo stick in the other.

Once on his daily rounds, some children took him for a madman and started hurling rocks at him. Some villagers even insulted him. Nonetheless, the women, who are the protectors of Indian civilization, always filled his bowl. How could a mother watch her son starve? Walking back to his cave with his bowl full of alms, Bhagwan was followed by stray dogs. He ate some of his food and offered the rest to the dogs. This play went on for months. While living in that cave, sometimes intense sadness would overpower him, and he would cry for hours. There was no one around to offer his aching heart solace. His yearning to meet the Divine Mother grew stronger and stronger.

Although going through all kinds of hardships, I never became hopeless.
I had complete faith in that "great unknown," the Divine Mother. I was
sure that someday the inner sight would illuminate me, the *Vaikhari*
would flourish, enriching my voice with confidence and inspiring the
truth to emerge.

One evening, sitting under a tree near the cremation grounds, he saw an old woman. She offered him roasted chickpeas in a small packet. She sat down with folded hands and told him her story. Her only son was very ill. Every treatment thus far had been unsuccessful. She was disconsolate.

Bhagwan Ram was moved by her sorrow, but he did not have a ready answer. He gave her a handful of ashes and said, "Mother, take this and apply it all over the body of your son. Go now."

Several days later, he saw the woman coming toward him. He thought, "Maybe she is coming to complain that her son was not healed." Instead, she flung herself at his feet. Her son was cured.

Soon the monk's beneficial presence in the area began to be known, and the villagers built him a hut outside of town. He agreed to spend some time there, but would not allow anyone to remain after 9 p.m. He lived off offerings people brought. More and more people sought his help, all with various worldly aspirations and sufferings. Sometimes they would promise him a permanent hut, new clothes or other material things, but Bhagwan Ram was not interested.

> Many rich and distinguished people began to arrive. I started to feel a sense of pride for my popularity. Then I became very fearful of this new-found pride. One night when no one could see me, I left. I found a place known as Dighwara Ghat on the banks of the Ganges, south of the town of Sonepur and I stayed there three nights. Experiencing a new sense of freedom, my heart filled with peace and calmness. I felt inspired to keep moving, to go to a more secluded place.

Bhagwan Ram crossed the river with the help of a boatman and wandered into a thicket of tall pampas grass. For miles he saw nothing but overgrown reeds with edges as sharp as blades. The nearest village was five miles away. Tying the tips of the grass together, he constructed a teepee as shelter. In the middle of the day he would walk to the village for his alms and then return to the seclusion of his teepee. A variety of wild animals also lived there. Poor people in the area earned a living by cutting the reeds and selling them.

> In this way I lived for a month or so. I was filled with happiness and contentment. I had many indescribable experiences. Thoughts of God would carry away my being, and my body would vibrate with joy.

Overwhelmed with contentment, one day I found myself walking toward
the village of Neelkantha Tola. On the outskirts of the village, by the Sone
River, I saw a grand pipal tree. I stayed under that tree for a while.
A local gentleman noticed me and asked me to stay at his place.
He said it was not safe under the tree because the river was rising and
the strong current was washing away the banks. He let me stay in the
stable where he kept his elephants. After three days, I moved on to
other unknown destinations.

ENLIGHTENMENT

In the cremation grounds of Mahraura, Bhagwan Ram continued his austerities, making his rounds for alms in the nearby village. Gradually he grew more
accustomed to living close to others, no longer disturbed by their presence.

Like many *sadhus* before him, he witnessed in the cremation grounds the
physical end of the rich, the poor, the hungry and the well-fed. He contemplated the truth that cemeteries are filled with people who thought the world
couldn't get along without them. No one escaped!

With the constant sight of dead bodies and burning pyres and the silence
of the forest broken only by the steady sound of the flowing Ganges, Bhagwan Ram experienced a deepening of his consciousness as he turned more
and more within.

Once I remained self-absorbed continuously for three days and nights.
I experienced myself as imperishable and *Urdhvareta*, as energy moved
upward and settled in. On the bank of the river in Mahraura cremation
grounds, I spontaneously became concentrated, self-absorbed. All my
sense organs found stillness in themselves. A circle emerged before my
eyes. Inside the circle, green, red, yellow, white, black, violet, blue and
saffron became visible. From eight different kinds of circles I also
witnessed the emergence of the deepest soul. My speech, all my limbs
and my inner sight received something magical from deep within.
A thought would arise within me about something, and before I
could speak, it was made available to me. A thought would come to me
to see a particular thing and before it was completed, it became visible
to me. A random thought might suggest that a certain thing would pop
up from under the ground, and as soon as I lifted my hand from the dirt,
it would spring forth. When I wished at times that no one should see
me while I was among the crowd, I'd become invisible. If a philanthropic
thought came to me, I'd say a few things to someone and it would
bring great benefits to that person. If I had the thought to heal another,

I would give whatever plant or shrub leaves I could lay my hands on and it would heal the disease. All this was the effect of the circle that had emerged before my eyes.

The *Yoga-Siddhi* was his now. Most of Baba's experiences were indescribable and cannot be set down here, but all the longings of the heart of the wandering *sadhu* were completely satisfied. His cries to the Divine Mother were answered, and she manifested herself to him in all her fullness. There would be much to contemplate and understand later, but the most stubborn door had opened. Now the blessings of discovering his own self dwelled within him in the form of great peace, light and bliss.

※ The bliss you procure
with the power of living
in seclusion in celibacy
is much greater than
the joy of possessing
all the gems in the world.

Water cleanses grime,
   light destroys darkness,
      and the *darshan* of a sage
purifies the heart.

Chapter 4　A New Life

MANIHARA

Folks from the towns of Mahraura, Kanwar and Manihara began to offer respect and honor to the *sadhu* in their midst, addressing him as Baba. They brought him whatever he needed. When people heard about his "miracles," they started coming from far and wide, telling Baba their problems. He saw the Divine Mother in each person he met, and a new concern for his or her well-being arose in him. At the villagers' insistence, he moved to the outskirts of Manihara, where they built him a hut near a pond. They wanted to keep this holy man in their presence for as long as possible.

Soon there was talk about performing a Vishnu *yagya*, a week-long fire ceremony and ritualistic celebration. People from the surrounding area contributed freely to make it happen. Thousands of visitors came every day. Devotional chants filled the air, with elaborate *pujas*, feasts and spiritual discourses by scholars taking place in the open air, while the sacrificial fire gave off plumes of smoke as *ghee* was offered to its flames.

As Baba's location became more and more popular, and people came for blessings for their material being, Baba saw it as a trap. Making a characteristic exit, he went to the village of Hariharpur, a few miles away. A shady tree outside the village became his new home. Since it was said to be a haunted spot, no one went near it, and Baba was able to continue his *sadhana* undisturbed. Some villagers still remember how he appeared to them at the time, "He would be in such a state that he would lie in the hot summer sun in the middle of the day, totally forgetful of food and water."

Soon a few people built a hut for him under that tree, overcoming their aversion to the location's reputation for ghosts. Slowly the crowds found Baba again.

HARIHARPUR

Kedar Singh, who spent many years in the company of Baba, wrote entries in his journals that spoke eloquently of his experiences with the "young *Aghor*" at that time.

> *Early in November 1953, I was visiting my friend in Sakaldiha. At my* friend's house some people had gathered and were talking about this young *Aghor* of Hariharpur who had a strange combination of sweetness and toughness in his nature. He had been seen at times running in a circle and at other times just sitting still. He accepted whatever was offered, but without speaking much. When he did speak, his speech seemed very clear and trustworthy. No one was able to get a whole picture of him.

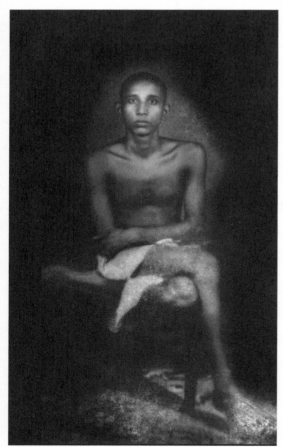

> A desire to visit this young *Aghor* grew more intense in me, even though *Aghor* ascetics previously had not been of any interest to me because of their strange appearance and unorthodox ways of relating to people.

> I arrived in Hariharpur, and as I drew near the hut, I saw no one. I peeked in and saw the young monk sitting very still. Without disturbing him, I sat on the mat outside. A combination of weariness, stillness of the atmosphere and warmth of the sun put me to sleep. After an hour or so, the murmur of people who had begun to gather woke me. I heard a

◘ Baba during his days at Hariharpur ◘

very sweet voice calling from inside the hut, "He is Thakur of Ish-wargangi." With this introduction, hastily I sat up.

Again the sound came from inside the hut, "Hello! How is Chedi Baba of Ishwargangi?"

I could not believe he knew about me or my caste. I thought per-haps he has seen me when he was visiting Chedi Baba. As we talked together about Chedi Baba, I was not convinced of his Divine insight, but for mere formality I bowed at his feet. As I bowed, his large eyes met mine, and I felt intoxicated, completely drunk. After a while, I asked for his leave.

He asked, "Won't you stay?"

"No, Baba, I have to leave."

"You will come back again, won't you?" was his sweet reminder.

His last words echoed inside me the whole journey home.

For the next three days I kept thinking about the simplicity and sweetness of this young *Aghor*. I decided to see him again and got on my bicycle for the journey, about 10 miles from my home. I arrived at his hut in the morning. Seven or eight people were sitting around him. I bowed and touched his feet out of respect. His large reddened eyes opened, and in a very sweet voice he asked, "Hello, Kedar! You came back?"

"Yes, Baba, I left early this morning."

"Have you washed?"

"Yes, Baba, I got that out of the way early in the morning."

"You will stay here today, won't you?"

"Yes, Baba, I think so." I answered, hardly knowing what I was saying.

After a while, I got up and left for my friend's house. That evening, I again appeared near Baba's hut. A group had gathered around him, but after a while only the two of us were left. We sat without saying anything for hours. The silence of the night thick-ened. Sounds of nature became more audible. Finally around midnight Baba asked me, "When are you going home?"

"When you wake up in the morning," was my answer.

"I do not sleep," he murmured.

His last words were like a lullaby to me, and very quietly I retired to my cot. When I woke up early in the morning, I found him still sitting by the fire. I offered my respect by touching his feet and prepared to leave. "When will you come back?" he asked.

"Soon, Baba. As soon as I find time, I will come."

"Come back soon." With these words his eyes smiled at me.

I left for home immediately. The long bike ride on dusty and

uneven roads seemed like smooth sailing as Baba's parting words echoed within me. This was the beginning of my addiction to his company.

After my return from Hariharpur, I got busy running my family business, the flour mill. On the third or fourth day, when I was repairing the mill, I heard a knock at the door. My mother opened the door

◘ Underground meditation cave in Hariharpur Ashram ◘

to find a young monk with a shaved head, wrapped in a worn cotton sheet, wearing wooden sandals. He was holding his bowl under his armpit. He asked my mother, "Is Kedar home?"

Nodding her head, she turned to call me. When Baba's eyes fell on me, he entered the house. Totally surprised, I collected myself and touched his feet. I introduced him to my mother, "Ma, this is the Baba of Hariharpur." Out of reverence my mother bent to touch his feet.

The young monk looked at my mother and said, "Please let me borrow Kedar from you."

I saw the hesitation in my mother's eyes, but she said, "Baba, this is my only son, the sole support for my old age, but whatever you wish."

Looking at her compassionately, he said, "Mother, do not worry. Kedar will always be under my protection and there will be no slack in his service to you." His reassurance consoled her.

That night he stayed at my house. Around four in the morning, I heard him calling me. As I got dressed, I heard his wooden sandals tapping on the pavement outside. I followed him to the river.

He bathed in the river, and I began to rinse the loincloth he had left on the bank. For drying the loincloth, I lit a fire by gathering dried leaves and twigs.

Baba was standing only a couple of yards from me without any clothes. All of a sudden he raised his right hand in the air. I could not believe what my eyes were seeing. A beautiful garland of marigolds appeared in his hands. He tossed the garland at me, and it landed around my neck. Spellbound, I kept looking at the garland. It was as fresh as it could be, filled with the fragrance of newly cut flowers.

For some moments I was lost in my thoughts, but when I collected myself I found Baba swinging by the aerial roots of a banyan tree. At that moment he appeared to be more a playful young boy than an accomplished *sadhu*. I went to him and said, "Please do not swing on those roots. They might break and you might get hurt."

With a smile, he stopped swinging. He returned to my home with me and had breakfast. Now he was ready to go to Hariharpur and asked me to come with him.

My bicycle became the vehicle for our journey. Baba sat on the carrier on the back. After a couple of miles, it became very difficult for me to pedal. The bicycle seemed heavy. I could not figure it out. The more I pushed on the pedals, the heavier it felt. I got off the bike and began to examine the wheels. Everything was in order. All of a sudden a thought came to my mind that it might be a trick of this young Baba." I said, "Look, Baba, this is not fair."

With a smile he said, "You think I am just a kid? You can't even pedal the bike. You haven't tried your strength. Why are you so irritated?"

I bowed to him, grabbed his feet and said, "Until now I considered you just a young lad, but now I recognize you."

After this little play, my bike began to run smoothly. We went a few more miles when a tire was punctured and went flat. Fortunately, I was able to busy myself getting the tire repaired at a nearby shop. In the meantime, Baba disappeared. Taking shortcuts through the fields, he walked to his hut a few miles away. By the time I arrived there, visitors from the village already had surrounded him. Totally irritated, I was about to shower a few words on him. Here I was a 41-year-old man and he merely a 16-year-old youth!

> ❀ The real work of
> a person of knowledge is
> to lead the world to a new light.

But Baba had something else planned. He had asked for a very comfortable cotton futon from the village. Placing it on a cot as I appeared, he smiled mischievously and asked me to sit on it. I was still upset with him for leaving me. He ordered me sternly, "Don't be upset, sit on it. I had it brought for you." The rest of the gathering was witnessing this play with amazement. He addressed them, "He is my guest, although he has a bad temper."

I could not take much more of this. With the excuse of visiting my friend in the nearby village I left and came straight home.

I arrived really tired and had a good night's sleep in my own bed. I got up early, but Baba's bittersweet memory remained with me. Although I wanted to return to him, my household duties needed attention. After taking care of them, I went for a long walk, then took a shower. All of a sudden a thought entered my mind. I lit an incense stick and began to wave it in a circular motion, thinking of Baba. This little act brought much peace to my restless mind.

In the afternoon the flour mill was running for customers who would bring their grains to be milled. I was weighing grain and returning it to them milled, in equal weight, in exchange for a small fee.

A few hours passed. Suddenly I heard a familiar voice saying, "You are looking at the grain, look at the scale!" My sight fell on Baba. I ran to welcome him and touch his feet.

"Why did you call me?" His voice was stern.

I stood speechless.

He explained to me, "Making circles with incense is very valuable. It is not good to call for no reason."

My eyes filled with tears, and I began to ask his forgiveness. But my prayer had been heard. My deity had come to my doorstep, heeding my call. Although my faith had been firmly established, my foolishness in inconveniencing my deity made me feel very small.

People who came in contact with Baba in those early days tell many stories of this nature. He would spend his time wandering from village to village, touching the lives of those he met in his own special way. All the time, a kind of play went on.

Back in Hariharpur, the locals wanted another *yagya*. Their enthusiasm was even greater than for the first. Baba agreed to be present. The neglected place shunned for so long transformed into an oasis of devotion, with continuous chanting, rituals and spiritual discourses. At the end of the celebration, the owner of the land offered it to Baba as a site for an ashram. Devotees constructed a boundary wall, dug a well and built a permanent brick hut with a verandah. At last Baba had a place where he felt inclined to stay. For many years, he spent a lot of time there, despite throngs of visitors.

One of these people was Thakur Meva Singh of Tajpur village, who was totally paralyzed. He had heard of Baba and had an intense desire to see him. When the visitor arrived, Baba was sitting in his room, eyes closed. The friends who had brought Meva Singh put him on the floor of Baba's room and left him. The paralyzed man pulled himself into a corner and waited for Baba to come out of his meditation. When Baba opened his eyes and saw a stranger in his room, he asked him to leave. Getting no response, Baba got up, grabbed Meva Singh's arm and pulled him to a standing position. When the old man realized he was standing, he began to walk without hesitation. Baba's compassionate grace had fallen on him. He was healed.

The ashram became a center where people came for healing, material success and better relationships with their families but also just to be in the powerful presence of a realized being. To their surprise, Baba no longer searched for solitude, as he had in the years of his relentless inward pursuit. With his inner state stabilized, Baba moved his attention in an outward direction to others. Once firmly established in that inner steadfast peace, he was ready to give from the deep well of his spiritual attainments.

Baba now wandered only to visit Varanasi or to walk along the Ganges, always coming back to his ashram at Hariharpur. When in Varanasi, Baba never stayed at Baba Kinaram Ashram, where he had been initiated.

A curious devotee once asked, "Baba, why don't you return to Baba Kinaram Ashram? After all, you are next as head of the lineage."

Baba replied, "Why bother with the old shawl? I will weave a new one."

Baba's Domestic Travels

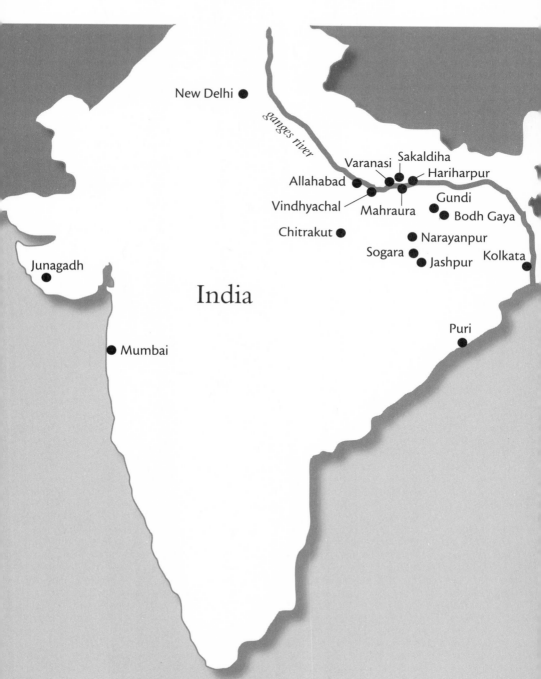

New Delhi

ganges river

Varanasi   Sakaldiha

Allahabad   Hariharpur

Vindhyachal   Gundi

Mahraura   Bodh Gaya

Chitrakut

Narayanpur

Junagadh

Sogara   Jashpur   Kolkata

India

Puri

Mumbai

One who is remorseful from within
should not be criticized further.

Chapter 5 The New Shawl

THE GURU'S GURU

The relationship between Baba and his guru was symbolic of all such relationships, even though many people misunderstood it for a long time. For example, after the *yagya* at Hariharpur, Baba Rajeshwar Ram, Bhagwan Ram's initiating guru, posted a flyer around town that read: "Beware of Bhagwan Ram! He is not my disciple!"

Seeing the flyer, one of Baba Rajeshwar Ram's longtime devotees remembered when he had first seen the very young Bhagwan Ram at Krim Kund. The devotee went to see his guru, who pulled him aside and confided, "Baba Kinaram has returned. Go and meet him." Then he pointed to Bhagwan Ram's room. Later that devotee would realize the meaning of those words. His guru had recognized Bhagwan Ram as another incarnation of Baba Kinaram from the beginning, but to maintain the integrity of the guru-disciple relationship, he had to play his part.

When they saw the flyer, most people assumed Baba Rajeshwar Ram did not want Bhagwan Ram to become too outwardly involved in the problems of society. The actions of gurus are often incomprehensible.

VISIT TO THE OLD GURU

Kedar Singh wrote about the mysterious relationship between the "old Baba" and the "young Baba."

> *After the* yagya *at Hariharpur, Baba spent the night at my home. I wanted* him to stay the next day, but he said, "I neither go anywhere nor do I stay anywhere. The ones who are running are forced to see me as running." He left, and I followed him with my bicycle.

My bicycle continued to be our chief means of transportation.
Sitting on the hind carrier, Baba would navigate, and I would pedal.
His destinations would be this or that temple or the banks of the
Ganges or Varuna. Asking me
to wait, he would disappear
for hours and then suddenly
reappear. We spent the next
three days in Varanasi like
this, staying at one place or
the other, but never at home.

※ Undisciplined conduct
   is the cause of all havoc
and frustration in life.

On the fourth day, as I was pedaling through the city, he jumped
off the hind carrier and got on a slow-moving bus. The bus sped up,
and I was left alone with my bicycle. Feeling empty and dejected,
I returned home. Mundane responsibilities awaited me.

The next day I had to go to a nearby village to take care of some
business. Of course, this village had to be near Hariharpur! On the
way I found out that Baba had camped on the riverbank in the village
of Sarsaul, a few miles from Hariharpur. The locals had erected a
small hut, and the usual scene was repeating itself.

Finishing my business, that evening I went to see what was
happening. I saw a small straw hut on the banks of the Ganges where
Baba was sitting surrounded by people. One of them was a friend of
mine. As Baba's eyes fell on me, a mischievous smile appeared on his
face. Gradually people began to leave, until only the three of us were
left. We cooked some food on the fire and retired for some sleep.
A stack of hay divided the hut into two parts. One part was for Baba,
the other for my friend and me.

The next morning, I went to the nearby town for some neces-
sities. On the way I met a friend who told me that Baba Rajeshwar
Ram had sent him. He said, "Brother, I have come straight from
Varanasi. Old Baba wants to see your Baba."

I said, "What are you talking about? Don't you remember the
leaflet that old Baba distributed just a few days ago? You must have
heard wrong."

He said, "No, brother, I am not deaf. Old Baba wanted to send me last night, but there was no means available to travel. He said very clearly to come here and fetch young Baba. As far as the relations and exchange between the two Babas are concerned, they are beyond the comprehension of our limited minds, so please just convey this message to your Baba and oblige me."

I said, "Since you have come so far, why not tell Baba yourself?"

He said, "I do not dare face your Baba since that incident at Krim Kund when he threw the keys in the well, then caused all the doors to open without them. It is better to bow from a distance to babas like this one."

We reached Baba's hut. The messenger, bowing to Baba, stood silent. Finally, I said, "He has come with a message; old Baba wants to see you."

Baba opened his eyes and looked at the messenger before moving his gaze to his own hands. He said neither yes nor no. I figured his silence meant yes. That evening 10 or 12 locals accompanied Baba on the overnight boat journey to Varanasi. I wanted to catch a good night's sleep, so I went home instead.

The next morning, I made my way to the Ganges and waited. Around 10 a.m. the boat docked near Manikarnika Ghat, where cremations take place. The "untouchable" caretaker of the cremation ground, Lakshmi Narayan, saw Baba getting out of the boat. He ran to greet him. Baba accepted his invitation to go to his palace. This "untouchable" man was very rich because he controlled the sacred fire used to light all funeral pyres at the *ghat*. Baba lay down in the caretaker's palace to rest. I whispered in the caretaker's ear, "He has to go to Baba Kinaram Ashram."

Baba opened his eyes and said, "I will not go. I have taken a vow not to take a step in that direction."

Hearing this, Lakshmi Narayan looked at me. I suggested to him with my eyes to somehow persuade Baba to go. Lakshmi Narayan was a clever man. After a pause he said, "Baba, if you have taken a vow not to take a step in that direction, it is necessary for you to keep your vow." After a short pause, he continued, "My horse carriage is ready to take you there. I will pick you up and place you in the carriage. Without taking a step on your own, you will reach the ashram."

This worked. Baba and Lakshmi Narayan rode in the carriage, and I followed on my bicycle. About a hundred yards from the gates of the ashram, Baba beckoned me to stop the horses. Letting my bicycle fall to the ground, I grabbed the reins. Sitting in the carriage, Baba said, "I will go neither in the carriage nor on foot."

Again Lakshmi Narayan's wit came in handy. He picked up Baba, put him on his back and entered the gate. Old Baba was reclining on his bed with half-opened eyes. Getting off Lakshmi Narayan's back near the eternally burning fire, Baba walked near his guru's bed. All the people sitting there hushed each other. Everyone was aware of what the leaflet had said.

As young Baba's hand humbly touched the lotus feet of his guru, the eyes of his guru opened. There was so much love in them, as if the child of a mother had returned home after many years. Tears of joy filled his eyes. Yet in a tone of complaint, he said, "I initiated you to take care of me, and you started wandering free on your own beyond my reach!"

Young Baba did not whisper a word.

The two spent some time together, but what they said was beyond the comprehension of the rest of us. After an hour, young Baba bowed again to the feet of his guru and left the ashram. The horse carriage returned Baba to Lakshmi Narayan's home.

THE GURU'S SANDALS

That day we spent at Lakshmi Narayan's palace. When I prepared to return home, Baba called me back and said, "I left a pair of wooden sandals in your house. Could you bring them to me by this evening?"

Without thinking, I got his sandals and returned them to him. When he accepted them, I noticed he had that mysterious smile on his face. A dozen people were sitting around him at the time. Baba announced, "The boat is ready to go to Sonepur for the fair at Chattarpur. Is anyone coming along?"

Everyone said they would join him on this weeklong journey, except me. I returned home and sent my uncle instead. After attending the fair, my uncle reported the incident that will constantly remind me of my foolishness in giving Baba those old sandals.

On the way to Sonepur, when the boat left the Ganges and entered the river Sone, the swift current made it impossible for the oarsman to maneuver properly. The boat tossed to and fro dangerously, and the high water splashed in. The boat began to go in circles. All the passengers except Baba began to pray for their lives. The oarsman called to God for intervention. Witnessing this, Baba stuck his foot in the water. A strong surge of the river swept against the boat, touching both of Baba's feet. Instantly, the boat began to move quietly in the right direction. Smiling, Baba said to his companions, "Kedar's entrusted property got washed away in the Ganges. The Ganges was rising, asked for the sandals and took them. What can I do? It is all right; at least the boat got out of the jam.

Kedar Singh never forgot his grand mistake of returning his guru's sandals. "What a fool I made of myself! I easily could have offered Baba a new pair," he said.

Those powerful sandals so casually left at his home could have been his most valuable possession!

VILLAGE LIFE

Everywhere Baba roamed, from village to village, he carefully observed the way people lived, and he became very sensitive to their practical needs. He was eager to understand more of what it means to be an ordinary human. He saw the hardships they endured—the result of inequities embedded in society—and his heart melted in compassion. Kedar Singh's stories reveal a lot about Baba's interest in common people during this time.

After the river journey to Sonepur, Baba left those who had accompanied him on the boat. He wandered alone for some time, then took a train to

Varanasi, where he stayed in a temple. One day a messenger came and said to me, "That *Aghor* Baba who visits you is calling for you at Hanuman's temple at Nati Imili."

I went, of course. Seeing me, Baba smiled like a child. After bowing, I began to massage his feet while he reclined. Smiling again, he said, "Kedar, your sandals got washed away in the Ganges, yes, but that helped the boat enter the Sone river."

☀ When your mind
    ignores your heart,
you are no better than an animal.
   But there is one remarkable
difference between a human
      and an animal:
   You can change your nature,
      ideas and mind.
An animal cannot.

I spent that night with him in the temple. I slept outside on the verandah. When I woke in the morning, he was gone. I waited, but he never returned.

Determined to find him, I mounted my bicycle and wandered the city. Some inner inspiration led me to pedal to where the Ganges and Varuna Rivers meet, and there I asked the boatman if he had seen Baba. He said, "Brother, *Aghor* Baba went across the river."

I shared a smoke with the boatman. He exclaimed, "Brother, this Baba is very strange. He took off his coat and gave it to my son in exchange for taking him across the river. It was such a nice coat; it is hard to find one like that in this country. I thought it was inappropriate to charge the holy being for a boat ride. If it is at all possible, we should give to such beings and not take from them."

I praised the boatman for his largesse of heart and gave him four times the normal wages for crossing the river.

I remembered the coat; it was an expensive one that a Kathak dancer of Varanasi had brought from Nepal for Baba. Many expensive gifts came to Baba, and, in the blink of an eye, he kept passing them along to those in need.

After crossing the river and dragging my bicycle on uneven tracks and through plowed fields, I entered the village of Kamauli. There someone related to me said that Baba had left for the village of Mustafabad on a male water buffalo. I followed, knowing that a ride on a male water buffalo could be wild. On the way I stopped in the market of Jalhupur and found out that Baba had left for the village of Sarsaul, riding on a camel. As I entered Sarsaul, I sighed in relief when I heard that Baba was at M. Singh's house. A large crowd had gathered around him, and food of all kinds was being prepared.

Seeing me, Baba turned his gaze in the other direction, although I did not miss the sweet smile that appeared on his face. That smile drove away all weariness and irritation of my long ordeal. After I rested a couple of hours, the host explained to me that his sister-in-law was a widow whose only son was dying. The doctors had given up hope. M. Singh wanted me to approach Baba to seek his intervention.

I asked, "Why don't you ask Baba yourself?"

"I do not dare to ask him again. Brother, please help me," he replied. When I mentioned it to Baba, all he did was murmur, *Rogia bhogia, bhogia rogia*—"The patient suffers, and the one who indulges is the patient."

After the *yagya* in Hariharpur, people had surrounded Baba for his intervention in their lives to obtain fame, fortune and material well-being. Baba would try to avoid such seekers and leapt like an alert lion to get away from their grip.

Once I asked Baba that if he could help people in these matters, why not do so. He replied:

> Man is the creator of the self. In the beginning he becomes intoxicated with the roar of his pride and indulges in lowly acts under its influence. The results of such acts will be his fate. Fate cannot be overcome. Divine intervention is the link to the unknown. You should not get involved in this at all. The Divine Mother is not a fool. Without her will, even a piece of straw will not move in this world. But people try to negotiate with God. By offering a few coins in the temple, they think they deserve favors from God. Everyone is looking for a cheap escape in this world. How could you find a ripe mango under a thorny bush? God becomes happy

by your remembering him, not by your asking him for things. If you really have to ask God for something, ask for such a thing that you never have to ask for anything again.

Despite this, I was moved by the tears of the widow and decided to approach Baba on her behalf. I waited for a suitable moment, paying attention to his mood and internally focusing my attention on him. Just then Baba called for me and asked me to go home. I did not move, but kept standing there in silence. He asked again, "Why don't you go? Why are you standing there as if gripped by a ghost?"

"Indeed I am gripped by a ghost," I replied.

"Then go to the river and wash yourself. The ghost will leave you. Are you afraid?"

"Sarkar, I am afraid to go alone."

"Well, should I accompany you?" Saying this, Baba got up and walked straight into the widow's house. He went directly to the room where her son was on the bed. Touching the boy on his forehead, Baba asked that all the charms and potions tied to the body be removed. Leaving the room like a storm, Baba headed straight to the nearby river and jumped into it. I had asked everyone present not to come to the river. I waited for him on the riverbank and watched him play in the water. An hour or so later he came out, and we left without returning to the village.

A few days later, I heard the boy had become well.

THE SHOE THIEF

The ashram in Hariharpur drew larger crowds every day. People were coming to get a glimpse of the young *Avadhut*, some to receive blessings to alleviate their worldly sufferings, a few just to be in his loving presence. When Baba was away in Varanasi and other places he frequented, the garden of Rai Panaru Das at Nati Imili became his camping ground. All types of people gathered there seeking fame, fortune or better health or just out of curiosity.

Kedar Singh, continuing his close relationship with his guru, told more stories about Baba:

A few people complained of losing their shoes. Someone was stealing them! I was intent on catching the thief.

I always sat in the back of the crowd surrounding Baba to listen to conversations. One day, another pair of shoes disappeared, and I saw the thief. The next day, I threatened him, telling him not to come around anymore. Baba overheard the conversation and called for both of us. He said to me, "Everyone comes here for one reason or the other with their own interests in mind. This fellow also comes here for his own purpose. Who are you to stop him?"

After this, most lovingly, he said to the thief, "You keep coming, come every day."

I was terribly insulted. The next day the man came and disappeared with a pair of shoes that belonged to a businessman. Before this incident, it was simple people whose shoes had disappeared, and not to cause a commotion, no one ever gave the thefts any importance for fear of displeasing Baba. But today this was a rich man of the city. He made a big scene and shouted, "Those shoes were so expensive. I just bought them." Baba heard the commotion and called for the businessman.

Baba asked him very sweetly, "You make jewelry, isn't it so?"

"Yes, Baba, and I also have a jewelry shop."

"In your business, isn't there some unscrupulous activity?"

"Yes, Baba, now and then."

"Isn't that a kind of thievery? Now for a pair of shoes you are making so much commotion."

The businessman had no words to answer and departed after bowing. The next day, the thief returned and sat next to me. When everyone left, he kept sitting there. Baba called for him and interrogated him about the shoes. He found out that shops would buy the stolen shoes from him for a few rupees. The man had no other way to support his family.

Finally, Baba asked, "Tell me, can you do some small business like a tea stall or something like that?"

"Why not, Baba, if I had the means to get started."

Baba ordered me to give the man 10 rupees. This request was fuel to my anger. Just a few days ago, Baba had scolded me on behalf of this thief and today he wanted me to give him money instead of a good beating. But it was guru's orders; I had no alternative. I gave him the money.

The worldy boat of this man had taken off. A few months later, I saw the man again visiting Baba. Now he was selling roasted peanuts on the street and providing for his family. He became an ardent devotee.

Be careful about your behavior
and make it so sweet
that the whole creation
may become your friend
and you may smilingly enfold
this wide world
into your heart.

Chapter 6   Baba's Adventures

VINDHYACHAL HILLS

Early in 1955, Haji Suleman, a Varanasi businessman, invited 18-year-old Baba to live in his garden of mango groves in Maduva Diha. This proved to be a good place for Baba, with enough room for him and enough open space in the garden for his visitors. Being in the city not only allowed Baba to keep in touch with his devotees, it also put him near easy transportation to the places he wanted to go.

While residing in Varanasi, Baba would make many trips to the Vindhyachal foothills. This area, only an hour's bus ride away, is part of a range of mountains dividing north India from south India. Ancient texts describe numerous caves along the streams and waterfalls in these mountains as the dwelling places of sages and saints who found them perfect for solitude and seclusion. At the base of the foothills in the town of Vindhyachal stand three very old temples. They are set in a triangle dedicated to the Divine Mother in the form of Ma Vindhya Vasini, Ma Kali Khoha and Ma Asta Bhuja.

Vindhyachal is now one of the major *shakti pitha* of India, holy places where millions of people make pilgrimages every year. They feel the presence of the Divine Mother the moment they set foot there. It is believed that many sages and saints still reside in these mountains, engaged in *sadhana*. Once in a while someone catches a glimpse of them.

Whenever Baba wanted to get away from the city, he visited Kali Khoha and meditated in a nearby cave. A few miles from there near Asta Bhuja, which is the original temple of the Vindhyachal Mountains, is a place called Bhairava Kunda. A stream of water flows there all year long. About 300 feet above this stream is a big meadow. On the edge of it, under a giant banyan tree, is a small cave that affords a view of the whole spread of the

Ganges in the plains, flowing in the form of a snake, winding around the foothills. This cave became Baba's favorite spot. Residents of nearby villages recall his presence with so much sweetness. He would eat whatever they gave him, although he never asked for anything from these simple folk.

Hundreds of Baba's followers would camp in the meadow during the nine nights of Navaratri. Eventually, the forestry department of the Indian government allowed Baba's followers to build a *kirti stambha*—pillar of victory—carved with Baba's teachings on four sides. Inside the cave where Baba used to sit, his sandals are cemented in the rock, and people come to pray for fulfillment of their wishes.

Baba felt close ties with the Vindhyachal Mountains and experienced many strange events there. He related one of them:

> One day, I was sitting under a tree near the Asta Bhuja temple. A *sadhu* who seemed to come from the town of Vindhyachal approached me and beckoned to me to accompany him. I followed. On the way, I noticed a few *hut-muts* with whitewashed walls. The narrow path ended at the lower end of them, and soon we were climbing into a wash. After a short walk, we came to an opening in the cliff. The opening had turned black with smoke but was covered with shrubs and vines and was not visible from outside. It was so well hidden that if you didn't know it was there, you would never have been able to find it.
>
> As we entered this opening, I noticed that for about 50 feet there was just enough space for one person to walk. Big boulders were blocking the way. At places we had to squat, bend and crawl to go farther. After another 50 feet, we could stand and walk freely. We walked about half a mile in this tunnel. At the end, it widened into a huge hall. It was both spacious and simple. Cut split wood was piled inside, and unsplit logs were stacked near the entrance. I noticed three or four *sadhus* walking around, and two *sadhus* cooking *puri* on a fire. The sweet aroma of this bread deep-frying with *ghee* filled the hall.
>
> My guide led me in another direction where on the bank of an underground stream, three *sadhus* were performing *havan*, making sacred oblations in the fire. Several pieces of broken statues were lying around and a few were resting against the wall. In a corner stood a whole idol of Bhagwati, the Mother. A clean natural light was falling on the statue, and a small *ghee* lamp was burning at its base. I did not get a chance to go near it and bow. It was about 12 feet from where I was standing. All of a sudden, the *sadhu* who was leading me disappeared from my sight, so I wandered through three or four rooms and came across more *sadhus*. I paid my respects, but they did not speak to me. They said neither yes nor no. Finding it very strange yet peaceful,

I wandered for hours. From time to time the impulse to leave would arise, but I had no recollection of the way.

A sweet light permeated the whole area. Sunlight fell in patches. As I paid attention to it, the light seemed to be entering from the south. Some light was falling on the stream, as well. The stream flowed swiftly with a soothing sound. Over the centuries it had cut its way through the hard rocks and was about seven feet wide. This was a Divine, peaceful place. A half-dozen or so *sadhus* appeared to be living there. Some were old, and some were 50 or 60 years of age. Possibly, a few were more than 100 years old; who knows!

There was a very small temple in the cave. Although it had no structure, a small *yantra* was placed near a big boulder with a few broken statues around it. Near the temple a *dhuni* was smoldering, but no flame was coming out if it. I noticed a book that seemed to be written in Sanskrit that the *sadhus* used to perform *havan*. The very sweet smell of earth like that of the first rain after a hot summer filled the atmosphere.

After two or three hours, I ran into my guide again. He led me toward his room on the other side of the stream. As I began to cross the stream, my foot slipped on a rock and I fell into the water. Again I lost contact with my guide. For a moment I lost hope of ever coming out of that cave and thought about never being able to return to my ashram in Hariharpur. I even cried for a moment. The water was no more than knee deep. I collected myself and looked for the stone I had slipped on. It was close, so I walked to it and sat for a while. While there, I felt helpless. The flowing water made it seem as if I were listening to a stringed instrument. As I looked up, I noticed cobwebs on the ceiling, but at least there were no snakes or turtles in the water! This place no longer seemed so fearful; in fact, it was very peaceful.

> ☀ After the mind resigns itself in exhaustion, it becomes easier to attain God.

Sitting on that rock in the middle of the stream, I closed my eyes. When I opened them, I could not believe what I was seeing. Sitting in the lotus position on a big leaf floating in the middle of the stream was a woman clad in a milky white sari playing a stringed instrument, a *vina*. Opening my eyes wider, I noticed her waving at me as if saying to go now. Although I did not understand her language, I could sense what she was telling me through her gestures. Witnessing all this, I covered my eyes with both hands and began to weep. I even forgot to bow to her or pay my respects. After two or three minutes, when I opened my eyes again, I found myself sitting under the same tree where I had met the *sadhu* in the first place. Five hours had passed.

Now I do not know when I will get a chance to visit that place again. I bow to the *sadhu* who led me there and to the Mother. May the Mother give me another chance to see her.

HAJI SULEMAN'S GARDEN

Baba always returned to Haji Suleman's garden in Varanasi before starting another journey. He was there in June, when the intense heat of summer can
scorch the whole city. On one of those hot days, Baba planned a *yagya*. At the
end of the ceremony, the custom is to feed many Brahmins and holy people, but
Baba decided this time he would feed the *domins* instead. These are the wives

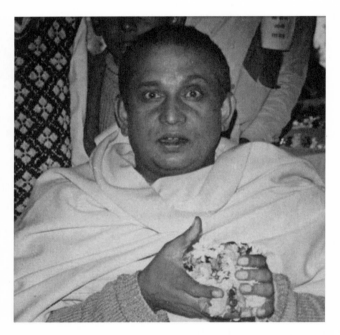

of the workers in the
cremation grounds, or
the lowest of the lowest
caste, the untouchables.
Then Baba included on
his guest list all the dogs
and donkeys of the area.
In other words, Baba
was reaching out to
the neglected, abused
and downtrodden. His
devotees knew how to
invite the *domins*, but
what about the dogs
and donkeys?

Baba's instructions
came to write out the
dogs' invitations and

◙ Baba in the early days of Parao Ashram ◙

take them to where people threw their garbage. He said to take the donkeys'
invitations and attach them to the stakes to which those animals were tied.
Twenty-five invitations were given to each group of guests in many places
throughout town.

First to arrive were the *domins*, who were greeted graciously. They were
escorted to a long floor seating, as is customary in India, where they were
served royally on fresh leaf plates with curries, rice and other delicacies.

After the *domins* left, there was no sign of the animals. Nevertheless, Baba had
us prepare 50 leaf plates in another floor setting, with 25 plates on one side for the

dogs and 25 on the other side for the donkeys. We waited. Some of us doubted they would come.

All of a sudden, in the gate they came. Quite spontaneously they went to their floor settings, took their appropriate places and enjoyed the feast.

In this way, Baba reminded us to care for those most neglected by society, but how it all happened so smoothly is still a subject for conversation. Strange phenomena always occurred around Baba.

Another time when Baba was at Haji Suleman's garden, a fancy car arrived with the chief priest of the golden temple of Kashi Vishwanath. This main temple of Lord Shiva in Varanasi, the City of Shiva, is a major attraction for pilgrims. To be head of the temple is cause for pride and a seat of recognition, so this chief priest was not exempt from vanity.

Sitting under the tree, Baba received the priest with much grace. They conversed on several matters concerning both spirituality and worldly aspirations. Eventually Baba asked him, "You are the priest of the holy temple of Lord Shiva. Shiva is the ruler of this city, and several guardians of the city are under Him. Kal Bhairava is the Divine Sheriff of the town. Isn't it so?"

The priest replied, "Yes."

"Could you help me offer a flower to the temple of Kal Bhairava?" Baba humbly requested.

"Not only one flower, Baba, as many as you want," the priest replied.

They took a flower from a rose bush nearby, and everyone got in the car and headed to the temple. When they were within a couple of miles of the temple, out of nowhere a thunderstorm began to pour over the city, flooding the roads, so it was impossible to proceed.

With an air of defeat, the priest said, "Baba, we cannot go there today."

"So, you cannot help me in offering a single flower to the servant of the Master whom you serve?" Baba asked. "Well, let us go back then." They had to turn around. As soon as the car arrived at the garden, the sky was clear.

GIRNAR MOUNTAINS

In March 1955, while Baba was attending a celebration organized at the temple of Dhumavati, a well-known poet of Varanasi, Pundit Devaki Nandan, also was present. He persuaded Baba to go to the Girnar Mountains at Junagadh in the state of Gujarat, where in ancient times Bhagwan Dattatreya wandered. It was as if Baba was already prepared to go. That very night he left alone, taking the midnight train from Varanasi. The next day he arrived in Agra, then went by way of Bharatpur to Pushkar. Every year, Pushkar organizes a grand *mela*, and people from all over India come to this holy place. Baba stayed a little while.

❁ Remember well
that in this world
you have neither a friend
nor an enemy.
It is your own conduct
that produces friends or foes.

In his meandering way, Baba went on to Ajmer, where he spread his blanket on the ground at a railway station to rest. A young man approached and asked for initiation. Seeing the man was hungry, Baba took his hand and consoled him, giving him what little money he had left. Baba now had nothing for his ticket to the next town. In the evening, he boarded the train to Ahmedabad, but with no money to pay for the ticket, he was put off in the middle of the night at a small railway station.

As Baba stood in the dark station, a young shopkeeper offered him a cup of tea. Baba sat on a cot and drank the hot tea. He recalled, "How good it tasted at that moment!" In the morning as Baba sat in the same place, another shopkeeper offered to buy him a ticket to Ahmedabad. Baba found himself standing in front of a restaurant with his ticket and also a bowl of food. Aboard the train, he found a five rupee bill tied to a corner of his shawl, most likely a gift from the gentleman who had bought his ticket. After reaching Ahmedabad, he bought another ticket to Junagadh for four rupees. The remaining rupee he spent on a horse carriage ride to the foot of the Girnar Mountains. There Baba met an old *sadhu* who gave him directions to the Bhagwan Dattatreya hillock.

Set on the western shore of India, the prosperous city of Junagadh is strategically located for trade. Its natural beauty is incomparable. On one side are tall mountain peaks; on the other side are wide expanses of jungle. The lions of this forest not only are well known in India but also are popular throughout the world for their strength and magnificence. They are known as the lions of Gir Mountain. Big families of black-faced monkeys with long tails also roam this area. Large flocks of vultures nest in these mountains. They can be seen gliding on their majestic wings above the peaks.

To reach the top of Gir Mountain, you have to climb 10,000 steps. On the way are many temples and caves dedicated to various deities and saints, one of them being the cave of Rajarshi Bhartrihari, known for his treatises on renunciation. Bhartrihari lived there after leaving his kingdom and receiving initiation from Gorakh Nath. Further on, a temple dedicated to Ambaji is right across from the place of Gorakh Nath. From there, 900 more steps lead to the place of Bhagwan Dattatreya.

Between two hillocks sits another called, *Aghor* hillock. A *dhuni* is always alight, and many *Aghor sadhakas* live near it, though people rarely see them. Some yoginis also live in these caves. These female *sadhikas* are highly accomplished but do not generally have public contact; nevertheless, a few fortunate people have been able to see them. The area is called Kamandal Kunda.

Baba stopped for a while at Kamandal Kunda. He said, "I arrived here on Thursday. The Mahant in this place was very hospitable to me. The Chief Mahant had just left his body. His appearance was very similar to mine, so all the *sadhus* living there were very attentive to me."

The young man who had been installed as the new Mahant was from Nepal. Later he came to Baba's ashrams in Parao and Jashpur and lived under his guidance for many years.

Baba moved on to Bhagwan Dattatreya's peak, staying in Ma Kali's cave nearby. After spending time there in *sadhana*, he returned to Junagadh. At the railway station, a very old but radiant *sadhu* wearing *rudraksha* beads and ashes smeared over his body approached Baba. This radiant being called Baba by his name in a soft endearing voice, asking him to come near. He didn't want Baba to leave. He wanted him to come back with him to the mountains. The sweet memory of this encounter remained with Baba for a long time. He said, "A part of me thinks that it was Bhagwan Dattatreya himself in disguise."

JASHPUR

Baba returned to Varanasi, making frequent visits to the Vindhyachal and Girnar Mountains, but always coming back to the gardens at Maduva Diha. One day while Baba was in Vindhyachal, the Prince of Jashpur state came to visit him. Baba described their meeting:

I was merely 20 years of age, spending some time in the mountains. One day while I was sitting on a giant rock behind the temple of Asta Bhuja, a man of about 35 years of age appeared from the thicket of the jungle. After bowing down, with great politeness he tried to strike up a conversation. Receiving no encouragement from me, he went to the bungalow nearby. Around noon his secretary appeared on the scene with trays loaded with fruit and all kinds of other food. He said, "Please accept this humble gift from the Prince of Jashpur state. He is aware of your presence here and also knows that you have not eaten for a while." It was true. My last meal was just a few potatoes that someone had given me several days before.

The thought came to me to accept this food that was made available to me, without asking for it, in the middle of the wilderness. Insulting this gift would not be appropriate. After some time, when I opened my eyes, I found the secretary still standing there with his gifts in his hands. I signaled him to leave the tray near me on the rock. He left promptly with tears of happiness. After eating the food, I remained on the rock.

In the evening, I noticed a young couple approaching. Their dog was right behind them. As they came closer, they removed their sandals, offered me flowers, bowed and sat at a comfortable distance. Their dog also sat at a distance; even the dog was still. I sat motionless for a while. Then I asked them, "Gentlemen, where have you come from? What is the reason for your being in this wilderness? What is your inquiry, O' Prince?"

This couple happened to be the Prince of Jashpur, Vijay Bhushan Singh called Ju Deva, and his wife, Rajmata Jaya Singh. All the man could say was, "To find the One, I came to perform a *yagya* in this *shakti pitha*, and I have found him on the very first day. I cannot contain my happiness."

"What did you find? What do you know about me? I could be the right person or a con artist!" Baba said.

"No, Maharaj. Your long arms, the lines of your forehead, your lionlike chest, your demeanor are the characteristics of a realized being. I am witnessing this right in front of my eyes. I am fully confident of my success in this *yagya*. Now the completion of this ceremony is a mere formality. I brought 101 Brahmin priests here for the week, but when I bid them farewell, I would like to come back to you. Do I have your permission to return and sit in your presence?"

"O' Prince, how long would you want to sit in my presence?" Baba asked.

"Until my heart keeps experiencing peace, vibrationlessness, one-pointedness, until the waves of happiness keep rising in my heart, I would like to remain in your presence. If it does not disturb your routine, I would like to remain near you. O' Great One, do I have your permission?"

"O' Prince, you may, but remember one thing: As soon as I indicate I am to be left alone, you must leave immediately with your wife because that will be the time for me to engage in my practices and I will withdraw unto myself."

"It will be so, Maharaj."

After this initial meeting, the prince left, but it was the beginning of a great friendship, as well as of three major ashrams that Baba would establish in the state of Madhya Pradesh.

The prince continued to visit Baba in Varanasi and other places. He also spent time with him at the Kumbha Mela of Prayag, now called Allahabad. He kept insisting that Baba visit his home state of Jashpur. Finally, in 1958, Baba accepted his invitation. The journey was hard, with no good roads and not much to speak of in the way of transportation. It took 16 to 20 hours by Jeep.

Baba was taken by the natural beauty of Jashpur. Surrounded by forests of lush green trees of sakhu and other trees with medicinal qualities, the area was very different from other places Baba had seen. The locals were simple tribal people. Baba's heart melted at the sight of their poverty and lack of education.

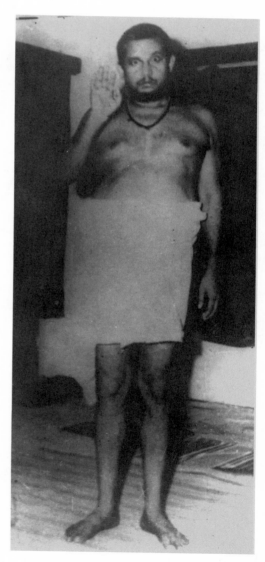

⊞ Baba at Parao Ashram ⊞

❒ The *Aghoreshwar* on his *asana* ❒

In early 1959, the prince visited Baba and expressed his desire to make available several hundred acres of land in five different villages for establishing ashrams in the Jashpur subdistrict in Madhya Pradesh. Baba declined his offer, but the prince quietly registered the land to Baba anyway.

Soon after, 30 miles from the palace of Jashpur, in a village named Narayanpur, Baba established the first ashram of Madhya Pradesh. He sent one of his disciples to initiate the project. First they erected a humble straw hut under a giant banyan tree and named it Abhed Ashram, the nondiscriminating ashram. The land around it was already cultivated, and they added a cowshed, storage room, kitchen and residence for Baba. Baba would occasionally visit. Many sadhus, sadhakas and a few helpers still live there and are of service to the local people.

After that, Baba established a second ashram called Shakradhara Gram in the village of Sogara. Sogara is known for its natural beauty, surrounded by hills like a pearl necklace. The government built a large reservoir for irrigation using water from a spring near the ashram. Adding to the compound, Rajmata Jaya Singh built a temple of Ma Kali. This became a favorite spot for Baba, who would visit this ashram often and spend time in solitude.

Baba founded the third ashram three miles from Sogara Ashram and one mile outside of Jashpur, in the village of Gamhariya. Called Aghor Pitha, Vamadeva Nagar, it stands on a hill with its buildings set in a triangle.

In addition to being ideal places for *sadhana*, all three ashrams engage in social work, helping the community in matters of education and health, as well as spiritual awareness. Recently, Gamhariya Ashram constructed a hospital on its grounds.

❀ Without having the light in your own eyes, outside light is of no use, no matter how bright or golden.

Baba's presence brought the attention of many government dignitaries to the area. Morarji Desai, the Deputy Prime Minister of India at that time, visited him there, and the result was a wave of new developments for the welfare of the locals.

This was the beginning of Baba's involvement with society on a large scale, working for the welfare of those who are often forgotten.

Spirituality is
    the complete truth.
Philosophy is
    only incomplete truth.

Chapter 7  Travels

CHITRAKUT

Journeys and wanderings were always part of Baba's experience. They started when he was only nine years old and continued throughout his life.

Legend tells us the story of Rama wandering 14 years in Chitrakut forest with his wife Sita and brother Lakshmana. Baba went to this same forest, a place of pilgrimage in Madhya Pradesh. Pundit Yagya Narayan Chaturvedi, a long-time devotee of Baba's, wrote about accompanying him on his journeys.

In 1961, Baba and I took a train from Varanasi to Allahabad. A bus from Allahabad to Sitapur brought us near Chitrakut. Following the river Mandakini on foot, we arrived at the base of a hillock known as Kamandal Giri. After resting for a while, we made our way to Chikani Parikrama, the circular path around the hillock where Rama had set up his hut. Pilgrims walk this path, visiting various temples and monasteries built along the way. The priest in one of the temples was very hospitable and gave us a nice place to stay. Close by was the temple where Bharata, the younger brother of Rama, had come to take him back to his kingdom. In this temple are the rocks that have melted with the intensity of the love of the two brothers, as the mythology goes. You can clearly see footprints on these rocks; they are not carved. Also near is the temple of Hanuman that Baba remembered in his later days with much fondness.

We stayed in Chitrakut several days visiting all the places such as the Ashram of Atri Muni and Sati Anusuiya, the legendary parents of Bhagwan Dattatreya; Hanuman Dhara; Gupta Godavari; Bharat Kup; and Sphatica Shila, a quartz slab by the river where Rama had worshiped Sita in the form of the Divine. The Ashram of Atri Muni and Sati Anusuiya is on the river next to the quartz slab. This ashram

is the birthplace of Bhagwan Dattatreya, the original expounder of
Aghor teachings, who had appeared to Baba Kinaram and also to
Baba in Girnar. No wonder Baba went there on the birthday of
Baba Kinaram. Chitrakut is a very special place with great historical
significance and unbounded beauty.

The Maharaja of Sonpura joined us. No roads existed in those
days. We had to walk on foot from one place to another. Baba asked
us both to ride on horses, but he would walk. The strange phenome-
non was that wherever we went, Baba would be there before us, even
though he was on foot. With various stories and jokes Baba kept us
entertained without letting us know how he was able to arrive first.

GHORA DEVI TEMPLE

One day during the spring Navaratri while we were still in Chitrakut, a radiant
Bhairavi arrived on the scene. This female *Aghor sadhika* asked Baba to
join her in *puja* at the temple of Ghora Devi in the wilderness. I wanted
to go, and the head priest of the temple of Bharat Milap also went with
us. We began on foot to Ghora Devi. Bhairavi had a complexion like
wheat, and her hair was matted. She wore sandals and a long gown that
was patched together. She carried by the handle a *kamandalu* pot made
from a coconut. She appeared to be about 55 years of age, yet she was
very sure footed on the uneven mountain paths.

It took about four hours to get there. A flat place close to the
temple was cleared for *puja*. Nearby was the hermitage of the Sarbhang Rishi lineage. We got some pots and buckets from a *sadhu* there.
Baba asked me to remain with the *sadhu* in the hermitage, but I
requested to stay with Baba. The priest of Bharat Milap temple got
busy with necessary preparations. Baba sat on a large rock, puffing
on his water pipe. A strange stillness was in the air. We heard nothing
except the chirping of birds and the sound of Baba's pipe. The moon
on the horizon was about to set. Darkness was deepening.

All of a sudden, from the thicket of the forest, an old but resplen-
dent being emerged riding a horse. Welcoming this guest as is the

custom, we paid our respects. It was Aghoracharya Someshwara Ramji. Baba said to him, "Maharaj, you took much time to arrive here." Aghoracharya said with a mysterious smile, "I left my ashram late." We tied his horse to a nearby tree and offered water. It was about 11 at night.

After a time, I saw that everyone was getting ready to do *havan*. One clay pot held fish; another held some liquid. Once the fire was going, the participants began making offerings of fish dipped in the liquid. The stillness of the night came alive with the sound of mantras. The whole atmosphere was charged. I noticed a bright light that appeared from the temple of Ghora Devi and, touching all the participants' hearts, disappeared into the fire pit. I thought maybe my tired eyes were seeing things, but at that very moment everyone laughed loudly. The sound of this laughter echoed in the wilderness.

A sense of fear engulfed me. I could not stay any longer. I picked up my bag and left for the nearby hermitage. I kept hearing sounds of "phat, phat, phat" coming from a distance. The next moment, the whole place filled with the chant *Shivo ham, Bhairavo ham, gurupada rato ham*—"I am Shiva, I am Bhairava, I am one with the feet of the guru."

In the morning, when I met the priest of Bharat Milap temple who was at this *havan*, he told me what happened after I left. As the *havan* went on, a flame rose from the middle of the fire pit and ascended as high as 40 feet. Then, as the flame returned to the fire pit, many yoginis appeared on the scene. Some of them had met Baba in Kalimath and the Himalayas. They were clad in blue gowns, wearing crystal necklaces. Each was carrying a *kamandalu*. It is possible they were attracted by the flame. The priest told me that these beings travel through space at will and arrive anywhere at will. To serve one of these beings would be a great accomplishment, but they are hard to find.

The next morning Baba and Pundit Chaturvedi bowed to Ghora Devi and returned to the ashram in Varanasi.

FOREIGN COUNTRIES

Baba's travel to other countries began with a trip to Nepal in 1968. After that, he journeyed to Afghanistan, Iran, Bhutan and Burma. Farther from home, he visited Switzerland, Italy, Mexico and the United States. He interspersed these trips with visits to south India and Sikkim, Assam and the Himalayas. If all the stories were told, they would fill volumes.

Baba's curiosity about the land and people of different cultures never ceased. His interest in establishing contact with other *sadhakas* and places of pilgrimage was ongoing. Baba's mind was always alert, his observations keen to study the religious, social and political situations wherever he went. He looked at the plight of the common man in every different set of circumstances. All these experiences provided the foundation for a social movement based on the ideals of *Aghor* to change conditions for humans wherever and whenever severe hardship afflicts them.

How can one who does not feel love
for living beings have love for
either a stone image in a temple
or the formless God in a mosque?

Chapter 8   Ideals of Social Service

SRI SARVESHWARI SAMOOH

By communicating with common folks in day-to-day life, Baba learned many things about their hardships. He saw how the place of women had fallen in society. The woman is supposed to be revered as mother, sister, wife and a symbol of *Shakti*, spiritual strength, but this was no longer always so, as she was often being misused. With the prevalent dowry system in Indian society, the birth of a female child had become a bad omen. Baba also saw how young people had no direction and were being lured to drug abuse.

The future of a formerly healthy society seemed dark. In the race to get ahead, the poor and helpless were ground down and neglected. Disharmony was spreading through discrimination and orthodoxy in the name of religion. Many undesirable practices had taken root under the guise of tradition. There was a lack of higher ideals to encourage people to live as real human beings. Baba felt a call to use his spiritual accomplishments to help people who wanted to rise above the restrictions of society.

He had just returned to the garden in Maduva Diha in Varanasi from a visit to his Jashpur ashrams. He was a mere 25 years old. His followers and companions had keenly felt Baba's absence from Varanasi. The need for a permanent place in the city for these devotees to help carry out Baba's ideals was very clear. A handful of his inspired and dedicated admirers gathered in his garden to confer on the subject. On September 21, 1961, they registered themselves as a nonprofit organization that Baba named Sri Sarveshwari Samooh. *Sarveshwari* literally means Divine Mother of all. *Samooh* means a group, a collective. Baba said, "I am proud to name this organization after womankind."

Sri Sarveshwari Samooh was formed with the following goals:

- ◆ To promote motherly reverence toward women in society.

- ◆ To promote harmony among all humans irrespective of race, religion, caste or social stature.

- ◆ To create a suitable environment for the proper education and wholesome growth of children.

- ◆ To serve the needy and neglected and help them return to society with dignity, and to educate people to accept their brethren without discrimination.

- ◆ To evoke the essence of true spirituality without much pomp and show, and to provide a secular stage for different ideologies to work together.

- ◆ To strive to eradicate the dowry system in India, as well as to eliminate the huge sums spent on marriage and other ceremonies, and to rectify the caste system.

- ◆ To establish additional ashrams dedicated to the ideals of Sri Sarveshwari Samooh and to help organizations of a similar nature.

By setting forth these goals, Baba took a wholehearted plunge into the correction of social ills. He gave those who sought his company very clear direction. The goals emphasize that the essence of all major religions is the same, that people can follow their own beliefs and allow others to follow theirs, thereby bringing harmony in society without needing to change anyone's spiritual practice.

In the name of religion, many unnecessary customs such as the dowry system had taken root in Indian society with ruinous results. These customs demand exorbitant spending for the basic ceremonies of life such as weddings and funerals. They take a heavy toll on people with meager financial resources in India and many other countries. Families often fall into a deep hole of debt, making it impossible to emerge without selling their land, home or possessions. Sri Sarveshwari Samooh provided an appropriate environment for such ceremonies, saving many families from ruin.

Other programs Sri Sarveshwari Samooh initiated inspired young people to take a more active role in the improvement of their society, as well as personal growth.

Serving the needy and downcast with respect became the main form of worship. Baba expressed such ideals as follows:

> Are you looking for God? Away from temples, churches and mosques; away from prayers, songs and praises; and away from places of pilgrimages, He must be flowing in the tears of the wretched and the poor.

To fulfill social ideals, Sri Sarveshwari Samooh formulated programs that all the branches implemented locally. As more and more people from different walks of life came in contact with Baba and his ashrams, they were inspired to carry these programs home. They received the full support of Baba and his companions in implementing these practices in their own lives and communities, thereby setting an example for others. In Baba's words:

> Sri Sarveshwari Samooh is neither a religious organization nor is it related to any particular tradition. It is not a place of politics either. Its doors are always open to all, and there is no obligation to practice or not to practice religious rituals or ceremonies. The main objective is to nurture a healthy society based on simplicity, equality and freedom. The greatest service is to give help and respect to those who have fallen back, without imposing your own ideas on them.

THE LEPROSY HOSPITAL

As Sri Sarveshwari Samooh became more active in social justice, Baba's attention was drawn to the lepers he had seen living in the streets. Not only had their own families turned them out, but society as a whole had insulted and abandoned them, too. Baba decided to dedicate his time and efforts to making a substantial difference in their situation. Mere rhetoric was not enough; concrete steps were necessary. Baba started a leprosarium.

First he needed land. Baba was still living on meager means in the garden in Maduva Diha. As his visitors became aware of his wish, they soon granted it. A businessman from Varanasi named Kamal Sahu had a small plot across the river in the town of Parao. It was a triangular parcel that sat between the railway line and Grand Trunk Road. Thorny bushes, thickets, big pits and mounds of rocks and dirt filled the derelict property. People would not go near it even in the daytime. Kamal Sahu had no use for the land and expressed his wish to offer it to Baba. To Kamal Sahu's surprise, Baba liked the land and accepted the offering. With Kamal Sahu's help, more land around the original grant was acquired, and clearing began almost immediately.

Baba would come from Maduva Diha and spend the whole day there. Although Baba had no financial means to tackle the project, with only his firm determination and the good of the lepers at heart, construction proceeded smoothly. Baba told the story of the beginning:

> We invited a great many dignitaries for the ceremony of laying the foundation for the hospital. The District Magistrate of Varanasi was the chief guest to place the first stone. I had only 10 rupees. Seven-and-a-half of them went for refreshments.
>   Fortunately a well-wisher of mine donated several truckloads of bricks on the spot, and construction began with the help of volunteers. I had only two-and-a-half rupees, but construction never stopped. With the grace of the Mother and the dedication of my admirers, we built a small building within two months and started functioning as a clinic for lepers.

The hospital was named after Baba, Avadhut Bhagwan Ram Leprosy Hospital. In the beginning, workers erected small straw huts for patients needing more intensive care. In due time the property had a 60-bed facility flanked by another building for women patients.

Well-trained doctors from town volunteered to care for these patients. Medical treatment used natural remedies such as Ayurvedic herbs—some gathered from the nearby forest and others cultivated in the hospital compound. Baba himself prepared herbal remedies and familiarized the doctors with their healing properties. Unprecedented cures began to occur. Everyone knew that it was the Divine blessing of Baba added to the Ayurvedic medicines that healed.

The story of miraculous cures spread fast. Many people came and received treatment. Some of the healed decided to dedicate their lives to helping other lepers and were trained as nurses and aides. With the number of lepers seeking help, it was necessary to branch out. Soon, another hospital, this one in Raibareli, about 200 miles away, opened with the support of Avadhut Bhagwan Ram Leprosy Hospital. Both facilities are still very active today in treating leprosy patients.

AN ASHRAM IN VARANASI

Once the hospital in Parao was up and running, it seemed logical for Baba to live nearby, since he was spending so much time there. Devotees made land adjoining the hospital available for building lodging for Baba. In early 1964, Baba moved to Parao, leaving his camping site in Maduva Diha.

Now the Parao Ashram became the center attraction, housing the head office of Sri Sarveshwari Samooh. A simple but attractive temple dedicated to the Divine Mother functioned as a place for worship, as well as an accommodation for weddings and other ceremonies that reflected Baba's ideals of simplicity and no dowry.

Many people came to receive blessings from the young renunciate who had returned to society. Although all kinds of miracles were happening in the lives of those who sought Baba's blessings, he never claimed them. Baba consoled people wanting the intervention of his grace in their difficulties with a few simple words or a wave of his hand. Sometimes he would just say words like, "It will be alright; now go home." Mere consolation worked as an elixir.

◙ Baba in his joyous moods ◙

Eventually, the compound installed a printing press. A few members of the ashram started a newsletter, the "Sri Sarveshwari Times," containing Baba's discourses. They also published books on the ideals of Sri Sarveshwari Samooh and Baba's teachings.

Today, the ashram covers 21 acres. In addition to the leprosy hospital, the compound contains a primary school, the printing press, an outpatient clinic, a pharmacy, cowsheds, staff residences, a meeting hall, a library and a place for guests to stay. Much of the land is left open for cultivating grains and vegetables. Hospital patients are encouraged to grow their own food. The ashram complex and the hospital complex are separate, and only those working in the hospital can enter that area. Former patients volunteer to staff the hospital's kitchen.

✻ The secret to life
   can be discovered only with
a well-balanced mind.

On numerous occasions people heard Baba say, "Residents of the leprosy hospital are my deities, and serving them is my worship." These sentiments for the poor and needy echoed those of Baba Kinaram, who established the seat of *Aghor* in Varanasi in the late 16th century. Baba presented the ways of *Aghor* for the modern day.

The fire of *Aghor*, buried under the ashes over the centuries, leapt higher with Baba's emergence as a shining star in the lineage of Kinarami Avadhuta Siddhas of Kashi. Many people went as far as saying that he was none other than Baba Kinaram himself.

One who uncovers the secret of life
    from within, from without
and from all around
        learns of God and Godhood, both.

Chapter 9 Tradition

BABA KINARAM

As legend tells us, in the 16th century, Baba Kinaram was making his way to the top of a hill in the Girnar Mountains when he met an old *sadhu*. It was a solitary place. The *sadhu* was eating a piece of meat and offered some to Baba Kinaram, who, being a Vaishnava, did not eat meat. After some hesitation, Baba Kinaram received the meat with grace and ate it. At that very moment he acquired omniscience. He knew by intuition that the old *sadhu* before him was Bhagwan Dattatreya himself.

In this story, Baba Kinaram is said to have been wandering in what the scriptures call the *"unmani state,"* searching for truth. Baba Bhagwan Ramji de-

▣ Baba Kinaram ▣

scribed this condition as "when the seeker is neither sleeping nor awake, neither conscious nor unconscious, neither accepting nor relinquishing and experiencing neither 'being' nor 'nonbeing.' At that time, being one with *prana*, the life force, the seeker is in ecstasy."

Baba Kinaram roamed for some time in this exalted state of consciousness. He came into the presence of the Master, Bhagwan Dattatreya, again
and again and received many teachings. As he meditated on the self, he experienced that nothing in the world is either big or small. In *samadhi*, the state
of self-concentration, he realized only pure knowledge, a harmonious view
of the universe, the oneness of everything. Bhagwan Dattatreya called this
knowledge the immortal seed. After knowing it, it is never lost, and no sorrows develop in the *sadhaka*, the seeker.

Knowing the difference between self and nonself, Baba Kinaram saw that
everything—the body, as well as the universe—consists of five elements and
three *gunas*. "The human body is a rare thing," he said, "and only when God
completed the creation of the human body was he satisfied."

Learning to transcend his mind with the help of *pranayama* and *pranava*,
Baba Kinaram reposed in his own inner self. As he resonated *Om*
continuously on the breath and listened to the internal sounds of the breath,
eventually awareness of breath, *prana*, and sound disappeared, and only pure
enlightened mind was left. Baba Kinaram had received the grace of Bhagwan
Dattatreya and absorbed his teachings.

He left the mountain and wandered farther. The Goddess of Hingalaj
appeared before him as a Divine Mother, offering him food as to a son, and
told him to go to Varanasi. There he should stay, she told him, as she herself
would be residing in Krim Kund.

Following her instructions, Baba Kinaram left the solitude of the forests
and set out for Varanasi. When he arrived, he walked along the banks of
the Ganges until he came to a cremation ground, a famous funeral *ghat*. He
saw a yogi, tall and dark skinned, feeding roasted chickpeas to the skulls of
skeletons lying in the cemetery. In a playful mood, Baba Kinaram ordered
the skulls to stop eating. They stopped. The yogi looked at him and said in a
rather sly tone, "I am hungry. Can you feed me?"

Baba Kinaram, facing the Ganges, said, "O' Ganga, please give us food
for three."

Three large fish jumped out of the river into the *dhuni*. When the yogi
saw the fish in the fire, he was silent for a moment. Then he pointed his finger and cried, "There's a dead body floating in the river!"

Baba Kinaram responded, "No, he's not dead. He's alive." He called the body, which slowly floated to the bank of the river and stood up.

The three persons now sitting together in the cemetery ate the roasted fish.

After their meal, Baba Kinaram told the so-called dead man to go to his village where his relatives had put him into the river because he had died of smallpox. Instead, the man requested to stay with Baba Kinaram, who granted his wish. The yogi, saying that his name was Baba Kaluram, took Baba Kinaram to Krim Kund, exactly where the Mother Goddess had asked him to go. Telling Baba Kinaram that the ashram was now his, Baba Kaluram disappeared.

Since Baba Kinaram was omniscient, he knew that this experience had been a test. He knew that Bhagwan Dattatreya had appeared to him again, disguised as Baba Kaluram, to be sure his teachings had taken root. During the long years of Baba Kinaram's life, until his *samadhi* at the age of 151, he always felt the close presence of the Goddess of Hingalaj and Bhagwan Dattatreya at Krim Kund.

Baba Kinaram's experiences took a turn at that time in history. The Moghul Empire was destroying much of India's culture. It was using the caste system to disempower common people until only a very rigid upper class had any social status. Baba Kinaram's sympathies were with the poor and disenfranchised. Witnessing their suffering, he became engaged in social movements to help them. A true visionary, he appointed people from lower castes to key positions in the various ashrams he established, upsetting the prevailing custom. Further, he introduced initiation of females into the *Aghor* tradition and welcomed whole families to do practices. In these ways he resisted the orthodox restraints that were causing so much suffering. His good works became legendary.

At Krim Kund, Baba Kinaram lit the *dhuni* that has been kept alive through the centuries and is still alight today. Many people find help by visiting the ashram and taking some of the sacred ashes from this fire. Baba Kinaram's influence was so great that many stories of his life still abound.

Today Krim Kund is a place of great spiritual energy. More than 60 richly elaborate *samadhis*, tombs of *Aghor* ascetics, are on the premises. Wide verandahs create lovely cool spaces all around them and overlook tropical trees and lush gardens. Anyone who comes to the ashram feels a sense of timelessness.

The intricate graceful designs of classical Indian architecture distinguish the two main buildings on the ashram grounds. Central to all buildings is a large pond from Baba Kinaram's time, which he charged with healing powers in answer to the needs of the sick. Even now, mothers bring their ailing children, or entire families come to bathe. Smooth rocks shore up this big square expanse of water so that it looks inviting from the verandahs. Profound silence pervades the water, the stones and the air itself.

This was the place to which the Divine Mother, whom Baba called Annapurna, directed the boy named Bhagwan.

BABA'S GURU

Years went by filled with Baba's multilevel activities. Whoever came in contact with him had a story to tell. In February 1978, Baba's guru, Baba Rajeshwar Ram, expressed his wish to install Baba in his place as Mahant at the Kinaram Sthal, another name for Krim Kund, Baba Kinaram's ashram and the seat of the *Aghor* lineage in northern India. Although the world didn't know it, it had always been clear to Baba Rajeshwar Ram that Baba was the reincarnation of Baba Kinaram. In response, very politely, Baba requested his guru not tie him down with this responsibility, for it could be a hindrance in his social work.

Both the old guru and the young guru were aware of the roles they were playing in this drama. The next day Baba appeared before his guru with a radiant child. He asked Baba Rajeshwar Ram to install the boy on the seat of *Aghor*. Baba Rajeshwar Ram looked at the child and nodded approval. All the necessary ceremonies and formalities were performed. The child was called Siddhartha Gautam Ram and installed on the seat of *Aghor*, becoming the 12th Mahant in the lineage of Baba Kinaram. He was only two years old.

On February 10, 1978, Baba Rajeshwar Ram left his body. He had already sent a messenger to Baba, telling him of his imminent death. The news spread like wildfire, and masses of people began to pour into the ashram to pay homage to the "great one." Following *Aghor* tradition, the ashramites

dug a rectangular pit in the center of the compound. In the presence of many saints, sages and admirers, they placed Baba Rajeshwar Ram's body in the pit sitting in lotus position, facing north. They filled the pit with salt and oil cakes, then closed it with slabs. They constructed a cement platform on top. A human-sized statue of Baba Rajeshwar Ram now sits on

> ☀ Discerning the beauty
> of our inner being
> unravels the secret of God.

the platform. This became the 61ᵗʰ *samadhi* shrine of the "great ones" in the compound of Baba Kinaram Ashram. People who were present still talk about the strange light, the lovely fragrance and the humming that permeated the atmosphere at the time of Baba Rajeshwar Ram's *samadhi*.

New responsibilities awaited Baba. Besides overseeing the upbringing of the very young Siddhartha Gautam Ram, Baba needed to turn his attention to the dilapidated condition of the old ashram. Since Baba Rajeshwar Ram had become introverted for the last several years, the walls, roofs and many structures were in disrepair. The garden had turned into a jungle. Very soon, with Baba's enthusiasm, new life breathed into this ancient place, and all structures were restored.

Siddhartha Gautam Ram resided across the river in the compound of Sri Sarveshwari Samooh with Baba. Many ashramites showered the young Mahant with love and respect. On the grounds, a school was flourishing where children from all backgrounds were receiving an education. Baba continued to oversee management of Baba Kinaram Ashram while Siddhartha Gautam Ram was in school and training under his guidance.

Although Sri Sarveshwari Samooh now manages Baba Kinaram Ashram, each retains its separate identity. The Sri Sarveshwari Samooh ashrams are active in social reforms and carrying out the organization's programs, and Baba Kinaram Ashram is a pilgrimage site for thousands of people seeking Divine intervention in their lives. *Sadhus* not only of the *Aghor* lineage but also of all traditions come for silent intensive *sadhana*. The legacy of Baba Kinaram and other *Aghoreshwars*, in the view of those who travel to his ashram, is to bring miraculous healing and grant boons. The power of the *samadhi* shrines lingers in their hearts.

No other place in India has more than 60 boon-granting *samadhi* shrines of enlightened beings. The sacred fire in the ashram compound, which has burned continuously from the time of Baba Kinaram, is witness to the continuity of this great lineage.

Sri Sarveshwari Samooh, with its hundreds of branches and centers engaged in social work, is like the arms and legs of the body of the *Aghor* tradition taking action in the world, while Baba Kinaram Ashram is like the womb in which its spiritual depth resides. This was the reason Baba chose not to change the nature of the established order. Shrouded with mystery and antiquity, Baba Kinaram Ashram calls to the true seeker as a source of inspiration for spiritual pursuits.

MAITRAYANI YOGINI

Lakhraji Devi, the mother of Baba, was heartbroken when her only son left the house years ago in search of the Divine. Not long before that, her husband had left his body, and then her only son, the support for her old age, turned his back to worldly aspirations. She remained in the ancestral home, hoping for her son's return. Baba was constantly aware of her feelings and tried several times to convince her of his destiny as a *sadhu*. But a mother's heart knows no boundaries. Although Baba would not reappear before her because of the pain of rekindling her sentiments, she did not give up.

After construction of the ashram in Varanasi, Lakhraji Devi would come to the gate and look at Baba from a distance. She would leave only after getting a glimpse of her son. She continued this routine for a long time. Slowly she came to grips with the reality of the situation. She had witnessed her son showering compassion on the multitude and understood he truly belonged to the world and should not be confined to the life of a householder.

When Baba was convinced that his mother's physical presence and sentiments would not be an obstacle, he agreed to have her move into a room at the ashram. By now she was old and weak, and some resident women took care of her needs. Gradually, Lakhraji Devi grew more distant from worldly matters and was happy to be where she could at least catch sight of her son from a distance. A few years later, she expressed the wish to be initiated as a renunciate. Baba declined. After several requests, on March 21, 1985, one of Baba's disciples, Gurupad Shambhav Ramji, initiated her and gave her the *Aghor* mantra. Lakhraji Devi took the new name Maitrayani Yogini, lovingly called Mataji.

After her initiation, Mataji sold all her jewelry and land holdings and donated the proceeds to build a school for girls and rest houses for travelers in Baba's birthplace. Her room became a place of pilgrimage for women visiting the ashram who needed solace. Spending her days in various modes of worship, prayers and quietude, Mataji consoled many women burdened with pain from the loss of a child or husband. Her simple words were healing, especially since she had suffered the same losses in her life. Her words were not lip service; they came from the depth of her lifelong agony and experience.

On one of my visits to the ashram, at the time I had become a monk, I went to pay my respects to Mataji. Someone had told her that I had served Baba when he was in the U.S. There was a sparkle in her eyes when she saw me. Caressing my forehead, she offered me sweetmeats and asked many questions about the States and Baba's routine while there. She was as simple as a child. When I began to take leave of her, she pulled a 20 rupee bill from under her pillow and with a gentle smile said, "Buy some sweetmeats with this for Babuva when he is in America."

I will never forget that sweetness. An ocean of love overflowed from her gentle eyes and mother's heart.

Greater than the light of the sun,
the moon and the fire
is the light of gracefulness,
the light of good conduct.
This shining light is pure,
transcendental and pervades all worlds.

Chapter 10   A New Turn

NEW DELHI

In early 1982, Baba visited New Delhi, staying with a devotee, Mr. S.N. Sinha, a member of Parliament. Baba arrived on a day when Mrs. Gandhi's secretary was at Mr. Sinha's residence. The secretary asked Baba to grant the Prime Minister an audience. Although tired from his daylong journey, Baba did not want to refuse this request, which was made with great humility. He left immediately for the meeting with Mrs. Gandhi. In commenting on these events, Baba said, "Whether one likes the policy of the occupant or not, one should always have respect for the seat." Baba was referring to the seat of the ruler of the country or the ruling authority. He was always alert to rules of conduct. He would say, "By honoring rules of conduct, you maintain peace in your society." In this simple way, he taught us how to live.

During this visit to New Delhi, Baba became ill. He spent 10 days in Ram Manohar Hospital. He was discharged, but within a short

■ Baba in New Delhi ■

time he was in another hospital, the Indian Institute of Medical Sciences. Regardless of his illness, wherever Baba went, politicians, business leaders and other well-wishers visited him. Baba decided to leave New Delhi and return to Varanasi. Everyone tried to persuade him to stay in the hospital long enough to complete treatment, but he had made up his mind. This period marked the beginning of the decline of Baba's health.

The doctors said that Baba had diabetes and should be treated right away, but he refused to take insulin, which was the only sure treatment. Many doctors and practitioners of alternative medicine, including homeopathic and Ayurvedic, came to see Baba over the next four years, but to no avail. His health did not improve. Nevertheless, until 1986 he continued to visit his other ashrams, but not as frequently. The doors of the ashrams were always open as usual, and Baba was available to visitors at certain times every day.

Many close observers were convinced that this was the start of a new stage of life for Baba. All kinds of rumors, theories, stories and concerns persisted. Some people felt that Baba had a calculated purpose in mind. With Sri Sarveshwari Samooh already well organized, with established ideals and successors appointed to carry out its mission in the future, they speculated that perhaps Baba felt it was time to withdraw a bit. Not many people believed he was ill.

An old-timer retorted to the questions of a worried skeptic: "You think Baba is sick? I have seen him touch the sick on their deathbeds and bring them back to life. I have seen him heal others by his mere glance or a few incoherent words mumbled under his breath, or even by a scolding. It is the same Baba, yet you tell me he is sick? It is his play, nothing but his play. Nothing happens until he wishes it to happen in a certain way."

Another eyewitness in the ashram said, "One day a medical doctor visited Baba and gave him some tablets, then a homeopathic doctor came who also gave him some small white pills and some liquid in a vial, then an Ayurvedic doctor came and gave him some powders and pills. After everyone left, Baba took all the pills, powders and liquids that were his supply for a week, put them in his bowl and swallowed them in a single gulp."

Baba listened to everyone and made each person feel as if he or she were his most important advisor at the time, but Baba always did what he wished.

No one knows any specific reason for his unpredictable behavior.

In early May 1986, all Baba's well-wishers conferred and decided to take him to the United States for the finest treatment available. Instead of agreeing, Baba gave up all treatment and decided to undergo his own brand of naturopathy. A straw hut was erected in the ashram compound where Baba would lie on a bed made of sand. All he wore were banana leaves and at times not even them. No visitors were allowed near him except a few caretakers. In the scorching heat, Baba continued this treatment for two months.

One caretaker related: "This was the most intense time I experienced around Baba. His behavior was most unpredictable. He would refuse to eat for days. For a whole week he said no one could enter his hut with clothes on. This restriction limited the number of people who were trying to come close to him! Sometimes his behavior made it seem as if he had gone mad, but no one dared to talk sense to him. A strange light emanated from his face. At times it was very difficult even to look at him. A fragrance from some unknown source permeated the hut."

To many it may have seemed just another play of Baba, but others saw it as illogical behavior resulting from an unstable mind. Without Baba's knowledge, a prominent psychologist was called in to evaluate him. When the psychologist came, he sat on the verandah to wait. Baba sometimes rested on that verandah after his stroll in the compound. When Baba sat on his chair, he acted surprised to find a stranger nearby. Without any introduction, Baba began to address the psychologist:

"You bought your car in Calcutta?"

"Yes, Baba," he answered.

"Was the driver of your car wearing a green shirt?"

"Yes, Baba."

"You had a new paint job done on your car?"

"Yes, Baba."

It was quite a scene to witness. The psychologist was shocked, for he could not understand how Baba was saying all this without having met him or seeing his car, which was parked outside the ashram, out of Baba's sight.

Baba continued: "In front of your ancestral home, there used to be a giant pipal tree where stray animals would graze."

"Yes, Baba."

Baba went on to describe events that had happened to the psychologist in the past. They talked about other things, as well. Finally the psychologist prostrated himself before Baba and asked for his leave. Coming out of the ashram he said to us, "You people called me to evaluate an ocean in fear of its overflowing! This ocean is self-contained. It never loses its grace."

In July, as Guru Purnima approached, attention turned for a while to the usual preparations for this annual festival. But Baba became worse. He went to Benares Hindu University Hospital, but on Guru Purnima, against the advice of the doctors, he returned to the ashram to be available for the masses who had gathered to pay respect to their guru. Baba sat for six hours in one place and gave *darshan* to thousands. A group of doctors remained in the ashram compound that day to look for any unprecedented turn in his health. In the afternoon, they advised Baba to rest and cancel the remaining program, but he would not listen. He gave an unforgettable discourse, speaking for an hour without showing any sign of poor health.

❁ Be afraid of yourself
and no one else.
It will lead you to greatness.

After the daylong ordeal, Baba was much worse. His kidneys were severely damaged. He went to hospitals in Bombay, Madras and Calcutta for treatment, but his kidneys failed completely, and he had to go on regular dialysis. There was a facility in Patna, but Baba's health was declining so fast that everyone knew something more had to be done, and soon.

The doctors advised Baba to go at once to the U.S. before his condition deteriorated even more. At first he was not ready to accept that, but many of his followers appeared before him in tears and said, "Baba, we know that you are not attached to your body, but we are! We still need you. Won't you go for our sake?"

Ever sensitive to the tears of others, Baba finally yielded, saying, "This is your body. Do whatever you please with it."

VISIT TO THE WEST

On October 27, 1986, Baba arrived in the U.S. A small group of associates escorted him, including a disciple, Gurupad Shambhav Ramji, and Dr. K.K. Tripathi, a nephrologist from Benares Hindu University Institute of Medical Sciences.

Waiting at John F. Kennedy International Airport were a few disciples who lived in the U.S. I was one of them. I had a travel business in Northern California. My visits to Baba in India invariably had been limited to a few hours, then Baba always sent me away, smiling gracefully at me as I went. Hearing that he was going to New York, I left everything to join him. I thought it was a perfect opportunity to be close to him for an extended period and to be of service. I wanted to be in his company day in and day out!

A few people from the Indian consulate in New York arrived at the airport, then other devotees showed up from New Jersey, Memphis and Washington, D.C. We introduced ourselves to each other while anticipating Baba's arrival. Rana K.D.N. Singh, who was Baba's host during a previous visit to the U.S. and Mexico, had been busy making the necessary arrangements for Baba's medical treatment in New York. His wife, Mrs. Kamala Singh, had traveled to India to accompany Baba on the flight. An ambulance was standing by to transport Baba to Brookdale Medical Center in Brooklyn.

Baba's plane landed but there was no time for ceremonies. The long journey had taken its toll on his body, which had swelled with fluid. He required dialysis immediately. He went directly to the hospital, where the doctors quickly determined that he needed a kidney transplant. Baba was to remain in the hospital and stay on dialysis until he was stronger, possibly a month or more, when he would be ready for the transplant.

The people who had escorted Baba from India and those who had come to be with him from different parts of the U.S. were staying at Mr. Singh's residence in Manhattan, which was quite far from the hospital. I asked Baba if we should look for a more convenient location.

He said, "That would be nice, but where are you going to find a place? If it were India you could go to a nearby temple and ask for permission to camp out for a while." He pointed out the window and continued, "Well, how about going to that church and checking to see if a place is available for us there?"

I looked, and sure enough a church was visible from Baba's room. I said neither yes nor no to his face, but I rejected his suggestion in my mind with, "This is the U.S., not India. Here you can't go to a church and camp out for a while!"

Rajendra Rai and J.P., two of Baba's disciples, walked the neighborhood with me for the next three days seeking a For Rent sign, but to no avail. During this long pursuit, they would tell me stories of Baba in the old days. How carefree, healthy and happy-go-lucky he used to be! These two people had known him for many years, and listening to their experiences brought tears to my eyes. My heart filled with the sweetness of their stories.

On the fourth day, I remembered Baba's suggestion about the church, and out of curiosity we walked up to it and rang the bell. A very pleasant lady opened the door and talked with us, showing a lot of concern. After listening to our story she said, "If you had come here just three days ago, we definitely would have given you the gardener's apartment in the complex. We were looking for someone to live there in exchange for gardening, but now someone has taken it and is moving in tomorrow." I was amazed and at the same time upset with myself for rejecting Baba's advice to look for a place at the church next door. First lesson!

The next day we went to a realtor and found an apartment nearby, but she told us we might have to wait, since someone else had first choice on it. Walking around for four days in the cold of New York had already put a strain on us, and our frustration was building. We entered a cafe and sat to have a cup of coffee to shake off the fatigue of the day before returning to Baba. I mentally asked Baba's help to bring this ordeal to an end. At that very moment, the realtor entered and sat next to us. While we drank our coffee, she said, "You people really need a home. Why don't you come to my office right now and we will finish the necessary paperwork."

Our eyes brightened. Within an hour we were walking back to the hospital with a key to an apartment where we all could stay and be near Baba. Baba called me into his room and said with a smile, "Is the place good enough?" How did he know that today we had found a place?

The next week, the doctors released Baba from the hospital, but he had to go back every three days for dialysis. Baba occupied the bedroom in the apartment, and eight of us made the living room our abode. A few days after we moved in, a local religious group rented the apartment below us and converted it into a church. Although it became very noisy with all the singing and drumming, Baba loved it. "I am living in a church building," he said to a devotee calling from India.

A SAGE IN NEW YORK

Baba never changed his way of dressing or his habits, regardless of where he found himself. In New York, he wore his old *lungi* and sandals, as he had in India, no matter the weather. He did wear a sweater, as well as his shawl, and carried a cane, which he wielded in a distinctive manner. He topped it off with a pair of large sunglasses. No one thought about attracting undue attention on the streets of New York, where hardly anyone takes a second look.

At first, Baba did not go about on the streets as he was regaining his strength. Later, he would see a lot of Manhattan and other areas, but for now he remained indoors most of the time. I had never had a chance to be with Baba so much. His body was weak, but his presence exuded a strange sense of strength and calmness. He barely slept. One of us had to be with him all the time to stroke his feet, help him out of bed or do whatever he needed. Three of us took turns throughout the night.

Something was always going on in Baba's room. Occasionally he requested a story or some narrative on politics, world affairs, the country and its people and so on, depending on who was in attendance. Sitting or lying on his bed, Baba appeared to be listening to the story, but at the same time he seemed somewhere else. At times he was very alert and said something pertinent, adding lines to the story or commenting on the narrative, then he would fall back into his state of absorption. If the narrator stopped, thinking Baba had fallen sleep, within a few moments Baba would say, "Oh, help me get up."

Sit up...lie down...sit up...lie down! Occasional laughter, mock scoldings, whispers, murmurs, a few words flung here and there—this was the way the whole night would pass. The attendant would be exhausted and starving for sleep when the shift was over. The next attendant would enter, and the scene would continue as before.

During the day many visitors came. Baba would meet each person and listen to his or her story. Most were seeking Baba's blessing in solving personal problems, and Baba gave freely of his grace. Devotees would call from India, and Baba would speak to them all, at any time. Days passed in this way as he slowly regained his strength for surgery.

Meanwhile, Baba was very interested in the U.S. and Soviet peace talks that were taking place. Every day his visitors employed at the United Nations briefed him. Often he could be heard murmuring, "Peace between these two countries is very important for the human race." Many of his followers speculated that Baba, to be an influence for good on world affairs, had chosen this crucial time to be in New York. With those major powers engaged in peace talks, the welfare of the whole human race lay in the balance.

For the first time, the two powers signed a pact for nuclear disarmament, and Baba seemed much moved and pleased. His body was suffering through various stages of illness, but who knows what was happening in his inner being, what work was taking place within?

Now the search began for a kidney donor. Baba was taken to Mount Sinai Hospital in Manhattan, where Dr. Lewis Burrows, a renal transplant surgeon, took charge of his case. Hundreds of people in India expressed a desire to donate one of their kidneys to Baba. Fortunately, an attendant who had come with Baba from India, Kaushal Singh, was found to be the most suitable donor. His blood type matched Baba's closely because he came from Baba's extended ancestral family. Kaushal Singh was grateful that an organ of his could be of use in restoring Baba's health.

On December 10, 1986, Baba received a new kidney. The transplant was a success. A wave of happiness spread through his followers and well-wishers, but Baba's stay in the hospital was not one of his favorite times. Hospital policy did not allow even a family member to remain there overnight. Baba insisted that one of us stay. With much effort, we were able to convince the administration to allow one of Baba's attendants to remain with him as a translator, for Baba did not speak English. Further, we had to be there to convince Baba to let the nurses routinely draw blood. Otherwise, he would throw a tantrum, behaving like a child.

One morning I arrived at the hospital and found Baba sitting on his bed. Pointing to a few drops that had escaped during the drawing of his blood, he said, almost in tears, "Early in the morning when it is time to meditate, they come collecting blood like the tax collector. She drew a whole jug full of blood from me! This is what happens when you are not around. That fellow who was with me last night is a coward. He can't even speak on my behalf. Send him home. I am so happy you are here now."

※ **The guru is not a body. The guru is the very life force.**

Looking at J.P.'s face, I could tell he had had a rough night. Baba's blood sugar had to be checked, and every time it was an ordeal. Nurses would complain, and the attendant had to reconcile the differences. Dr. Burrows would say, "Baba is at war with the nurses." Nonetheless, all the nurses loved him because once in a while he would greet them with a gracious smile that was enough to win their hearts forever.

Mr. Krishna Verma, one of Baba's devotees living in New Jersey, offered his home for Baba's recuperation. Straight from the hospital, he brought Baba and the entourage of eight people to his home. This created a problem for Baba, however, because he had to go to the hospital for routine checkups, and the 70-mile trip was very uncomfortable for him.

One day as we were sitting in the hospital waiting room, Baba said to me, "Go and find an apartment nearby while I wait here. I won't be returning to New Jersey; it's too far. Make sure the apartment is not too far from the hospital and the river is visible."

This request seemed totally off-the-wall to me.

Noticing hesitation in my eyes, Baba said, "At least try. Doubting before you have even tried is a weakness in the makeup of your personality."

I left the scene with a bow. I knew how difficult it was to find an apartment with neither references nor a job in the city. Now he was asking me to find an apartment in the next couple of hours. But I had experienced the way our last house hunt had gone. "Listen to Baba and do not discard his suggestions so lightly," I told myself. Lesson two!

J.P., a friend named Rosemary and I went to the hospital cafeteria to have a cup of coffee and figure out a way to find another apartment while Baba waited, ready to move into a place we hadn't even located yet. We were at a complete loss as to where to begin. I went to the restroom while J.P. got more coffee for us.

In the restroom, my eyes fell on a discarded hospital newsletter on the sink. Out of curiosity I picked it up and skimmed through it. In the classifieds section, I noticed a listing that read, "Apartment for sublet, immediate occupancy, walking distance from the hospital."

Rosemary called the number, and a man answered and said, "If you come right now, we could talk about it; but I am leaving for Europe in the morning." We practically ran there. A young doctor had moved into another apartment complex and was stuck with two months' rent still to pay on his old lease. While checking the place, I looked through the bedroom window, and to my surprise I could see the river. The man asked for a $500 deposit and handed over the keys. We were amazed at the way events had unfolded.

When we returned to the hospital, Baba was finished with his checkup and asked with a smile, "Did you find the apartment? I am tired and could use a nap."

Mr. Verma had a piece of foam in his van and a sheet to cover it, so we took it with us as we rode to the apartment. Baba was very pleased with the place. He did not forget to notice the river through the window. As he reclined on the make-do bed, he covered himself with his shawl and with an innocent smile said, "I am going to take a nap; you people take care of the rest." He fell asleep, and within a few moments loud snores echoed throughout the apartment.

The apartment proved very convenient for follow-up visits to the hospital and was walking distance to the doctor's office. Baba's health improved rapidly. He began to go for walks and take short rides. Amar Singh would come every evening and drive Baba around the city.

Picking up his cane as he left the apartment, Baba asked, "Amar Babu, where are you taking me today?"

Amar answered, "Baba, I would like to show you Fifth Avenue, Central Park and other rich neighborhoods of the city."

"What does a poor *sadhu* from India have to do with Fifth Avenue and the neighborhoods of the rich and powerful? Show me where the poor live," Baba said in a very soft and sweet voice.

Baba loved touring Harlem. He would often remark, "See how lively the inhabitants of this area are? There is a sense of community here, and people don't seem to be scared of each other." In contrast to this, at the apartment complex where we were staying no one seemed to know or acknowledge the next-door neighbors. Harlem seemed much friendlier. People would wave and smile at each other, walk hand-in-hand or with arms wrapped around each other's waist. Baba loved the fact that no one seemed to be rushing to get anywhere. He also noticed the homeless and the derelicts in the streets. He noticed the attractive but empty buildings boarded up, condemned for habitation even though the homeless were visible hauling their grocery carts loaded with their belongings or lying on the streets exposed to the intense winter.

Baba was surprised when he heard that some of these buildings could be had for a token one dollar provided they could be brought up to code and taxes paid. "With so many resources available in this country," he asked, "why wouldn't someone or some agency tackle the problem of the homeless in the city or let them live in some of these buildings? They could not be worse off or less safe than in the open streets!" No one seemed to have an answer to his innocent inquiries.

Sometimes Baba would take Ashok Choubey, a student studying in the U.S., along for a walk and then board a bus. As the hours passed, the others at the apartment would begin to worry. After a time Baba would return filled with stories. Ashok would relate, "Baba just wanted to get on the bus and go, not knowing where it was headed. We stayed on until the final stop and then turned around and came back. We never got off."

Baba loved to watch people in an unobtrusive way. He enjoyed this kind of anonymity. In India, by contrast, everywhere he went, crowds were waiting to fling themselves at his feet.

Often Baba would sit in the lobby of our huge apartment complex, alone or with an attendant, and watch people rushing to work in the morning and returning home in the evening. The rest of the day the building would seem empty. "Where are the children of these people?" he would ask. "What about their parents and grandparents? Where do they live? Who takes care of them?" There seemed to be no answers to the questions asked by this simple and caring person.

One day, Sarah Lewin, a resident of the complex, approached Baba as he was sitting in the lobby. I was standing by his side when she stopped in front of us. As she stood there silently, Baba looked at her and smiled. She said to me, "I feel so much peace just by looking at him. Who is he?"

I explained Baba to Sarah in a few words and invited her to visit us for a cup of tea. From then on she would come with her husband and daughter almost every evening to sit with Baba.

One evening as Baba was in the lobby, Sarah entered holding X-rays. With her was her eight-year-old daughter Rachel on crutches. She reported that Rachel had fallen in her dance class and fractured a bone. Rachel was standing very close to Baba. He reached over and touched her shin, saying, "No, she does not have a fracture. The X-ray machine must be faulty. Go home and give her some warm milk."

❀ Speech is the best weapon in the armory of the self.

In its wise use lies the success of life.

It was time for Baba to go and have a cup of tea himself.

Within half an hour Sarah entered our apartment, totally surprised, saying, "Rachel is walking and jumping around as usual as if nothing happened." I smiled and without saying anything led her to sit near Baba and brought her a cup of tea. Baba acted as if he had nothing to do with Rachel's miraculous recovery.

During the conversation he asked Sarah about her mother. She said, "We don't get along and have not spoken to each other for the past five years."

"One should maintain a good relationship with one's parents," Baba murmured.

Sarah returned to her apartment and in the morning came to see Baba to report that her mother had called, and they had a good conversation. Much seemed to have healed between her and her mother with this call. Baba's unconditional grace showered Sarah and her family.

Rachel came to Baba one day with her mother. She wanted to ask him some questions. Baba encouraged her, saying with a smile, "What do you want to know, baby?"

"Baba, I have heard people like you can perform miracles, is it true?"

The word miracle does not exist in my vocabulary. This word exists only for those who think they cannot do certain things. You can do anything you want to do as long as you do not doubt your success. Doubt inhibits us from performing certain deeds. Being doubtful of our abilities, we label certain deeds as miracles.

"Baba, can you be at two places at the same time?" was Rachel's second innocent question.

"It is possible, baby," was his short reply, then he fell into one of those quiet moods with his eyes closed and body swaying.

Events like these would happen all the time, but Baba would never take credit for unusual occurrences, acting if he had nothing to do with anything at all. Baba's disciples in India tell numerous stories about his direct intervention in one form or another in times of dire need. "Baba always responds in different disguises when a devotee in need summons him, irrespective of time and place," claimed one of his devotees.

Eventually we had to find another home. One day as we were sitting in the lobby of our current apartment building, a man holding two little puppies approached us. He introduced himself as Bernard, the caretaker. Referring to Baba, he said to me, "I have been watching him from a distance ever since I noticed his presence in this complex. He exudes so much peace."

I translated these words for Baba who looked at Bernard with so much compassion in his eyes. I find it hard to describe his look with words. I told Bernard of our need for another apartment in this vicinity for a couple of months. He said quite a number of apartments in the complex were left empty by previous occupants who still held leases on them. When we parted, he said that maybe he could arrange for us to shift to another apartment. The next day he gave us a key to one in the same building and said, "There is no need to pay any rent."

Events like this made one think, "How do such things happen?"

Days passed, then weeks. Every moment with Baba was distinct. There was never a dull moment. If nothing was happening, you could be sure you would be sent to the hospital to talk with Dr. Burrows about Baba's questions and concerns.

Baba was feeling better, but the doctors advised a very strict diet. We had to track his caloric intake. In addition to drugs to prevent his body from rejecting the newly transplanted kidney, Baba was taking medication for high blood pressure and diabetes. His eating habits were subject to his moods, and this caused great concern for the attendants. Some days he would eat enough, some days nothing. He would eat only Indian food, which had no recorded measurements of calories, sodium, potassium and so forth.

Baba would listen to the results of his blood tests very intently. Although the doctors would say not to worry if his numbers were a bit up or down, Baba would express concern and find another excuse to send us to the hospital to talk to Dr. Burrows.

Sometimes just two of us would be attending Baba. A few nights in a row could pass without our getting any sleep. Somehow during these days and nights I never felt tired. I had a strange feeling of lightness and freshness. Baba would tell stories of the days when he used to wander on the banks of the Ganges. He would hum an old song or even crack jokes.

Sometimes he would behave like a child and at other times like a mother, father, brother or friend. He would talk about *sadhana*, practices and mantra, and at such moments you had to be very alert, for his voice would be very soft, almost inaudible. His words seemed to be coming from his very depths. If asked to repeat his words, he would never respond.

At this time Gurupad Shambhav Ramji, who had accompanied Baba from India, was monitoring Baba's blood sugar and giving him insulin, and I was administering his other medications. Baba's health seemed stabilized.

Although the doctors advised spending more time in the U.S., Baba wanted to go back to India.

RETURN TO INDIA

Baba and his party of friends arrived in India on March 19, 1987. I was fortunate to make this journey with him.

A large crowd of devotees and well-wishers met us at New Delhi airport and took us to Mr. Sinha's residence on Akbar Road. It was a government building allotted to members of Parliament, with a gatekeeper on duty. After Baba had a night's rest, his morning began with a flood of visitors wanting *darshan*. Among them were politicians, bureaucrats, businessmen, office workers and housewives. Baba obliged them equally.

All of a sudden he called me and said, "Outside the gate an old man is sitting. He is hesitant to come in. Go and fetch him; he is an old attendant of mine."

The gate was not visible from where Baba was sitting. I thought maybe he just wanted me out of the room for a while and this was his way of asking me to leave. I casually walked to the gate. To my surprise, an old man in a khaki shirt was sitting under a tree, smoking a *bidi*. I inquired where he was from and if he was here to see Baba.

He said, "Yes, but I was hesitant to enter a building where big officials live."

I escorted him in. Seeing the old man, Baba addressed him in such a sweet voice that the man burst into tears and flung himself at Baba's feet. "This is Banshi Dhar," Baba said. "He has served me well as my attendant in the past." I offered Banshi Dhar a cup of tea, and when he left, I escorted him out of the complex.

I sat with him under a tree while he smoked another cigarette and told this story:

> I have known Baba a long time. It is hard to believe that is the same body. In the old days, three or four of us would massage Baba's body at the same time with all our might, and he would keep daring us to use more strength. Someone would take his arms, someone would take his back or chest, and two people would work on his legs. He had a body

of iron. He looked indestructible. Seeing the same body in such bad shape, I could not help but cry.

I was very poor. Four of my children had neither education nor direction for a career. I went to Baba in despair, running away from my problems. I was in his service for some time without ever telling him of my needs. One day he asked me to go home. I was hesitant. Noticing this, he asked, "Do you have any skills?"

I said, "Baba, if I had any skill why would I wander like a runaway?"

"Do you have any hobby?" Baba inquired musingly. He was in a very good mood.

I did not answer.

He gave me a flower and said, "Go, keep this flower with you when you start something."

Putting that flower carefully in my shoulder bag, I left. A few days later I visited an old friend. He was going to a betting place. I joined him and gambled with a few rupees that I had. Fortunately, I won. I thought maybe this was the effect of the flower in my bag. The next day, I went back to the gambling place and won again. I kept winning. This went on for a month or so. One day my bag mysteriously disappeared; probably someone stole it while we were gambling. After the disappearance of the bag and the flower Baba gave me, I began to lose. From then on, I always lost. I stopped gambling. By now I had saved enough to start a weaving mill for my sons. They are doing very well. It is all the grace of Baba. I am here because of him.

Finishing his story, Banshi Dhar prostrated himself in Baba's direction and bid me farewell.

The next day, Baba moved to another government building on Mathura Road, this one allotted to a member of Parliament who would come there only when Parliament was in session. A doctor in New Delhi took charge of Baba's regular checkups for the next month. Baba began to take walks in the morning and evening, even though many visitors would come all day long to have his *darshan*.

Politicians would gather in the evening and discuss national issues. Baba would listen to them putting forth their points of view, mostly sitting in silence except for an occasional word or two. His presence would work as a buffer for their heated arguments. At times the politicians would heed Baba's suggestions and reconcile on matters of national interest.

In the crowd of *darshan* seekers would be *sadhus*, journalists, lawyers, industrialists, scholars, students, laborers, the rich and poor. Fortune-seekers would come, as well as people who just wanted to get married or receive Baba's approval or mediation in personal matters. He treated everyone equally. Baba did whatever he could to help them all. At times a wave of his hand or a glance would be sufficient consolation.

One night Baba called me into his room and asked me to write these words in my notebook:

> The poor think that riches will make them happy, and the rich think popularity will make them happy. The ones who are popular think more power will make them happy, and the ones in power worry how to stay in power. The unwed think that marriage will bring happiness, and the married ones have their own set of problems. Everyone is unhappy in this world. Oh, God, where is the end of sorrow?

One morning the gardener of the complex came with a bull to pull the lawnmower. After mowing the lawn, he tied the bull to the tree and left. None of the residents or visitors paid any attention to the animal. Baba was sitting on the verandah, receiving people. Around noon, he called one of the attendants and said in a very soft voice to bring water for the *bail*, which means bull in Hindi.

The attendant thought Baba said to bring water for the *vaidya*, which means doctor in Hindi. He brought a glass of water with some sweetmeats on a plate and stood near Baba, trying to figure out who was the doctor among the visitors. Finally he asked Baba.

Stroking his head, Baba said, "Oh, fool, it is not the *vaidya*, but the *bail* that is thirsty." The bull drank three buckets of water. Baba's ever-watchful vision did not fail to notice the needs of the *bail* tied to a rope in the corner of the garden.

At the end of the month, Baba returned to the Varanasi ashram. Before going to his quarters, he went to console the family of Ramji Singh, the main doctor of the ashram hospital, who had died while Baba was away. Then he went to greet his mother. With Baba's return, the ashram began to radiate as before. In his absence, some activities had tapered off, but now the whole machinery went into gear with new energy, and the ashram started several new projects.

Baba chose the young monk Anil Ramji for the doctors to train to take care of his routine medication. Anilji would check Baba's blood sugar several times a day and give him insulin, record his blood pressure at intervals and keep an eye on his food intake. For me, watching Anilji's devotion and alertness to his duty was a lesson in itself. Although at times Baba would pout like a child during blood sugar checkups, Anilji would not give up until he had completed the task. He would make sure Baba had a proper diet.

Several cooks came and went in this process because in trying to please Baba with the taste of food, they would add more fat and salt than prescribed. Baba cleverly played Anilji against the cooks, but I knew it was only to strengthen the young monk's endurance and ability to cope with difficult situations. Anilji would stay firm in his convictions about the things that concerned Baba's health. He would follow Baba like a shadow.

As time went by, with Baba healthy and happy, a new wave of optimism washed over the ashram. Throngs visited every day to receive his *darshan* and Divine intervention in their lives.

However, this relaxed period did not last. In October 1987, Baba's health suffered another dramatic turn, and his doctors in New Delhi concurred that he once again should seek treatment in the U.S.

▣ Baba giving *darshan* ▣

If you feel joy,
      lightness of the heart and mind
    and think of God after meeting someone,
      it is worth keeping
the company of that person.

Chapter 11 Glimpses of Baba in the U.S.

Escorting Baba this trip were senior disciple Priyadarshi Ramji and the young monk Anil Ramji. As before, Baba was rushed to the hospital. Dr. Burrows and Dr. Finegold of Mount Sinai Hospital in New York kept him there for a week, finally deciding that the transplanted kidney was no longer functioning. Baba had to go on dialysis for a couple of months.

Baba stayed again at Mr. Verma's house in New Jersey, where he could have dialysis at the Jersey Shore Medical Center. Dr. Burrows advised a second kidney transplant. The search for a new donor was in progress. Many people were ready to donate a kidney for Baba. Some people even sent blood from India for cross-matching.

One day, Baba said that if Anilji was willing, his kidney might work. Anilji was overjoyed with the prospect of being able to do something for his guru. Baba was right; they found that Anilji was the best match of the whole lot. One could call it a coincidence or a miracle that both times Baba's donor turned out to be someone he had taken with him to the United States.

Poor health did not stop Baba's curiosity and creativity. In addition to being available to see people, he dictated two books in two months. He would be up most of the night contemplating various matters of social reform, as well as dictating material to me for the new books. I finished compiling a book for him in Hindi called "Aghoreshwar Anupranit." After dinner Baba would sit up straight on his bed and start speaking. My job was to note it all down during the night. In the daytime, I read it back to him and then gave the final touches to the book. Sometimes he would have me read scriptures to him as he sat or lay in bed.

At other times Baba would talk about details of various practices, mantras and different views on spiritual understanding. His ways were very unconventional when imparting teachings. He reserved the mornings for long walks,

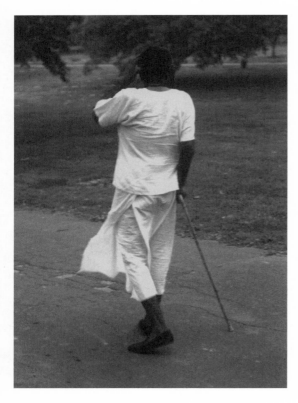

■ Baba in New York City,
taking a stroll in Central Park ■

and in the evenings, he went out for a ride seeing the sights in New Jersey or sat with visitors. His health had stabilized during these months, so the doctors were preparing for the second transplant.

One day we were all sitting around Baba after he had his dialysis. One of us asked, "Baba, it is hard for us to see you suffer so much. We know that you can be well if you wish, so why don't you get well?"

He replied, "Why should I heal myself? If your guru has given you strength to heal, you can do it for this body."

On January 29, 1988, Dr. Burrows transplanted one of Analji's kidneys into Baba's body at Mount Sinai Hospital. The operation was successful, and Anilji was discharged in good condition. Siddhartha Gautam Ram, the young Mahant of the Baba Kinaram Ashram in Varanasi, arrived from India to be with Baba. Now Priyadarshiji, Gautamji and Anilji were all together with the rest of us in Mr. Verma's residence. It was one of our happiest times.

Baba developed a taste for *churra*. This dish of crushed rice and yogurt remained his favorite food, one we could rely on to satisfy him. He seemed to be in much better health, and we were all grateful.

In the night, I was most content sitting on the floor next to Baba's bed when everyone in the house had fallen asleep. Baba would ask me to read to him. Sometimes I would ask him questions, and he would answer in a very soft and sweet voice. Some of these conversations ended up in my notebook that I always kept under his bed. One night, noticing him in a good mood, I asked about *Vaikhari*, a type of speech in Sanskrit that does not emanate from the mind or from heartfelt emotions. Baba gave an example:

> The Master's words are *Vaikhari*; they are the reflections of the deepest self of a realized being. From whatever instrument this power flows, and there are not many such instruments to be found in this world, its effects are irrevocable and irresistible. It always achieves its end sooner or later. The Master's words are not academic, poetic or even philosophical, but even one word from him is capable of redirecting the entire course of one's life.

I was curious to know more "Baba, how does the *Vaikhari* flourish?"

A silence settled for a few moments. At last Baba said, "I can only speak from my own experience." I waited patiently while he seemed to look inside himself. Then Baba went on:

> When the mind acquires stillness, that is the first stage. After the mind begins to stay in stillness, the knowledge that there is a complete stillness within also fades. As long as we are aware of the stillness, there also has to be the awareness of its polar opposite, the restlessness! This is known as the second stage. In the third stage, everything disappears. What remains is nothing.

"Oh, it is the 'void' then," I said.

"No, it is not." Baba waved his arms at me as he spoke. His graceful gestures, the look in his eyes, told more than words.

"What then?"

Baba looked at me with compassion and said:

> It is a state between yes and no or the interlude between happening and nonhappening. It is beyond the understanding of the mind. The limited mind can explain only so much. The higher levels of consciousness can only be experienced, not described. You may call it the fourth stage. It is like a page all written out and yet a page on which something can be written out again. *Vaikhari*, a subtle speech, emerges at this point. A person may say something that appears to be very trivial, but its impact will be farreaching in the life of a listener who has a peaceful and pure consciousness.

Baba was feeling so well that I suggested we might visit Northern California, where I lived before I came to New York to be with him. I thought it would be a good change for Baba to spend time in Redwood country, where the air is clean and the weather is pleasant. To my surprise, Baba agreed. On May 3, 1988, six of us left for San Francisco. En route to Redwood country, we spent two days in Berkeley.

The first day we explored the Marina and Tilden Park. We then drove along Telegraph Avenue. As we neared the University of California campus, Baba asked me to stop. He got out of the car and strolled toward the campus.

⊞ Baba in Garberville ⊞

Then he strolled back, got in the car and asked, "Who are those people digging food from the trash cans? They all look healthy and capable of living a good life." He also noticed young people in strange clothing and with outlandish hairstyles dyed in many colors sprawling along the footpath we had followed. He remarked, "These kids need a lot of attention. They seem to be angry with themselves, as well as their society. This is a world-famous educational institution. Isn't there anyone here who could give a little attention to these young people?"

I said, "Professors at this university are very learned and hardly have time for anything besides the subjects they teach."

"Yes, teaching their subjects they have forgotten themselves, not to mention the young people who need their care and guidance," Baba remarked.

During the next two days, Baba visited the de Young Museum, Golden Gate Park and the Golden Gate Bridge. He was delighted with his expedition. Then we took off north for Garberville, a town in the heart of the Redwoods, near the city of Eureka. After a day of rest, Baba saw the Rockefeller National Forest, where the sight of these majestic trees captivated him. He remarked, "Like austere sages, these trees stand in one place for hundreds of years enduring the sun, rain and storms. Their austerity is great. In such places Divine inspiration enters your being."

While we were in Garberville, many people would gather every evening to meet Baba, ask questions or just imbibe his energy. One day a few people brought some musical instruments and sang *bhajans*. Afterward, Baba encouraged everyone to enhance their practices:

> Singing and chanting cleanse your mind and save you from spending your time in other meaningless activities. It is good. In the beginning I also used to look for God in singing and chanting, but I did not find God there. I found God on the doorsteps of the poor and in the tears of the helpless. It was very easy.

Two weeks passed quickly. On the final day, Baba addressed the gathering, saying:

> You live in a very nice place. Mother Nature is spreading her grace in many ways. Your lakes and rivers are filled with clean water, the air is fragrant and clean, deer roam unafraid. Such places are where seers and sages dwell. To strengthen your society you must inspire in your children a feeling of respect for womankind. If you are able to educate yourselves and your children to have that kind of respect for mothers and for all women in your society, you will prosper, and your culture will be worthy of imitating.

In days to come Baba would refer many times to what he had seen in California.

When we returned to New Jersey, a small group of people arrived to sit with Baba. They were listening to his deeply resonant voice, hoping to speak with him about their problems, but most of all they were basking in the light of his presence.

At Baba's bidding, Anilji and I offered the guests a cup of tea. Some of these people had dropped in from nearby, and others had come from New York, Boston and Washington, D.C.

Baba had been quiet for some time, eyes half closed, his body swaying gently, forgetting himself. He would collect himself now and then to softly murmur, "Oh, hmmmmm."

Someone asked, "Baba, please tell us about Sarveshwari. Who is she? What is her mystery? How should we contemplate her?"

Baba became very silent. Swaying back and forth, with eyes half closed, his deep voice emerged from the very depths of his being. At last he spoke:

> Sarveshwari is the name of the Divine Mother of all. Contemplate her as the absolute whole. She is absolute peace. She is everywhere, in everybody. If we say we can understand her omnipresence, we are wrong because her omnipresence is boundless, limitless. How can anyone measure through speech something that is immeasurable? She is without measure.

Another person asked, "What is her form?"

> Sarveshwari is neither a word nor a form. Manifesting as a mother, she gives birth to all creatures, men and women. Manifesting as a wife, she becomes loveable, soothing, pleasing, auspicious and the source of inspiration to all. She is never depicted holding weapons as other Gods and Goddesses are. Bare of any symbols of violence, her hands are always granting boons and fearlessness. She never produces enemies; instead she inspires all humans to behave toward each other in a friendly manner. She is not an icon of any particular religion. Away from all limits of religion and Gods, she exists on her own. Contemplate her; she is the giver of peace and happiness.

The guests sat quietly, absorbed in stillness.

Sometimes it was quite entertaining to watch Baba as he listened to questions and then answered them patiently. Each person seemed to get what he or she needed most. A gentleman talked during his entire stay about his various spiritual experiences. He kept mentioning the names of different *swamis* he had met and titles of books he had read. He seemed to have a question on his mind, but took a long time getting around to it.

Finally he asked, "Baba, in my meditation I hear all kinds of sounds in my body. Isn't that a sign of the awakening of my kundalini?"

Baba said very sweetly, "I don't know much about the awakening of the kundalini. You must be suffering from gastritis. Take some medication for it."

On one of his daily walks in the suburb where we were staying, Baba kept eyeing the many plastic bags filled with cut grass piled on the curb in front of each house. Ever inquisitive, he asked me what was inside them. I told him that people had mowed their lawns, and a dump truck would come to collect the bags.

"Where does it all go?" he inquired.

I told him that it would probably end up in a landfill.

"People spend so much time, money and energy on growing this grass only to cut it and throw it in landfills? Even the plastic bags look so sturdy," he said.

In a country like India where every green blade of grass is used to feed cattle, it was hard for Baba to comprehend such waste. Finally he said, "Well! It is a sampling of the way people live. They work hard, earn money and spend it on unnecessary things. They practically throw away that hard-earned money on things they could do without."

In May we received an invitation from Dr. Rajendra Rai to visit him in Memphis. Dr. Rai had spent many of his student years in Baba's ashram in Varanasi. His wife, Neelam Rai, grew up there, receiving a lot of love from Baba. In some crucial moments in New York, Mrs. Rai had come to take care of the kitchen, and both husband and wife were a great help during Baba's time in the U.S. Baba, Anilji, Gautamji and I left for Tennessee on May 26.

No matter where Baba was, he adhered to the same routine of long morning walks and an evening drive in addition to making himself available to visitors in the afternoon. In Memphis he visited churches of many denominations. They all fascinated him.

During one drive, Dr. Rai pointed to a building saying, "This is a synagogue."

"What is that?" Baba inquired.

"That is where the Jewish people of our neighborhood pray," Dr. Rai explained.

"Oh, then let us go there." Baba's eyes lit up.

Dr. Rai felt very uncomfortable and said, "You can't just walk in. You must be invited by some members."

Baba could not buy this answer. He said, "If it is a place of worship, why do you have to be invited? If you feel uncomfortable, drop me here." He turned to me and said, "Hari, you will come with me, won't you?" Saying this, he got out of the car and started toward the entrance. We had no choice but to follow.

Baba entered the gate and stopped to look around. No one was in sight, but we could hear sounds coming from the lecture hall. He noticed a basket of yarmulkes and picked one up. Securing the skullcap on his head, he walked in the direction of the sound. We followed suit. Dressed in his *lungi*, a shawl on his upper body and the cap on his head, Baba was quite a sight. We were embarrassed and hesitant, but Baba had no qualms about appearances.

As our party of three entered the lecture hall, all eyes turned to us, and there was pin-drop silence. Baba found an empty chair and sat down; we followed. The rabbi continued his lecture. Afterward, all the worshippers got up and read some prayers. Baba also rose and copied their gestures. It happened several times: getting up, saying prayers, sitting down. Baba followed and so did we. At the end of the service, everyone went to light candles in the other room. No one came to us. We left the hall and went outside.

Dr. Rai's annoyance was clear as he said, "I told you so. See, no one acknowledged us."

To this Baba remarked, "They are busy doing their prayers. Why should they waste time acknowledging us? It is a good place."

The next day Baba wanted to return to the synagogue. In spite of the resistance we put up, he made sure we went. The same thing happened. No one came to say hello. On the third day, Baba insisted we go again. Dr. Rai stayed behind; he had had it. This time, though, the rabbi came to meet us and inquired about us.

I introduced Baba saying, "He is a holy man from India and he really likes this place, enough to come three days in a row."

The rabbi was very moved and introduced us to other members of the congregation. They invited us to come back whenever we wished.

Emerging from the synagogue, Baba was as happy as a child. When we returned home he called Dr. Rai and said, "I have been in this city for only four days and have made more friends than you have made in the last seven years. If you wait for someone to issue you an invitation to get to know each other, thinking that you are different, you will never get to know anyone. How could a meeting happen? Someone has to break the barrier. Your inhibitions keep you from making new friends. They are all just people like you and me."

During our stay in Memphis, whenever Baba would go for a walk, people would wave at him and exchange smiles. Although he did not return to the synagogue, it did not matter. Members of that synagogue lived in our neighborhood and had come to know of him. After we left Memphis, Dr. Rai said they would ask, "When is the holy man coming back?" Dr. Rai has many friends in his neighborhood now.

Baba went back to Memphis on a couple of occasions, and the neighbors who had come to know him in their synagogue always greeted him on his walks.

After the trip to Memphis in 1988, Baba's health stabilized enough to leave for India for some months. He returned to New York in 1989 for more checkups. While there, he stayed at the corner of East 46th Street and 2nd Avenue in Mr. Amar Singh's apartment, across from the United Nations. I made sure I was there as soon as Baba arrived.

As usual, Baba took his morning strolls. One morning, he spotted a very unkempt woman digging through trash bins, collecting beer cans and bottles. She dragged her large plastic bag behind her as she moved from one bin to the next. Baba stopped in the shade of a tree and sat on a bench.

"Go and talk to her," he said to me.

I hesitated and said, "Oh, she is just a street person, Baba, probably under the influence of drugs."

"At least you could go and talk to her. Why are you so hesitant?" He looked at me with his eyes very big.

I was also in a playful mood, so I walked up and said hello with a smile on my face. "There is a holy man from India and he would like to talk to you." I opened the conversation with her in this way, and she looked at me as if she might or might not acknowledge my greeting. "He would be very happy if you gave him a few minutes," I continued.

"Oh sure, why not?" she said as she walked with me to Baba and, coming close to him, sat on the ground with her bag of cans. The stench of stale beer from the bag was almost unbearable.

Baba smiled and joined his palms to greet her. He told me to ask her, "Why are you walking around in such poor condition in such a rich society? You look intelligent and healthy; couldn't you find a job?"

She looked surprised at such a straightforward inquiry, but did not react against it because an innocent foreigner was asking it and, besides, he was a holy man. "I don't believe in this social system. That is why I don't want to contribute to this system by working in it. I make my living by selling what others have thrown away."

"What kind of education do you have?" was the next question I asked at Baba's bidding.

"I have a master's degree in social sciences," she replied.

"Do you go to a church?" Baba continued with even more curiosity.

"No, I don't look for God. I look for the spirit of God," was her indirect reply.

"Yes, Mataji, I agree, that is good," came Baba's rejoinder.

Right then a guard from the hotel appeared on the scene and requested that the woman sit on the bench, not the sidewalk. She was furious and got up saying, "See why I do not believe in this system? I am happy sitting here on the street, but he wants me to sit on the bench." Saying this she bid us farewell and walked off dragging her plastic bag behind her.

Baba also got up and started toward the apartment humming, "I do not look for God, I look for the spirit of God." Reaching home, he asked me to write this sentence in the little notebook. He did not forget to remind me, "See how wise that woman was, and you were discarding her because of her outer appearance."

Later when I shared this incident with some people in the ashram in Varanasi, one of them exclaimed, "You never know who meets Baba in what disguise! That may have been Ma Kali herself having *darshan* with him in New York."

One day I called a cab to take Baba to the hospital for his routine checkup. It was a 15-minute ride from our apartment. The cab driver was in a grouchy mood. He had been on the night shift. At first he got angry and honked at every possible hindrance in his way. By the end of our ride he was quieter and refused to take money from us saying, "I don't know what happened, but I feel very calm. It must be this gentleman sitting beside you. He is so grounded. This world needs more people like him." We thanked the driver and parted. Entering the hospital Baba remarked, "That poor man is over-worked."

You could set the clock by Baba's punctuality in maintaining his schedule. He would go for his walks at exactly 5:30 in the evening, rain or shine. On these walks across from the United Nations, he would notice all the home-less people sitting on benches, leaning against walls or lying on makeshift beds they had devised by flattening cardboard boxes. Although he received no responses in the beginning, he would stop and give them a smile or wave. This went on for a week or so, then he changed his route. When Baba re-sumed his old route, he continued giving the homeless the same attention as before. This time, not only did a few of the people return his glances and waves, they asked, "Where have you been, man?"

Baba responded with a smile, "Oh, I was walking in the other direction." Later it was obvious that some of his "friends on the street" would eagerly await Baba's return at his set hour. You could see them watching for him, looking in the direction from which he usually approached.

"See! Just a few days ago, these people were indifferent. They seemed to have forgotten themselves. Now, with only a little attention and care, they seem not only to stand on their feet, but wait for you to pass and exchange smiles," he said to me.

Strolling the sidewalks of New York, we noticed many abandoned pen-nies, nickels and dimes. Whenever Baba came across a coin on the ground he would move it with his cane and ask me to pick it up. He also would point to nails, glass or any sharp object and have us dispose of them in the street bins.

We would drop all the day's collected coins in the donation boxes of peo-ple who had booths set up across from the United Nations for one cause or another.

Among all the things Baba attended to, he answered letters from devotees in India. In reply to one letter, he had me write:

> Guru can give you everything except experience. He can give you his material wealth, teachings and knowledge, but as far as experience is concerned, you have to earn it by yourself. Knowledge received in the company of your guru and your own experience are the two wings that will help you soar in the sky of time. Following the scriptures and imitating your guru are not enough to solve a particular problem because situations change according to time and place.
>
> Life does not go backwards, nor does it get stuck in the past. It always remains in the present moment heading toward the future. Guru cannot paint the exact picture of the future for you. Yes he can give you a rough idea or a glimpse of it, but in the days to come and the situations that will arise, you will have to make your own decisions with your intellect, which comes from a combination of knowledge and experience. Therefore, you must strive for experience through your own efforts.

In reply to another letter from India, Baba dictated the following:

> Dear Mr. Singh,
>
> Blessings. I received your letter dated June 27 today, July 13. I am still in the United States. Yes, I do have an attachment to the land where the familiar melodies of my childhood are disappearing. Your country is divided into various classes and castes, which makes it very unappealing for a conscious person to dwell there. Nonetheless, on account of its being my motherland, I have great love for India. Although I know that people of India have become aloof to their culture and the melodies of the past, adopting the modern ways of living will prove to be nothing but deception with themselves. Our ancestors are the descendants of Rama and Buddha, but now, not understanding the *atma*, the spirit and soul of Rama and Buddha, people are infatuated with the body, which is changing every moment. They are confused and perceive the descending to be the ascending. It is this that one should understand, but most fail to do so. All are running toward the half-truth, ignoring the Absolute Truth, which is the soul of Bhagwan Ram. A person should take to be one's own only those who are permeated with the virtues and characteristics of such ancestors.
>
> With the hope of listening to the sweet melodies that start before the arrival of the sun every morning, of coming among you in the near future, I have saved this *prana*, this life force, in this body. If I can be of any other service, please do let me know. Convey my good thoughts to all my well-wishers.
>
> Yours,
> Bhagwan Ram

Baba suddenly complained of excessive heat in his body and became very restless. We took him to the Jersey Shore Medical Center. After being admitted, he complained of intense headaches and asked us to apply almond paste to his forehead. Hearing this, Dr. Strauss asked a few questions and, after a test of the spinal fluid, determined that Baba had suffered a minor capillary hemorrhage in the brain. While in great pain, Baba went on answering phone calls from India and talking to visitors. Amar Singh's younger brother Vijay was visiting his family in New York, and Baba called him in to chat. He asked Vijay about his job managing a bar at a reputable hotel in Philadelphia.

▣ The *Aghoreshwar* with Baba Harihar Ram ▣

Vijay asked Baba, "Why don't you visit me in Philadelphia?"

Baba said, "I was there three nights ago at your bar, but you wouldn't serve me any drinks." Saying this, he smiled at Vijay.

When Vijay came out of Baba's room, he asked me, "How is it possible? I refused drinks to a young woman at the bar three nights ago because she was intoxicated, but how did he know that?"

There were no obvious answers to such questions, of course.

The Supreme mantra of life is peace.
Only on the foundation of peace
can you construct the
joy-giving monument of life.

Chapter 12   Final Travels

GURU PURNIMA

Guru Purnima is one of the most important events celebrated in Baba's ashrams. People from all over India come for this three-day celebration paying respect to the guru who has given a new direction to their lives. Although the main

◘ Guru Purnima scene at Parao Ashram, 1990 ◘

event is *darshan* of the guru, Guru Purnima has other functions, with representatives from the various branches of Sri Sarveshwari Samooh meeting to report on their progress. In July 1989, Guru Purnima was approaching with Baba still in the United States.

Baba really wanted to return to India for the festivities. He had recovered from the "minor" brain hemorrhage, but he was still very weak. Dr. Burrows thought he should stay in the U.S. for close supervision. Baba said, "How can I disappoint people who come to the ashram from such distances for this occasion? As long as I am able, I must be there for those who need me."

Dr. Burrows answered, "You are not really strong enough to endure such a trip, with all the pollution, climate changes and other hardships of such a long journey."

Finally we talked to Baba about sending a videotaped message instead. This worked. He recorded his message for Guru Purnima, and we sent it to be shown in various locations in the Varanasi ashram compound. It was a great relief for the people in India to see their guru.

While the day's festivities were occurring in India, it was the wee hours in the U.S. Baba sat in his room the whole night. He had asked us not to disturb him. Although his body was in New Jersey, he seemed elsewhere. Sitting in a state in which he forgot his surroundings, from time to time Baba mumbled words that did not seem to make sense to us.

In the morning, a handful of devotees gathered at Amar Singh's residence in New Jersey, where Baba was staying. In India, thousands of people would gather on such occasions, trying to get a glimpse of the guru. Here, the occasion was so small and intimate that everyone felt it to be very special. Baba was relaxed. He gave each guest a personal *darshan* and afterward inquired about the menu for *prasad*. First he suggested we cook the food outside on an open fire. Then he gave us recipes. At times he would appear at our side and give further directions for preparing the food.

After we finished cooking, we served the guests as they sat in a line on the floor, Indian fashion. Yes, it was very special. The taste of that *prasad* is still fresh in my mind.

One year later, in 1990, Guru Purnima drew even larger crowds than usual in the ashram compound. Baba was there! He had returned to India, his health much improved, and everyone's spirits rose to a record high. The first day of the celebration always is dedicated to cleaning and preparation, the second day is for the main functions, and the third day is for people to visit with each other. People from all walks of life poured into the ashram to pay homage to their guru. Even the then–Prime Minister of India, Mr. Chandra Shekharji, a devotee of Baba, came with his entourage of politicians and security guards.

In the morning, the line of *darshan* seekers stretched a mile long. Baba sat patiently until the last person received *darshan*. Everyone had one-on-one contact with Baba, as it was his practice to be guru to individuals, not the masses, no matter how many people came.

Those in charge of the arrangements had been preparing for days. They erected many tents, straw huts and other shelters all over the compound for visitors who had traveled from afar.

Numerous volunteers helped prepare meals. People donated freely, whether it was food, money or labor. As was customary, the joint effort made it possible to host this huge festival.

In the afternoon, after a short break, Baba emerged from his room to address the gathering. Everyone had been given a chance to express views and concerns. Now Baba spoke about those same concerns, adding his blessing and a message for the times ahead. Afterward, people with outstanding performances in various social activities were acknowledged and rewarded with tokens of appreciation.

In the evening, the youth wing and women's society of

▣ Baba giving *darshan* during Guru Purnima ▣

Sri Sarveshwari Samooh held their meetings in Baba's presence. They spoke of the need to improve the social system, what the ashram was doing about it and what more could be done. At the end of the meetings, Baba counseled those involved on the issues that concerned them.

On the third day, representatives from various branches met to set their agenda for the following year. They called a press conference to talk about the social work the ashram's branches were doing around the country. Everyone mingled freely. This was the day for it, an opportunity for people from other branches to get to know each other. It was like a big family reunion. Baba said:

> Sri Sarveshwari Samooh is a family of friends. On many occasions we gather to share our views and concerns, our joy and sorrow, our freedom and dependency. We gather to strengthen our love, devotion and trust in each other. If there is unity, mutual admiration and cooperation among all members, there is the seed of a healthy family. We start our practice at home. From a healthy home, a healthy society can be formed, and from a healthy society, a healthy nation is formed.

This Guru Purnima ended with a great sense of renewal. All active branches of Sri Sarveshwari Samooh felt the breath of new inspiration. Many representatives stayed longer at the ashram to seek further audience with Baba. He obliged everyone who sought his company.

As a result of this Guru Purnima, the youth wing of Sri Sarveshwari Samooh had a new program on its agenda. Young people from various branches organized locally and traveled on bicycles from village to village holding meetings and distributing literature to raise consciousness about drug abuse, the dowry system and senseless communal tensions. Wherever the riders went, they found a welcoming audience. They spread Baba's simple teachings, such as:

> Before we become a Hindu, Muslim, Christian or Brahmin or untouchable, we should strive to become a human.
>
> Womankind is our mother and sister, not a curse.
>
> A drug abuser is like a walking tomb.

Today, this program is still active and effective. Whenever the riders returned to the ashram from their travels, Baba greeted them with love, sweetmeats and praise for their efforts in helping eradicate the social evils of their time.

In the months that followed, Baba maintained his usual daily routine with frequent visits to New Delhi for checkups. He also would visit his other ashrams now and then.

◨ Meeting with Prime Minister Chandra Shekharji
and cabinet ministers at Parao Ashram ◨

Meanwhile, the Indian political and social scene was undergoing trials and tribulations, with religious extremists causing an uproar for political gains. A politico-religious party was mobilizing the masses to take over a much publicized mosque in Ayodhya, trying to return it to the Hindus, claiming it to be the birthplace of Lord Rama. Tension between Hindus and Muslims was at a record high. Riots had erupted in various cities, claiming many lives.

Baba was saddened by the violent turn of events and often would say:

Who is going to feed the families of those killed in these mindless riots? Is Rama or Allah going to console those in mourning? How senseless and selfish people can become, intoxicated with power and religion. There are so many neglected temples and mosques where no one goes to pray, and now for one temple or mosque, so many lives are being sacrificed.

In the name of temples, churches and mosques, so many people are losing their lives. It is better to have a simple place, void of idols and symbols, to express your devotion.

A delegation of these leaders visited Baba to ask for his blessing for their movement, but he politely declined to endorse such activities. In fact, he had a temple that used to sit in the middle of the ashram compound removed and replaced by a very elegant but simple platform for worship and prayers. On one side of this platform workers erected a decorative rock structure shaped like a mountain peak. Baba had a plaque on the wall behind his seat that read, "All the addresses (of God) told by priests, temples, churches, mosques and all the religious texts have proven wrong."

Long before the next Guru Purnima, Baba was focusing more and more on the youth of the country. He called a meeting of the board of the ashram and made a dramatic change. He suggested that all the old–timers withdraw their power and titles and bring young managers into the limelight. Although the old–timers would continue to supervise day-to-day activities, the young people in management were included in decisionmaking.

All the monks, most of whom were younger than 30 years old, were given more responsibilities and importance in the social and religious endeavors of the ashram. Energetic and dedicated young men and women now were to run the hospitals, schools, social programs, eye operation camps and relief works in disaster-stricken areas, as well as to spread Baba's teachings in mainstream society. These changes brought a whole new group nearer to Baba. People who had been around him for many years were encouraged to withdraw a bit and pursue their inner journey.

These changes definitely indicated preparation for a new era. Baba himself began to withdraw from his social calls and sent young monks instead.

AN ASHRAM IN THE U.S.

On a beautiful summer morning in New York, while walking in the United Nations park, I tried to express to Baba how I was no longer content with running a business. I had all the money and worldly things I needed, but I still felt there had to be more to life. He said:

> As long as you are living for yourself, you are not going to find happiness. Look for it in the smiles of others, particularly those that are caused by your actions.

These words hit home. A deep desire welled up within me, and I asked Baba on the spot to become a monk. He did not respond. I talked with

Anilji, the monk who had donated a kidney to Baba and continued to be in his company. He encouraged me to persist. But another year passed without any words from Baba to give me hope.

In mid-1990 Baba returned to the U.S. once again for medical treatment. I made several attempts to communicate my wishes to him, without any response. One day we were riding home from the hospital in a cab when, all of a sudden, he turned to me and said, "You think being a monk is easy? It is very difficult. If you want to become a monk, you will have to renounce everything that you have accumulated so far. After you have done so, you must go to a new place, penniless, where you do not know anyone. For three days you will be tested and tried. If you remain firm and steady in your conviction, I will have some hope for you. If you are on the right path, on the fourth day you will find a place to set your foot, and this will be the indication of the approval of the Divine Mother for the next phase of your life."

While he was saying this, I felt as if I were being drained completely. I felt empty. Baba's large eyes were fixed on my eyes, and I felt as if I were not there anymore.

By the time I collected myself, the cab had delivered us to our apartment. I was calm and composed, but speechless. I had been granted what had been preoccupying my mind for the last two years. Anilji, sitting in the front of the cab, had been listening to what Baba was saying, and he smiled at me with an expression of congratulations. Deep inside, I felt different from then on, although my outer appearance and duties remained the same. Baba never referred to the subject again during his visit, and I could never muster enough courage to bring it up.

Baba and Anilji left for India in June 1990, and I returned to Northern California with a new agenda. Very quickly, I found a way to dispose of my land, house and business. The whole transaction went so smoothly as if predetermined. In a couple of weeks, I was free to walk the path of a renunciate.

On July 2, I had a big breakfast and got a full tank of gas for my car. I drove out of the town where I had spent the past 10 years living the life of a businessman, but this time I was penniless. I had no idea where I was going. All kinds of emotions welled up within me: fear of the unknown, where and how I would find my next meal, where I would sleep. But a consoling thought would follow: "Baba's blessing is with me; something will happen." Then I would feel a newfound sense of freedom and excitement in thinking of the life ahead. It is very difficult to describe those moments in words.

Along the banks of the Eel River, I made several stops, sitting in contemplation, searching for guidance. By the time I arrived in Santa Rosa, the sun was moving toward the western horizon. On the freeway was a sign indicating that I was approaching the town of Sonoma. All of a sudden, my mind was made up: I was going to Sonoma. I took the exit. What was running through my mind was that *sono* means listen in Hindi, and *ma* means mother. Not knowing where to go, making a call to the Divine Mother seemed more appropriate than anything else.

Downtown Sonoma has a beautiful central plaza and park. I sat in the park not knowing what to do next. For two days I wandered around the town, hungry with no money for food. I slept in the car and lived off water from the fountains in the park. When hunger became unbearable, I decided to call a friend to ask if he knew anyone in Sonoma. Fortunately, he gave me the name and address of a couple who turned out to be very hospitable and hosted me for the night.

At that couple's recommendation, the next morning I left their house to meet Mrs. Patricia Westerbeke, a generous and civic-minded mother who had just returned from India. When I arrived at Westerbeke Ranch, Patty Westerbeke greeted me by saying, "I don't know who you are and what you need. I am very busy now because I am throwing a Fourth of July party. But you are welcome." Then she handed me a glass of champagne. This was the first gift I had received since leaving everything. How auspicious that this new phase of my life would begin with a glass of champagne!

That was followed by a meal of roast chicken and mashed potatoes, my first full meal in three days. After spending the night as Patty's guest, she suggested I meet Father Dunstan Morrissey, a Benedictine monk who had a humble monastery in the hills around Sonoma called Sky Farm.

Father Dunstan welcomed me with a graceful smile and, after listening to my story, said, "God has sent you here; what can I do? You can live here as I do." Attached to his house he had two spare rooms with separate entrances for guests. I occupied one of them. Just as Baba had told me, when I found a place to set my foot on the fourth day, I knew that the Divine Mother's blessing was with me.

Father Dunstan lived the life of a hermit. He had a library filled with books on all the different traditions, Eastern and Western. His company was the most precious gift for me at that time. He poured his love and wisdom unceasingly upon me. Just the two of us were living there, and we spent most of our time in silence, reading and meditating.

After a few months of seclusion, I decided to teach yoga and meditation classes in town to help with my expenses at the hermitage. Although Father Dunstan did not expect any money from me, Baba had warned me not to be a burden on anyone. I should at least do something to support myself, he said. Within a few weeks my classes became very popular. I would make $50 to $100 for each class, charging $5 per person.

I was very happy with the developments. One day I called Baba and related all that had happened during the past two months. After listening to my story, he said, "You are opening a shop again? You should not be charging for your teachings! Yes, you can leave your bowl there for whatever is put into it as a donation. You should find your contentment in that. The Divine Mother who has given you a stomach will also fill it. Aren't you convinced of that yet?"

After a few months at the hermitage, I left for India. At the Varanasi ashram, I undertook various practices as Baba instructed me. When I asked for a new name, customarily given by the guru when one becomes a monk, Baba said, "What is wrong with the name your parents have given you? A new name is not necessary. Look at my name. My parents gave it to me. You do not need other people's recognition to be a monk. Most of all you need your own recognition and the recognition of your guru. That you already have. It is your actions that denote you are a renunciate, not your name or appearance." After four months, he sent me back to my hermitage in California.

Six months after I returned to Sonoma, I was informed that Baba was coming to the U.S. for a checkup with his surgeon, Dr. Burrows. Although Baba had been doing very well, I thought it best to make sure no complications were developing. I went to New York to be with him and his other attendants while he took the necessary medical tests. One day as we were waiting for Dr. Burrows in the hospital, Baba said to me, "Let's go, Pandey Baba."

Surprised, I asked, "Where?"

"Let's go to Sonoma, where you live. There is not much to do here now, and I want to see the place where you have started your hermitage."

After becoming a monk, I had constantly entertained the idea of inviting Baba to Sonoma but had not been able to make up my mind because I didn't have a suitable place for him to stay. I was living in the hills outside of town. The arrangements at Sky Farm would not have been comfortable enough for his frail body, I thought. Now I had no choice. I mentally asked Baba to help in securing a suitable place for him in Sonoma. Just then, my friend John Painter's name popped into my mind. He had built a new house in Sonoma

🔲 Baba blessing the ashram in Sonoma, September 1991 🔲

and often was away on flying missions. Hesitantly, I called John and explained my need. He was more than happy to offer his home during Baba's stay.

On September 19, 1991, Baba, Anilji and I flew from Newark to San Francisco and arrived in Sonoma in the late afternoon. John's house was perfect for Baba. He could just walk out the door and take a leisurely stroll on Fifth Street East and other neighboring streets. Baba was impressed with the calmness, cleanliness and natural beauty of the town. Although he had asked me not to publicize his presence in

Sonoma, some people found out he was there and gathered in the evening for *satsang*.

September 21 was the day we traditionally celebrate Sthapana Divas in India in recognition of the date in 1961 that Sri Sarveshwari Samooh was started. I thought this would be a perfect opportunity to receive Baba's blessings on the first anniversary of the ashram in the U.S. Baba wanted to celebrate at Sky Farm, where I was living and had registered our organization. When we arrived at the hermitage, Father Dunstan greeted Baba with much respect. We all walked over to the Sri Sarveshwari Samooh flag flying there. Anilji lowered the flag and wrapped flower petals in it, then raised it. Baba had me offer flowers, incense and a lamp, which I placed on the base of the flagpost. Baba then pulled the cord attached to the flag. It burst open in the wind, showering petals all over us and the ground. We paid our respects to the flag by bowing and then lit some camphor to do *arati*. This simple symbolic ceremony touched me deeply. I felt deep within as if Baba's blessings had been bestowed for the beginning of an ashram in Sonoma. The ancient lineage of *Aghor* had officially arrived in the U.S.

◘ Baba in Sonoma ◘

Baba thanked Father Dunstan for providing accommodations for me on his property when I arrived as a penniless monk. Baba walked into Sky Farm's beautiful library and, while looking at the books, asked our host, "Will you share the taste of the butter that you have accumulated by processing the milk of all the cows kept in the library?"

Father Dunstan smiled and answered, "Baba, the taste of this butter pales when compared with the butter you have tasted by living in the company of God. Books are just the guideposts, not the destination."

After some time, we all returned to my friend John Painter's house in town. In the evening we took Baba for a ride to see the scenery around the central plaza and then along the Napa River where there was not much traffic. He loved seeing the trees and vines loaded with fruit and flowers, as well as open fields, vineyards, dairies and cows grazing in the pastures. On early morning and evening walks, he would point out various herbs growing along the river footpath and their medicinal properties.

Once I asked Baba, "Since these plants don't grow in India, how do you know their medicinal properties?

He looked at me, smiled and said, "Herbs and plants constantly are telling us of their healing properties if we are still enough to listen."

In the evening in Sonoma, many people came to be with Baba. Certain nights, people would chant and do a short meditation followed by questions and answers. The whole evening would be spontaneous and without structure.

Baba would recline on a sofa in the living room with his eyes closed or half open, and people would drift in and sit on the floor in silence. The only sounds came from pots and pans in the kitchen. Once in a while Baba would open his eyes and greet the visitors. Now and then he would invite someone to ask a question. Jishnu Shankar, a student who was studying in the U.S., or I would be at hand to translate. Some questions Baba answered in great detail and some he answered by a wave or gesture of his hand or by a mere glance. Often his eyes, gestures or facial expressions told more than any words could say.

After a few questions, Baba would fall back into his half-dazed state and ask me to lead the group in simple chanting or guided meditations. His body would begin to sway or even droop to the side and rest. It would appear as if he had fallen asleep. In the next 10 or 15 minutes Baba would collect himself and sit up. If someone had a question, Baba would ask me what the visitor wanted to ask. After I translated the question, Baba would give a precise answer that I would then translate.

Here are examples of *satsang* in Sonoma:

Someone asked, "Baba, what could we do to save the earth?"

Baba replied, "Save yourself, brother. The earth will take care of itself."

Another person asked, "Baba, I want to be a healer. How could I take away someone's pain?"

Baba responded, "Sister, why do you want to get involved in that matter? Look at me. I used to roam like a lion, carefree. Then I got involved in that profession and now see the condition of this body. If you pick up something from somewhere, where are you going to put it? If you really want to heal someone, give them good advice for proper living, herbs or medicines."

Another visitor said, "Baba, I am a mother of two children. Trying to keep up with my busy schedule, performing all my responsibilities, I hardly have time left for sadhana. *My practice requires at least two hours every day and, when I don't have it, I feel guilty. What can I do?"*

Baba answered, "Sister, for a householder, only practices that can be done without causing any conflict in the flow of family life are fit to be called *sadhana*. Even five minutes spent in that direction by a householder is more valuable than hours spent by a renunciate. Instilling good mental impressions in your children and maintaining harmony in your family is your *sadhana*. Do not feel bad about not having enough time for a set regimen."

One evening, a prominent cabinet minister in India called. Afterward, our host John Painter asked Baba, "How do you feel about politicians seeking your advice?"

"Oh, they ask my advice, but do whatever they want to do anyway," he said with utmost simplicity.

John MacKay, a friend, asked, "Do the thoughts of the lower nature like anger, greed and jealousy find their way into the inner world of a realized being like Baba? And if they do, how does he deal with them?"

"Yes brother, they do come, but I don't act on them," Baba replied.

Another person asked, "Baba, my mother is in the hospital. I wanted to visit her, but my work schedule does not permit me. I feel bad. What can I do in such a situation?"

"Send her your love and concern through the vibrations of your heart. Spending your time in such a way would be more healing and meaningful to both of you instead of feeling bad about it. Rest assured, she will receive it," were Baba's consoling words.

One day an Indian man claiming to be a swami *visited Baba. Hesitatingly he asked, "Baba, during my meditation when I focus my attention on the third eye, all I see is the image of a* yoni. *The harder I try to push it out of my mind, the stronger it comes back. I feel very irritated. What can I do about it?"*

"What is wrong with that? After all, it is the gate through which you entered the world. Meditate on it, concentrate on it with reverence. There is nothing impious about it," Baba said sincerely. Those of us sitting around found it hard to contain our smiles.

A week later, the visitor returned and reported that the image of the *yoni* was no longer coming in his meditation.

Baba liked Sonoma and the people who lived there. He encouraged me to continue my services in the town. After 10 days, we returned to New Jersey.

VISITS TO ITALY AND SWITZERLAND

Navaratri was approaching, and arrangements were being made at Amar Singh's residence in New Jersey where we were staying. Baba was feeling well and took an active role in the ceremonies, addressing the gathering every evening. The sweetness of this time with Baba deeply enriched the people in this small group. After Navaratri came to a close, Baba decided to return to India. Dr. Burrows assured us that Baba's kidneys were maintaining a normal condition and gave permission for us to leave.

Baba accepted the invitation of his followers in Italy and Switzerland to visit them en route, with Anilji and me escorting him as usual. In Italy, Biffi Umberto's residence in the village of Mezzago outside of Milan became Baba's temporary home. Biffi Umberto and a few of his friends had come in contact with Baba in early 1976, and he became a staunch devotee. Over the years a number of other people in Italy had made regular visits to the Varanasi ashram. Together they had started a center at Biffi Umberto's home.

During Baba's 10-day stay, people gathered as they did everywhere to be with him. This time we needed two translators, one to go from Italian to English, and one from English to Hindi, and vice versa. But it didn't make a difference. Everyone who came was deeply touched by Baba's presence and the peace that permeated the atmosphere around him. Baba enjoyed visiting all the monuments and places of interest in Milan and surrounding areas.

In Switzerland, we stayed at the home of Harsha Varshan Singh. On our train ride to Geneva, Baba pointed out the scenic beauty to us as we rolled along the grand lakes and mountains and through long tunnels. Harsha Varshan Singh met us at the station and took us to his residence. Many Indian people working at the United Nations in Geneva came to visit Baba, who was enjoying everything.

One day Baba developed a toothache, which concerned us because every little thing had a tendency to escalate into a big health problem. It was very easy for him to contract an infection. Harsha Varshan Singh took Baba to a dentist. Noticing the long list of medications that Baba was taking, the doctor hesitated but then gave him something mild for the toothache. Fortunately it worked. Baba liked the way doctors practiced medicine there, he related to me later. We returned to Milan after four days in Geneva, rested a few days and then resumed our flight to New Delhi.

Stay away from conceit.
    Beauty is defeated by age, life by death,
wealth by anger, modesty by lust
        and endurance by pessimism.
But conceit seeps into every corner of life
    and destroys it entirely.

Chapter 13　Last Days

SEVERE TRIALS

We spent the next few months in India as quietly as possible, with Baba suffering occasional minor infections. With Baba on immunosuppressant drugs, his attendants had to be very careful. Pollution and the crowds of visitors who sought out Baba did not help the situation. During observance of Navaratri in March 1992, Baba contracted an infection in his sinuses, and traces of blood were coming out of his throat. After treating him with no success, the doctors in India advised Baba to return to New York.

Before leaving, Baba called all residents and prominent well-wishers of the ashram and bade farewell saying, "I am not going to come back. I will leave my body in the United States. Each and every one of you, continue your assigned duties. I leave the ashram and its activities in your hands." He called an elderly gentleman to him and entrusted the keys of the ashram to him. Although Baba had never acted in such a fashion before, no one in the ashram could believe he was not coming back. They all heard his words but dismissed them as if Baba were just trying to tell them they should be more mindful of their duties in his absence.

Baba and Anilji arrived in New York on Friday, May 19. A few of us received them at the airport and went to Mr. Amar Singh's apartment in Manhattan by the United Nations. After the long flight, Baba was very tired. All he said to me during the ride from the airport to the apartment was, "Pandey Baba, my throat is bleeding. I have lost a lot of blood. I feel very weak and dizzy." Entering the apartment, he went straight to bed to stretch out. I contacted Dr. Burrows and made an appointment for the following Tuesday.

After a short rest, Baba questioned me about the appointment with Dr. Burrows. "Why not tomorrow?" he asked. I called Dr. Burrows again and requested that he see Baba as soon as he could, since Baba was intent on being admitted to the hospital. The next two days were the weekend, so we fixed an appointment for Monday. Soon Baba became very restless and said, "Take me to the hospital right away. My heart is pounding." His expression and demeanor were alarming. Somehow we got him downstairs and rushed him to the nearest hospital, NYU Medical Center.

The doctors there contacted Dr. Burrows for consultation, releasing Baba when tests indicated he had not had a stroke. Dr. Burrows asked me to bring Baba to his office the next morning, where tests found that Baba had an infection in the chest. Pneumonia had affected his lungs, and he was not able to breathe fully, causing a kind of suffocation and making him very restless. Baba was admitted to the hospital immediately for treatment. He was still restless, so the doctor gave him a sedative. This calmed Baba, and he appeared to have fallen asleep. They biopsied Baba's kidneys and in the process noticed the incoherent state Baba had slipped into. They put him on a respirator and took him to the Intensive Care Unit. A doctor explained, "His lungs collapsed, and he was barely breathing. Malfunctioning kidneys were not able to filter the drug he had taken, and it may have acted as an overdose."

This was the beginning of a long difficult ordeal. Things had never gone so badly so fast before. From the very first hour Baba landed in the U.S., events took their course rapidly. We all were taken by surprise, as everything was happening unexpectedly. When Anilji related to me how Baba had said farewell to the ashramites and told them he would not be returning to India, it only intensified the anxiety building in me.

Baba was to remain in intensive care until his lungs had regained their normal state. Although visitors were not allowed, we obtained special permission to be in his room. After a week Baba's lungs returned to full capacity, and he wanted out of the ICU. The rules were too restrictive for him.

One day Dr. Burrows and a transplant coordinator named Mary visited him on their daily rounds. Seeing the two familiar faces, Baba sat up in bed and complained about all the different shunts in his arm and at the collarbone. He practically pulled one out while they were there. Blood gushed out. Mary immediately patched it. Resting one arm on Mary's shoulders, Baba got out of bed and, under the pretense of taking a few steps, walked out of the ICU and headed to the elevator. He refused to sit on a chair but stood at the elevator while relying on Mary's shoulders for support. Mary could not let go of him nor steer him toward the waiting room, for he was determined to leave.

Dr. Burrows, who saw this, said amusingly to the puzzled doctor in charge of the ICU, "Well, Baba has discharged himself from your floor. I will take care of him on my floor; don't worry." Fortunately, a room on Dr. Burrows' floor was available. Baba sat in the waiting room while they prepared it.

A few days passed. Baba's health stabilized. The kidney biopsy indicated that this second kidney transplant also had failed and he needed to be back on dialysis. Baba murmured, "The kidney might be restored to at least 25 percent capacity. May God give wisdom to Dr. Burrows." He did not give up and continued the medication to prevent his body from rejecting the kidney. Reversing the prescription of regular dialysis, Baba went for intermittent dialysis, giving the kidneys a chance to regain their strength.

Dr. Burrows said, "We might get service out of this kidney for another year or so. Let's hope for the best." All the nephrologists seemed upset that Dr. Burrows was so obstinately optimistic.

Anilji and I were at a complete loss, not knowing what to do. We called the ashram in India and asked Shambhavji, the eldest monk, for suggestions. Shambhavji immediately arranged for Dr. K.K. Tripathi, Baba's personal nephrologist from Benares Hindu University Hospital, to come to New York. After Dr. Tripathi arrived, Anilji and I felt some relief from the responsibility of having to make decisions regarding Baba's kidney. Jishnu Shankar also arrived to help Anilji and me attend to Baba.

The wound from the biopsy was not healing. To prevent clotting, they were irrigating Baba's kidney. They placed a catheter in his urinary tract, but the fluid coming out of it was blood red. Baba was writhing in pain. Every 10 minutes he would want the catheter to be suctioned clean for fear of blood clots in the tube. Whenever a clot or air bubble blocked the flow in the tube, the excess fluid buildup would cause Baba to moan with pain. This intense trial went on for 10 days or more. Not a single hour went by when he was not suffering.

Many nights, both the lack of sleep and the excess buildup of ammonia in the body due to the malfunctioning kidney took their toll on Baba's nervous system. He began to mumble incoherently. Giving Baba any kind of medication was a feat in itself. He finally said he would not take any medicine. Nurses would leave his medication with Anilji or me, and it was our job to give it to him. Somehow we managed to make sure that he took it all on time.

In the midst of all this, people from the Indian Embassy, Nepalese Embassy and U.N. would visit, as well as his local devotees and well-wishers. Although writhing with pain, at moments Baba would be very alert and present. He even gave a visiting Nepalese politician a few moments of instruction on how to meditate. As soon as she left, Baba reverted to his cries of pain.

I had never witnessed anyone suffer so much. My heart felt as if it had been wrenched, and a strange sadness and emptiness welled up from deep within me. Sitting next to Baba's bed one night, I was lost in thought. He opened his eyes and, in the midst of moaning and groaning, said quite clearly, "Everything...everything...nothing." Seeing tears in my eyes, he proclaimed the same words several times.

I asked him, "Sarkar, why is this happening? Why so much suffering?"

"You think it is all mine?" Saying this, he slipped back into his pain, mumbling incoherent sentences. He whispered, "I have called on all the names of God in all different languages and traditions. Is anyone there to listen?" Days went by like this.

Seeing that Baba was not improving, Dr. Burrows cautiously prescribed strong sedatives. They worked, and after many sleepless nights, Baba was able to get some rest. When he woke from his daylong sleep, he felt much better. The mumbling stopped. By the end of the second week, the wound in the kidney had begun to heal. To everyone's happiness and surprise, blood tests showed much improvement. Dr. Burrows announced that Baba's kidney had regained strength and started to function at 30 percent capacity. I remembered that when Baba first heard that his kidney had failed, he said it might regain at least 25 percent capacity.

With all catheters and tubes removed, it seemed as if Baba was on his way to recovery. Those around him breathed a sigh of relief. Baba was still complaining of pain, but it was much milder than previously. This pain was from irritation in the collarbone caused in the ICU when they were trying to locate a place for a shunt.

However, after only one day of relief, a large amount of blood starting coming out of Baba's stool. Again a wave of fear swept through our hearts. What was to happen next? This occurred three or four times during the night, and every time it was more intense. In the morning a specialist was called in, and he determined that an ulcer in Baba's stomach must have ruptured. He added another medicine to Baba's long list. On the fourth day the bleeding stopped, and Baba felt much better.

In addition to pain in the collarbone, Baba was suffering from dizziness, weakness, nausea, lack of food and blurred vision. We were all used to these complaints. As long as nothing major was occurring, we thought these conditions were manageable. We were relieved to see Baba returning to his old complaints. After a couple of weeks, he was stable enough to go for short assisted strolls, and then Dr. Burrows said we could take him home.

In the meantime we had managed to rent a two-bedroom apartment on Madison and 91st Street, a block from the hospital. In addition to Anilji, Jishnu and me, a few more guests would always come from different parts of the U.S. or even from India and Italy to visit Baba. We had no trouble accommodating our visitors. Baba occupied one bedroom, and we gave the other one to women visitors. The rest of us slept on the living room floor with our blankets and sheets.

The muggy summer of New York City mixed with the sounds of cars and wailing sirens was not the perfect place for Baba's recuperation, but we liked the security of being so close to the hospital. After a week in the apartment, Baba began to venture out, sitting in a wheelchair. We would take him to Central Park, which was only a block away. After a few days, Baba began to get out of the wheelchair and take a few steps, resting his hands on someone's shoulders. This routine continued for a month or so. He would go to the park four or five times a day and gradually began to take longer walks. Someone would push the wheelchair behind him in case he wanted to rest. In addition to walking in the park in the early morning and evening, Baba would go there at midnight and a couple of times before dawn. He cherished nighttime, when the weather was cooler and the streets were empty.

Baba was recovering well. His kidney was functioning properly, he had begun to put on weight, and his spirits were up. The pain at his collarbone continued to be a nuisance. He would be sitting in his bed or walking around with one hand placed on it. The old routine of sitting up all night returned. Someone would stay up to rub his back, someone else would read him a book, and Anilji would be called several times during the night for intermittent blood pressure readings and medications. One kind of drama or another would happen all night. Jishnu and I took turns being with Baba while the others slept. Although Baba's overall health was much better, I do not recall a single day during this time when he was not in pain. Baba, who was known to push all boundaries to the extreme, was now pushing the boundary of withstanding pain to the extreme. Often I would reflect on the words he had said to me in the hospital, "Do you think it is all my pain?"

THE LAST GURU PURNIMA

The full moon of July was approaching, and again in the Varanasi ashram, the multitudes would pour into the compound to pay respects to the guru. Baba used to be very enthusiastic in making plans for this celebration, but this year when we suggested he send another videotaped message, he showed little interest. When we brought the camera and requested that he record something for the people in India, all he said was:

> Dear friends, I am in a very far land at this time. I have grown tired of carrying these old bones around. I feel extremely lonely. At this time only two of my children, Anil and Hari Pandey, are near me, and the rest have left me. Even my doctor has left me (Dr. Burrows was vacationing in Australia). I feel even my bones have dried up. Now I will end my life in this country. When my body reaches India, offer it to the fire by the Ganges. I give this responsibility to elders in the ashram, Chandra Shekharji, Rajwant Singh and Hari Sinha. My old mother is in the ashram and as long as she does not find out, let it be so. I leave it in your hands. May you all keep prospering and growing with your progeny as long as the waters of the river Ganges keep flowing on earth. I take leave of you all.

After this he became silent. When I protested this kind of message for

Guru Purnima, Baba waved his hands at me to indicate I should leave him alone, saying, "Keep it for the record then."

We all discounted this comment, thinking it was just one of Baba's moods and we had caught him at the wrong time. When we asked him to tape something the next day, although he was in a good mood, he declined.

On the day of Guru Purnima in 1992, in addition to the locals and a few visitors from India, people gathered at the apartment from Memphis, New Jersey and Washington, D.C. We had a humble but sweet celebration. Each person present paid heartfelt respect to the guru and received his blessings.

It was suggested that we all spend the day in contemplation and repetition of our mantras. We prepared food for the visitors, and all received *prasad*.

In the evening, after the local visitors had gone, Baba left his room, and six or seven of us went to Central Park with him. We spread a sheet on the grass, and Baba reclined on it, basking in the light of the full moon. Everyone was silent. The atmosphere was saturated with sweetness. Sitting silently in the presence of Baba in the stillness of the night drove us all deeper within. We exchanged no words, yet the grace of the guru was overflowing. This moment was far different from any previous Guru Purnima we could remember.

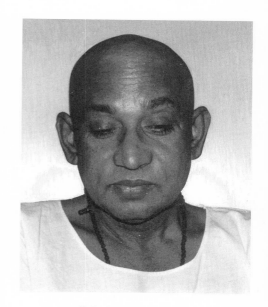

▣ Baba in contemplation ▣

FURTHER TRIALS

Another month passed. Anilji, Jishnu and I were the only ones left in the apartment with Baba. His health was improving except for the pain in his collarbone and general weakness. Baba decided to go to New Jersey for a while.

We locked up the apartment and went to Amar Singh's residence. We were still taking Baba to Dr. Burrows for weekly checkups. His kidney had begun to function normally, but now Baba began to complain of headaches. For the two weeks we spent in New Jersey, Baba took only minor painkillers.

Once we returned to New York, Dr. Burrows gave Baba a shot of cortisone that took care of the collarbone pain. But now the headaches were a constant problem. Dr. Kantu, an ENT specialist and a devotee of Baba, said that Baba's sinuses had swollen and needed draining. Treatment helped temporarily, but the problem returned in three or four days. Dr. Kantu arranged for an MRI of the sinus area and drained it again. Draining eased the intensity of the headaches, but the pain continued.

Mrs. Nozomi Williams of Syracuse had been requesting that Baba visit her home. She had been quite generous with her financial contributions toward Baba's treatment in the U.S. Although Dr. Kantu had arranged for another set of MRIs to make sure there was no fluid buildup in Baba's sinuses, Baba decided to take the five-hour trip to Syracuse instead. I protested, but he was determined and became irritated with me. He did not speak to me the entire next week.

In Syracuse, in addition to having a mild headache, Baba began to complain about irritation in his eyes. After spending four days at Mrs. Williams' residence, we returned to New York. I wanted Baba to have the MRI that Dr. Kantu had scheduled, but this time he decided to go to New Jersey instead, to the home of Mrs. Meera Singh. An unceasing headache and sore eyes became Baba's constant companions. Although he saw an eye specialist who gave him drops, they did not help.

We took Baba to the Jersey Shore Medical Center, where the doctors knew him from previous visits. After a week's treatment with no improvement, we contacted Dr. Burrows, who ordered an MRI of the sinus area, including the eyes. We took Baba for the test with Dr. Kantu in charge. When we entered the doctor's office the next day to get the results, we could see the doctor was alarmed. The infection had spread all over the sinuses, and the fluid had built up, causing oozing of the eyes and headaches. It was Saturday, and Dr. Burrows was not available, but Dr. Kantu wanted Baba to have an operation right away before the infection reached the eyes and brain.

Now it was one problem after another, and each one was worse. Dr. Kantu drove us to Mount Sinai Hospital and got Baba admitted through the emergency room. He consulted with the ENT surgeon on duty, who agreed with his opinion and scheduled an emergency operation on Baba that lasted four hours. When they brought Baba to the recovery room, the surgeon reported, "This is a very strong fungus and hard to clean up completely. Let's hope it is all out and his eyes are not affected."

I wanted to go to Baba in the recovery room, but the nurses were very strict about visitors. Finally after much pleading and persuasion, they gave me a gown and cap to cover myself and allowed me to go near him.

After half an hour or so, Baba opened his eyes and found me sitting next to him. I had been looking at his face, which was all swollen, his nostrils stuffed with cotton gauze. Traces of bleeding were visible all over his neck and ears. He wanted to sit up to clear his throat and rinse his mouth. The nurses gave me some water and helped me clean him. They asked me to feed Baba some gelatin, and he agreed and ate it.

After a while I went out and sent in Anilji. We took turns while other visitors waited outside the recovery room, eager to hear news of Baba.

After a few hours Baba returned to the renal floor, where the nurses and doctors were familiar with us all. The intensity of the headaches had lessened. Baba was given mild painkillers to cope with this. Then he had a new complaint. The index finger of his right hand had lost sensitivity, and he could not straighten it. The doctor explained that maybe a nerve was damaged during the operation while putting in a shunt, but sensitivity should return soon. Baba was not able to eat by himself because of the pain in his finger. Anilji and I helped brush his teeth and feed him. After a week, the doctors removed the stuffing from Baba's nostrils, and he began to breathe through them again. It was a great relief to see him in more comfort.

The fungus that had infected Baba's sinuses was hard to fight, but the constant headaches had turned into an intermittent occurrence. After three weeks, the headaches finally were under control. Since Baba was not eating food from the hospital cafeteria, we would cook Indian meals, mainly *khichari*, a dish of rice and lentils, for his dinner, and crushed rice with yogurt for his breakfast. Despite improving, Baba seemed to have lost all enthusiasm to get well. Whether brushing his teeth, bathing, taking medication or eating, he never would initiate these daily activities. He left that to Anilji and me. He would lie in one position in bed and not shift unless we made him sit up or took him for a walk around the floor.

INTIMATE MOMENTS WITH BABA

Once, around 3 a.m., Baba sat up in bed and started telling me, "I want to leave this body now. I am tired of dragging these old bones around."

The tone of his voice brought tears to my eyes. I said, "Sarkar, please do not say such words. We are all still very young and need your guidance." Saying this, I began to sob.

He reached over and patted my head, saying, "Why are you crying. I am not going anywhere. I am just leaving this body. I still have much to do, and this body has become an impediment in my free movement. When you need me, call upon me and see for yourself." He then became silent and, after a few moments, sent me to fetch a nurse to check his blood pressure.

Another night Baba mumbled, "Everyone is telling me about their pain, who should I share my pain with?"

An assistant nurse who had come to know Baba said amusingly, "Baba, praise the Lord! Accept Jesus as your savior, and He will save you."

Baba replied, "Yes, mother, I sing the same song, but in a different language."

It was time for the next month's newsletter that we were putting out in the U.S. I asked Baba for the message of the month, which he usually included. After I'd tried three or four times in a week to get a response, one day Baba said, "Do you have a pen and paper?"

"Yes, Sarkar," I said, ready to write. He began to hum:

> Who is the One present everywhere...
> Who is the One present everywhere...
> Who is omnipresent in all beings...
> Who is the One ever ecstatic...
> Who is the One ever ecstatic...
> Can anyone tell me?

Baba fell back into a deep silence. I was happy, as well as puzzled in translating these multidimensional poetic words that had just flowed from Baba's mouth. After much effort, the above translation was the closest that Jishnu and I could offer in English.

A couple of days later, sitting next to Baba's bed, I had begun to nod off when I was awakened by his call to help him go to the bathroom. I looked at my watch. It was 3:30 a.m. Returning from the bathroom, Baba sat on his bed and began to hum. I was taken by the sweetness of this sound and tried to understand the words he was humming. Pulling my diary from under the chair, I began to write the words as I heard them:

> I, *Aghoreshwar,* move freely everywhere, in all times.
>
> I, *Aghoreshwar,* am present in the rays of the sun, in the rays of the moon, in the atoms of the air, in every drop of water.
>
> I, *Aghoreshwar,* am present in all the beings of the earth, in the trees, in the vines, in the flowers and in the vegetation.
>
> I, *Aghoreshwar,* am present in every speck and every atom of the empty space between the earth and the sky. I am in light and I am in darkness, too. I have a form and I am formless, too. I am in happiness and I am in sorrow, as well. I am in hope and I am in hopelessness, too. I roam at the same time in the past, the present and the future. I am knowable and I am unknowable, too. I am free and I am fettered, as well. In whichever form you search for me with your friend, your faith, in that form you shall find me.

This combination of prose and poetry answered the question he had posited a couple of days before. Little did I know this would be his last message for the many people who awaited news of the well-being of their beloved Baba.

By the middle of November, Baba was doing much better. He was on a long course of antibiotics to fight the fungus infection of the sinuses. Dr. Burrows felt it would be better for Baba to return to the apartment. One morning when Dr. Burrows visited Baba in his room, Baba smiled at him and said, "I am very content and assured." Dr. Burrows took it to be a signal that Baba wanted to leave the hospital. The next day the hospital discharged Baba with some medication to continue the course of antibiotics at home.

When Baba returned to the apartment, life became almost normal again. We were doing all the things we had done for Baba in the hospital, such as feeding him or helping him brush his teeth. Baba refused to use his right hand, as his index finger was still numb, but he began to take short walks inside the building and seemed to be gaining strength.

November 21 was as normal as any other day, except that Baba emerged from his room and sat on the sofa in the living room for a long time while we busied ourselves with our duties. After breakfast he went to his room to rest and later returned to the living room. He was unusually silent that day, but we did not disturb him. In the evening, he called me and asked for some puffed rice cereal. After finishing a small serving, he said, "I have been sitting here for a long time, my waist has become stiff."

I suggested he lie down. Jishnu escorted him to his room, and Anilji took his blood pressure and gave him his routine medication. Anilji said, "Baba did not ask what his blood pressure was, which is very unusual."

Sitting on his bed, Baba seemed very quiet. All of a sudden he straightened his spine, took a long deep breath and fell on his back. Alarmed, we tried to speak to him, but there was no response. Anilji tried to give him oxygen while I called an ambulance.

In the emergency room, they put Baba on life support right away. After seeing him, the doctor in charge told us, "He has had a massive brain hemorrhage. I have never seen such a hemorrhage before. We will have to wait and see if there is any improvement in the next 48 hours."

Events had taken such a sharp turn that the three of us were stunned. We were back in the hospital, and this time it was more serious than ever. Even Dr. Burrows, who had seen Baba through so many crises, seemed to offer no hope now. We called Shambhavji in India and asked him to come immediately.

Those 48 hours passed with no sign of progress. Baba's well-wishers had begun to pour in from all over the U.S. and Italy. Doctors at the hospital had completely rejected any hope of recovery. Dr. Burrows told us, "His body is there, but he is not there. We can keep the body functioning for as long as we wish, but it is of no use. You should make a decision so that we can take him off life support."

I told Dr. Burrows that no one could make that decision for Baba. Baba himself would make that decision. We were all waiting for Shambhavji or someone from India with the necessary responsibility to answer Dr. Burrows.

Two days later, a group of doctors asked us to sign the release for taking Baba off life support, but at that very moment his right arm moved, and everyone was surprised because it was not simply a reflex. The doctors looked in Baba's eyes and noticed some sign of light. They decided to wait.

A few weeks prior to this, Baba had told Anilji in the hospital that if something happened to him, we should light a lamp in the apartment and keep it burning as long as we were there. Anilji did so the very night Baba was taken to the ER. We had kept it alight by pouring more oil in it.

Shambhavji and Pankaj Singh arrived on November 28. They put their baggage in the apartment and went to see Baba. After briefing them, Jishnu escorted them to Baba's bedside in the ICU. They both returned after a short interval, and we all gathered in the waiting room. Within five minutes, a nurse came in and reported that Baba's vital signs were disappearing rapidly. Our hearts sank and a deep silence blanketed us.

Shambhavji, Anilji and I rushed to Baba's bedside, but it was all over. Baba had decided to go, but characteristically had waited until some people from India arrived on the scene to take responsibility. Everyone, including Dr. Burrows, was surprised at the timing of this event.

The lamp in the apartment went out on its own at that moment, although there was plenty of oil in it.

We transported Baba's body to a nearby mortuary. We arranged for a casket to be designed to transport Baba's body sitting in lotus position, since it had stiffened that way. Many people poured in to pay their homage and respects to the *Aghoreshwar*. Dr. Burrows said, "He was a remarkable man. I have treated many people in my life, but I never met a person like him. Although he was beyond our medical science, he followed all the rules. Now I know why you gathered around him so faithfully."

The next day, we flew on Air India to New Delhi with Baba's body. People from all walks of life filled the airport to receive us. Chandra Shekharji, erstwhile Prime Minister of India, took us to the compound of Bharat Yatra Kendra. Inside was Bhuvaneshwari Ashram, one of our ashrams in New Delhi. The next morning an Indian Air Force plane took us to Varanasi.

News of the arrival of Baba's body in Varanasi spread throughout the city. The airport was jam-packed with devotees when we arrived. The casket was placed in a truck decorated with leis and a big photograph of Baba on top. A caravan of cars, scooters, jeeps and motorcycles followed the truck. Wherever the truck passed, people flung leis and showered the casket with flowers. Many people even tried to jump in front of the truck. The procession wound its way through the holy city that had been blessed to have a giant of his magnitude in its midst. The streets were full of people who expressed their mourning in so many different ways.

◙ Baba granting fearlessness ◙

Baba's body went first to Baba Kinaram's Ashram, Krim Kund, where his spiritual journey had begun. After the *arati* and initial ceremony, the caravan left for Baba's main ashram in Parao. His body was taken out of the casket, dressed and decorated with ashes and flowers, then placed on a platform. For the next 24 hours a constant stream of devotees and well-wishers paid their respects and farewells to Baba, their beloved guru, mother, father and friend all in one. The whole time you could hear a continuous chant of *Aghoranna paro mantro, nasti tatvam guru param*— "The very name of *Aghor* is a mantra above all other mantras. The presence of the guru is the highest presence in one's life."

The ashram purchased 10 acres on the banks of the Ganges just across from the tree where Baba used to sit in his early days. Volunteers cleared the land overnight. They built a solid hexagonal platform of bricks for cremating Baba's body. It was 12 feet high and 12 feet across. The next morning, in the presence of approximately 60,000 people, Baba's body would be offered to the fire on the new platform.

I read Baba's final message to the gathering, and then pin-drop silence fell. All we could hear was the sound of the flowing waters of the Ganges, as if the river were singing a lullaby to the son who had roamed carefree on her banks for so many years at the outset of his spiritual quest.

Siddhartha Gautam Ramji, the young Mahant of Krim Kund, lit the fire to the pyre. As the flames leapt higher and higher, so burned our attachments to Baba's body. People began to circumambulate the hexagon platform while Baba's body returned to the elements from which it had arisen. The crowd burst into the chant of *Aghoranna paro mantro, nasti tatvam guru param* as they walked around the platform. The atmosphere turned very magnetic. This went on for six hours. As the sun began to set and the western horizon was turning red, all that was left on the platform were glowing embers. As was customary, a combination of milk and water was poured on the embers to cool them down. As the liquid touched the glowing embers, a cloud of steam arose and took the shape of Baba's body with arms extended toward the sky, granting fearlessness. The onlookers roared, *Hara Hara Mahadev*—"Glory to the great God Shiva." Then all was silent.

After most people had left, those of us remaining sat around the platform through the night and stared at the Ganges, lost in thought. The body that we had respected, attended, cared for and loved over the years was offered to the fire right in front of our eyes, yet we felt Baba's presence even more strongly. His words kept echoing in my mind:

> Guru is not the body. I am not going anywhere. I am just leaving this body. I still have much to do.

I don't remember how we passed the night. All I know is that I did not sleep. It was the fourth night in a row since we had left New York that I had been awake.

The next morning devotees collected Baba's ashes and placed them in many small copper containers and sealed them. Baba's ashrams would receive these containers to use as the centerpiece of memorials they would build dedicated to their guru.

On the sixth day after cremation, the ashram fed a large number of people and gave away hundreds of blankets to the poor.

Within days, Mataji, Baba's mother, suddenly fell ill. She was admitted to the hospital but insisted on leaving almost immediately, saying, "It is all useless. Let me go to be near Babua." Ashramites brought her from Parao Ashram to Krim Kund, which was closer to the hospital. Within a few days she also left her body.

A few yards from the platform where Baba's body was cremated, the ashramites constructed another six-pointed platform in the shape of a star, *sri yantra*. In the presence of thousands of people, the ashram offered Mataji's body to the fire.

The loss and shock devotees experienced within a two-week period were indescribable.

※ Take refuge in the guru of the self.
It dwells within you.
Look for it egolessly.
You definitely shall find it.

REFLECTIONS ON LAST DAYS

Many people sought us out to hear the details of Baba's final days. Listening to our story, an old *sadhu* said, "I am not surprised. Saints of this tradition have always chosen the time for their departure. They determine when to leave their body. It is also customary for the *prana* of *Avadhutas* to leave through the skull."

As the doctor had reported that he had never seen such a massive hemorrhage, the *sadhu* was right. The crown chakra was the gate through which Baba made his exit.

The more we reflected on past events, the more it became evident

※ If you want
to cast a spell on the world,
don't suffocate the truth
within you.

that Baba was aware of everything that was to happen from the very beginning. Although he tried to alert everyone, no one was willing to accept the bitter truth. He could easily have left his body in India, but to avoid the mass hysteria and tears of his devotees, he chose a faraway place and left silently.

The *dhuni* of Baba Kinaram's Ashram at Krim Kund in Varanasi has burned continuously for 400 years. During this time, the *Aghor* lineage has produced many great beings. When society's need has been greatest, an *Aghoreshwar* has emerged. In the tradition of Baba Kinaram, Aghoreshwar Bhagwan Ramji emerged during the chaotic times of our modern world.

When a creature wishes
    to keep itself in darkness and deception,
it clings to an attitude of disbelief
    and narrow outlook.

Chapter 14 *Aghor* Then & Now

WHAT IS *AGHOR*?

Aghor literally means "that which is not difficult or terrible." It is a simple and natural state of consciousness that recognizes the Divinity in everything. A person who lives with this awareness is an *Aghor* ascetic.

    Aghor is a mystical tradition that dates back to the farthest reaches of time. One of the five faces of Shiva was known as *Aghor*. The "Shiva Purana," among India's oldest legends, contains a hymn to the glory of Shiva that includes the verse, *Aghoranna paro mantro, nasti tatvam guru param.*

    This translates as "The very name of *Aghor* (Shiva or one who has attained the state of *Aghor*) is a mantra above all other mantras. The presence of the guru is the highest presence in one's life."

AVADHUTS AND *AGHORESHWARS*

For centuries, the *Aghor* path took seekers into jungles, mountain caves and even cremation grounds in the quest for deep solitude. *Aghor* ascetics chose these places not to avoid society but to find the seclusion needed to transcend limitations caused by anger, fear, judgment and disgust. When some seekers overcame these obstacles and found their true self, the public viewed them as holy and sought them out relentlessly. This drove many *Aghor* ascetics deeper into solitude. Others stayed behind, lured by the recognition and attention. They posed as the real thing by displaying whatever magical powers they had acquired. Still other *Aghor* ascetics remained in society but assumed a fearful unkempt appearance to keep the public at bay.

    True *Aghor* ascetics renounce magical powers as mere trappings of illusion, taking no credit for them. They are known as *Avadhuts*, those who live in a blissful carefree state. Many such beings have inspired us with their clear simple teachings, which seem to come from their pure being rather than from any intellectual storehouse of scriptures. These teachers are very few in number at any given time, are very difficult to find and usually impart their wisdom only on a one-to-one basis.

An *Avadhut* who has completed all stages of *Aghor* and then returned to society for the benefit of others is known as an *Aghoreshwar*. The term comes from *Aghor* + *Ishwara*, meaning Lord of the state of *Aghor*. An *Aghoreshwar* remains above and beyond all social and material illusions, distinctions and categories and can effect many social reforms. Realizing their Divine nature and staying established in the unattached *Aghor* state of being, *Aghoreshwars* may appear to observe contemporary social norms on the surface while remaining a recluse in the heart.

THE *AGHOR* LINEAGE

After the prehistoric association of *Aghor* with Shiva, the ancients considered another legendary being to have realized the state of *Aghor*, as well as to have taught it to others. This was Bhagwan Dattatreya, worshipped as an incarnation of Shiva, as well as Brahma and Vishnu, the principal Godheads in Hinduism.

Many other saints and *mahatmas* who embodied this *Aghor* state arose at their destined times in history, while the lineage became dormant at other periods, like embers hidden under ashes. Eventually guru–disciple relationships began communicating the methods and means to achieve this *Aghor* state. However, the practices continued to be shrouded in mystery and available to very few individuals who renounced the world.

In the 16th century, a great being called Baba Kinaram was recognized as an *Aghoreshwar*. Stories tell of his wandering for years until he attained complete knowledge after meeting Bhagwan Dattatreya in the Girnar Mountains, a holy place in the Gujarat state of India. Later in life, Baba Kinaram wrote a book called "Viveksara," the most authentic treatise on the principles of *Aghor*. In the book, he stated that when he understood what Bhagwan Dattatreya was saying to him, he saw that the whole world—the whole universe—was in this human body, a vast world perfect in all respects.

Baba Kinaram founded an ashram called Krim Kund in Varanasi, India, the city of Shiva. He initiated many social reforms during the tumultuous times of the Moghul invasion and persecution of the Indian people.

The direct lineage of the *Aghoreshwars* that began with Baba Kinaram extends to the present. When Baba Bhagwan Ramji became the 12th *Aghoreshwar* in this lineage, he was likened to Baba Kinaram for his strong sense of social responsibility, identification with human suffering and compassion to help people in their struggle against injustice.

In 1961, Baba Bhagwan Ramji renewed the socially expansive spirit of Baba Kinaram when he established a new ashram in Varanasi called Sri Sarveshwari Samooh dedicated to helping the poor and afflicted. The embers buried under ashes leapt into flame again, fed by the spiritual fuel of another great *Aghoreshwar*.

To maintain the seat of the *Aghor* tradition as a continuum, Baba Bhagwan Ramji initiated his own disciple, Siddhartha Gautam Ram, as head of Krim Kund so he could be free to follow his social callings, which he did until his *samadhi* in 1992.

AGHOR TODAY

Krim Kund and Sri Sarveshwari Samooh still stand on opposite sides of the Ganges in Varanasi, living *Aghor* principles to effect social improvement. In addition, disciples of Aghoreshwar Bhagwan Ramji have established many ashrams throughout India and in other countries, including the United States. All locations work cooperatively to maintain the ancient tradition while adapting to contemporary needs. They provide social services as well as guidance on integrating *Aghor* practices into the daily life of their communities. (For information on Sonoma Ashram and Bal Ashram, please see Resources on page 271.)

Aghor is timeless. It remains simple in concept and practice. One is absolutely whole and in union with the Divine. The essence of the practice is passed on one-to-one by a guru through initiation with a mantra. The expression of the practice is both internal and external. Through *sadhana*, a daily spiritual practice, one connects to the Divinity within; in turn, that fullness overflows as *seva*, selfless service in the world. These are the cornerstones of a meaningful life.

The Teachings of Aghoreshwar Bhagwan Ramji

Baba regularly spoke to householders on how to live a meaningful life. In addition, he gave discourses to his monks that delved deeper into the principles and practice of *Aghor*.

Baba shared these teachings in various locations, most often at Sri Sarveshwari Samooh, his main ashram in Varanasi.

Without having the light
in your own eyes,
        outside light is of no use,
no matter how bright or golden.

Chapter 15 — Baba Speaks to Householders

WHO ARE WE?

Dear mothers and brothers, life is a mystery. Who are we? What are we? Why was this life-form given to us, and what are we doing with it? What is happening now, and what will happen tomorrow? None of us knows the answers. It is said, *Sub din hota na ek samana*—"All the days of one's life are never the same." Even Rama, considered the ideal and worshipped as a Divine being, fell into calamity, spending part of his life roaming the jungle. This life is bound to go through ups and downs. That is irrefutable.

A person who has access to all types of food and amenities falls prey to sickness more often than a person who lives in poverty and often goes without food. If the latter has any hunger, it is for food. But for the one who has everything, there is a hunger for all kinds of things. There is a great difference in these hungers. In spite of having everything, if one does not possess a healthy *citta*, the heart-mind, all is meaningless. All is in vain. Even living in a palace such a person is subjected to all kinds of pain and suffering. Lying in a cozy bed, the person keeps tossing and turning. On the other hand, a manual laborer with simple needs enjoys a good night's sleep after a hard day's work. Which of the two has a better life? It is up to us to ponder this.

Friends, we always want to become something, to accomplish something, but we remain totally unacquainted with our own selves. We remain unable to mold ourselves into what we think we should be. In the limited time that we have in this life, we not only manage to get farther away from ourselves, but we also invite fear, hatred, jealousy, disgust and restlessness into our lives. To rid ourselves of these, we pray to that "unknown" about whom we know very little, but who knows everything about us. For this reason it is advisable to call upon that "unknown" repeatedly to enable us to live a life of wisdom. A guru teaches monks to call upon the consciousness—God, Goddess,

Divinity or whatever form is acceptable to them—to give them the favor of that precious wisdom. This wisdom cannot be purchased nor created by ideas; austerity is the only way to obtain it.

Austerity, though, is not related to any kind of hardship. The true meaning of austerity is to keep a constant guard on one's mind, actions and voice. We have to remain alert at all times and remember what we have been taught. The grace of the teachers or the guru liberates us from the darkness of illusion and enables us to reclaim the gem we have lost but are unable to find by ourselves. Although it is right underfoot, we cannot gain hold of it. How can we reach it? We constantly receive subtle directions. We must listen to those directions, which remind us that we must have compassion on the self and warn us to save ourselves from perpetual self-inflicted deceptions and misunderstandings. This inner voice repeatedly asks us to save ourselves from these miseries. Being saved from them, our state of being becomes like that experienced in the company of Divinity.

For this very reason we worship the so-called God or Goddess. The *Para Shakti*—the eternal power, the Almighty—is not male, female or hermaphrodite but, rather, beyond gender and form. Nevertheless, it becomes illuminated as a form, in full consciousness. That is why we behold it as bluish light in the heart, just as during meditation we behold the guru seated in the center of the forehead clad in milky white clothes. Holding the sweet bluish light in the heart during meditation gives us immense peace. The Almighty does not belong to the category of male or female, neither a combination of the two nor in the middle of the two. Furthermore, we cannot call that light by any name.

That is why in the beginning of "Devi Bhagavata," the author Vyasa said, "O' God, I know you are formless, you are beyond being seen with the eyes; nonetheless, for teaching others about your presence, I am going to call you by name and form. Please forgive me for this contempt, but it is impossible to tell others about you without giving you a form and a name. If I do not make others understand all this about you, they will waste their precious lives in the darkness of ignorance."

Thus the saints and holy beings keep teaching others by giving examples from treatises and texts, together with their own experiences. But the real thing is very different. Only you can experience the truth. You can experience the taste of hot pepper or sugar only by putting it on your tongue, not by reading books or being taught about it.

Sitting silently, being centered and attentive, repeating your mantra with the sound of your heartbeat, imagine vibrations emerging from every pore of your body, from the big toe to the crown of your head. Immense joy will permeate every cell of your body. In such a state, happiness and peace descend, followed by auspicious thoughts. The good thoughts that arise have not been experienced by anyone else, nor have they been found in any holy text or treatise.

We all know how transient this life is. There comes a time when all the things that we once considered irreplaceable start to repel us and seem meaningless. Everything appears like a dream that we see in the darkness of sleep. When we observe Navaratri—*nava* means nine and *ratri* means night—those nights are different from the rest of the nights. They are not nights of sleep, but nights of alertness. During this time the seekers, remaining alert, submerge themselves in contemplation, meditation and reflection on teachings received from their guru or teacher. As a farmer sows seeds and in due time reaps a beautiful crop, the seeker having sown the seed mantra in this favorable season procures happiness and peace. Having all the wealth in the world cannot compare with the great peace and happiness obtained in spirituality and in such Divine moments. Deprived of the knowledge that dispels ignorance and ensures happiness and peace, the seeker roams hither and thither looking in all the wrong places.

Today that "unknown," that friend of mine, was visible only from a distance. I was unable to have a conversation as I had yesterday. Otherwise I would tell you more about our dialogue. I did not want to meet that friend today because I was preoccupied. I hope you will understand what that "unknown" friend of mine is. That "unknown" is everything of substance in this life. I will proclaim it from the housetop. "Everything, everything and nothing, nothing—and yet everything!" Nonetheless, human beings, being deluded, get involved in all kinds of mundane affairs. What is the truth? The truth is a matter beyond our intellect. If our heart-mind were able to grasp the message of that "unknown" friend, we would comprehend that God and Goddess are very close to us. It is we who are far from ourselves. We are so far from ourselves that we are unable to cast ourselves in our true mold.

Human beings are capable of producing other human beings similar to them in size and shape. But good mental impressions and behavioral patterns are established by teachers and social environments. Disciples are recognized by the characteristics, virtues and behavior that resemble those of their teachers. In the same fashion, a seeker who worships a deity obtains the characteristic of that form of Divinity. Finding identity with our teacher or guru is like meeting that "unknown" friend. Cultivating identity with the object of our contemplation, our adored teacher, deity or guru, is an important aspect of our practice. During Navaratri we worship the Divinity in the image of the Mother. We certainly will enrich our lives by acquiring her attributes of unconditional love, compassion and attentiveness.

With these words, I bow to that "unknown" residing within you and take leave of you.

THE MANTRA AS A FRIEND

Dear mothers and friends, the mantra your guru gave you is the indicator of a friendship that permanently unites you with your guru. Mantra is not a cheap thing any babaji gives in passing. When a guru initiates you, he takes responsibility for your being. An accomplished guru, when giving you a mantra, is giving you a friend in the form of a mantra. This friend will remain with you always, coming to your aid during hard times in your life. Without such a mantra, you might become terrified and scattered, and your life might become unbearable.

A good friend should be like the earth, which keeps going around the sun looking for light. Because of that light, the creatures on earth are nurtured and able to accomplish many things. The darkness is removed from their lives. There is great need for a nurturing friend in our lives, as the sun is to the earth.

But many so-called friends come just to cause us pain. In the name of friendship, they encourage us in various lowly acts, perhaps in gambling, drinking or using drugs. While luring us into practices that cause poor health and weak minds, they still call themselves our friends. We should be aware of what kind of friends they really are.

In our families as well, it is not always possible to find friendship. Sometimes we are like the wounded deer who indicates its whereabouts to the hunter by the blood dripping from its body. Like this deer, our own blood, our children, can defeat us. Parents should treat children older than 16 years of age as friends. Otherwise, parents invite great pain into their lives. Despite other victories, we can never win if we haven't made friends with our children. If we continuously harass them, they become our enemies. If you have two or three children and have not made friends with them, they start to fight with each other right in front of you and then they fight with you. You become a dysfunctional family.

Mothers should understand that just bathing and feeding their children does not relieve them of the duties of motherhood. They also must nurture their children with good *samskara*—mental impressions—and friendly emotions, as well as encourage them to keep good company and stay away from the wicked. If the children ask for water, give them milk. Try to give more than they ask for because the mother is the giver of *piyusha*, nectar in the form of milk. A woman who does not practice this kind of friendship in her family invites a miserable situation. It is for this greatness that the mother is revered in India. A guru teaches his monks that after renouncing the family you may not bow to anyone except the mother—whether she is the physical mother or the Divine Mother—because it is the mother who nourishes you.

Fathers are equally responsible for the character of their children. The father is and should be the best friend of a child. A father's character and daily routines mold his children. For this reason, the father should show affection and reverence toward the mother of the child. If he treats her otherwise, it is disruptive to the family environment. Under some circumstances, if parents are entertaining undesirable guests, they should be careful about exposing their children to them. Later on, children may start behaving like those guests, and then it is too late.

In every situation of life we need a friend. We can find God, guru and children, but we don't seem to know where to look for a good friend.

Actually, the friend we are seeking is God, and the guru mantra has the same meaning as friend. When we meet a good friend, we experience boundless joy, and upon parting, we experience immeasurable sorrow. The situation is quite the contrary when we meet a wicked person. We must understand this difference and practice discrimination in our lives accordingly.

A guru instructs his disciples to behave in a noble manner. The disciple who crosses the boundary between noble and ignoble action is never considered a true disciple. A true disciple will not behave in an offensive manner, spreading disharmony. Standards of nobility also exist for all the spiritual practices, as in meditation and contemplation. Instead of meditating by closing our eyes, paying attention to everything in life is the greatest worship of all. Remaining alert to our behavior is propitious to the self, as well as to others. This is the greatest friendship with ourselves. If the company of certain people rattles our minds and drains us of our *shakti*, we should definitely terminate our association with them, no matter how dear they are to us. If we practice this kind of discrimination in our lives, we obtain great happiness and peace.

Where ethics and discipline have to be maintained, passive politeness has no place. You will have to practice *hridaya priti muh vachana kathora*— "maintaining love in the heart but speaking firm words." Keep love in the heart, but use words strong enough that by listening to them, the misguided persons may come back to their senses. In such a situation, passive politeness would be dangerous and could cause great harm. You would be responsible for the sufferings that result. Just talking about this will not work; you have to practice it in your actions. You will have to remain very alert to your own behavior and thus obtain peace and happiness. As others observe this behavior, you will be an example for them. They also will obtain peace and happiness.

The *sadhus* of this ashram are constantly tested and tried like iron blades in a furnace. Living in the midst of society, they constantly have to pass through fire. All kinds of people surround them, but they are always alert because they know that by deviating even a bit from their path they will be thrown out like a fly from milk. You as a householder cannot test and try your children like this if you have not made friends with them. You may face a big revolt.

Dear friends, these two words, friend and friendship, have a wide definition. A true friend always encourages you toward good deeds. Instead of becoming involved with losing propositions, you are always propelled toward winning propositions. The day our youngsters come to understand this, they will set out to find true friends. The question of violence toward anyone will not even appear. Even violent animals will be tamed in their presence.

The friend that the guru imparts to you in the form of a mantra is more than a mere sound or word. Those who receive and practice a mantra become virtuous, steadfast and stable. The floods and storms of human life never deter them. They remain immovable and stable like the Himalayas. There is no rise and fall of the tides in their nature, only the calmness of the deep ocean. The proverb *Kshudra nadi bhari chali utarai, jas thore dhan khal baurai*—"A shallow river floods with a little water, as a wicked person is intoxicated with a little wealth"—does not apply to a stable person. A person like this is never arrogant, talkative or impertinent.

When you have received that friend, the mantra, you will find out how stable you can be. Although exotic seductive situations may appear, you are never affected by them. The excitement does not arise. Once your *manas*, your heart-mind, experiences this state of stability, you should know that you have found that friend. You have found the company of God. You have reaped the benefit of your mantra. On realizing this, instead of being vain about it, you should practice humility. There should be stability in all your actions. It is only then that you can remain a rightful possessor of this secret. As long as you do not gain control over yourself, it is all worthless.

In the company of an *Aghor* ascetic, an *Avadhut* or an *Aghoreshwar*, your behavior is given more importance than your religion, race or color. *Aghor* monks give importance to renunciation and celibacy rather than caste and religion. They are well versed in making friends with themselves, as well as with others. Thus they share this knowledge with the people who come in contact with them so that they may live in peace and let others live in peace.

We should be very careful in choosing our friends. All kinds of wicked characters may pose as noble beings, with little difference in outer appearance. At times no one will seem more sympathetic than these characters. Paying attention and being alert to this hypocrisy is a type of *puja*. We should avoid food and gifts these people offer because they pollute our intellect and health. Simple food offered by saintly beings is much more pleasing than delicious food offered by the wicked. If your health and intellect are being polluted, try to dive into the heart of the matter and find the truth.

Being compassionate to yourself, I hope you will try to learn about friendship and seek the suitable friend. The day this happens you are no less than the Divine itself. Whatever the Divine does, you yourself will do. Whatever you wish, it will happen. Your determination will be firm. You will be endowed with noble character. This is the way of saints. Everyone is looking for peace, prosperity and happiness, which only this friendship makes possible. If we do not obtain peace along with material wealth, we remain very poor. I hope you will definitely strive to be your own friend. With these words, I bow to the "unknown" residing within you and take leave from you.

ARROGANCE

Dear mothers and brothers, today is Sankranti, the festival of the harvest. Most of us are farmers of one kind or another. Whether we are *sadhus* or laypersons, we all have come from the same sort of place. Nonetheless, many of us possess much arrogance and put on airs. If we do not replace them with extreme politeness, we constantly will be rebuffed. The result of arrogance can be a curse on our nation, our society and our personal well-being.

We have just harvested our crops and gathered them into the barn. Now our attention will be drawn from our fields to the threshing floor in the barn where our grain, our livelihood, is stored. We all know how important this livelihood is. In its absence, we experience much hardship. In the same fashion, we have another kind of livelihood for the other aspect of our lives that consists of politeness and straightforwardness. If we lack these, others insult and ignore us, and we are forced to feel sorry for ourselves. As long as we harbor arrogance, cunningness and excessive cleverness, we will continue to face troubles of various kinds in our lives. These traits are a kind of sickness. We should be aware of the nature of these tendencies, pay attention and work to be rid of this sickness.

When dominated by our sensory organs, we experience dreams, restlessness and pains within ourselves. Our desires and expectations overpower us, and we forget our true nature. We start behaving arrogantly, and a strong urge to become something different arises within us. If we are not able to maintain whatever we already are and pretend to be something else, disorder is inevitable. Therefore, if we do not pretend to be something that we are not, there is no possibility of chaos in our lives. If we do not climb a peak, the notion of falling does not even appear.

In difficult situations, if we lack endurance and tolerance to abusive language, we lose control of our emotions. Cruel thoughts and anger arise within us when we face obstacles and afflictions. We know that although a situation may actually be very simple, we are distracted by our desire to be something else and are unable to maintain our balance. In this unbalanced state we are apt to create great misunderstandings.

We are hindered by undesirable situations because of our arrogance and vanity. If we do not have the strength of forbearance and tolerance, we should at least refrain from trying to be something we are not. Even if we have the strength to bear it all, we should not set ourselves up to be a target for other people's barbs. As long as we remain in our true nature, others cannot disorient us with hurtful comments, and then people will abstain from labeling us as good or bad.

A few inches of skin and cartilage in the upper body—the tongue—and in the lower body—the genitals—give birth to all kinds of weaknesses in us. If we contain and discipline these two organs, we can avoid much of the suffering they cause for us and others. It is said in the "Bhagavad Gita," *Yukta aahara viharashch*—"Diet and sensual pleasures should be in moderation." Once we observe moderation, we obtain the beauty and joy of stability and bliss.

No matter how much money we spend on erecting big houses or how many big books we read, if we roam about carrying the weight of them in our minds, we do not find stability. It is our silence that enables us to obtain it. Once our sensual organs become silent, we are able to achieve balance in our lives. Until we come to that state, we will keep running into chaos and irregularity.

Many temptations keep us from gaining anything of real substance. We think that a good bed and fine clothes will bring us happiness, but as soon as we get them, they start asking for our attention. They say, "If you do not keep us clean, we will stink and become unhygienic; either you wash us or have someone else do it. This is your punishment." In this fashion, all the little things that are supposed to bring us comfort add up and become a big burden.

In such a situation, how can we obtain a centered and balanced mind? All the methods discussed in those big *shastras*, those treatises, are of no help because we are constantly moving. In the day, in the night, while eating or sleeping, we are constantly on the move. Even now, because you are sitting in silence, you might think you are centered, but you are moving around. Some might be running toward sounds, some toward words, some toward a vacuum, and some toward an unknown direction. Nobody is stable, but stability is needed for sainthood.

It is stability or remaining in our true nature that is *Aghor pada,* the state of *Aghor* or enlightenment. Just like our crops, it does not remain in the fields, it comes into the barn. A person belonging to any sect, race or religion can obtain this state. *Aghor* is a state of being. It is not a cult or tradition. It is separate from any tradition or ideology. It is the essence of all the great traditions. To obtain this state, one must be void of arrogance. One has to have maximum ability for forbearance and tolerance toward the arrows and swords of words.

Socrates was such a person. His wife was always angry with him. One day while he was standing outside his home, she got tired of calling him names and dumped a pot full of urine on him.

Socrates looked up with a smile and said, "Oh, rain always follows the thunder."

His wife fell to his feet and said, "You are a great being. Even after so much abuse you did not get angry or excited." If Socrates were in our country, he definitely would have been called a *mahatma*.

As long as we host arrogance in our lives, it is very difficult to obtain the state of *Aghor*. Arrogance is born out of various bad habits. We must abstain from the habits that weaken us. Our lives are going downhill. No one knows how long we are going to stay on this road of life. If we are able to do something of substance, we can attain the highest goal during this short life.

Please do not lose heart by looking at your long past life. A person lost in the morning who comes back home by the evening is not listed as a missing person.

When we compare things today with things in the old days and find we are farther away from ourselves than ever, then we have become our own enemies.

In such a situation, by visiting monasteries and ashrams, we can try to learn about these things. If no activities are planned there, you can still learn by paying attention to the behavior of those who live there. Being in the presence of holy beings and saints, witnessing their balanced state of being in different circumstances, we come to understand that arrogance and airs are undesirable qualities.

You can learn by asking yourself such questions as: What kind of place is this? In what pose did I stand? In what manner did I present myself to others? What are the daily activities of the place? What expression does the sky have? What does the land express? What do the trees and shrubs tell me? What do the dust particles tell me? Are the birds and animals of the place quarreling with each other or rejoicing? Is there any vibration in the place or is it silent? Are the people of that place running around or self-absorbed in their nature? Is the environment self-contained or not? By paying attention to such questions, you will discover many things.

Dear brothers and sisters, once you go near good people, you are touched by good vibrations. Everything is transmitted in silence, without words or voice. If the voice is used, it expresses only a little. The medium to tell it all is silence. The company of such persons is worth seeking, thus saving ourselves from the ill effects of the lowly company we usually fall prey to. As the proverb goes, *Sangat se gun hota hai, sangat se gun jaya bans phans aor mishri, aikai bhava bikaya*—"Because of the company we keep, we earn virtues or lose virtues, as the bamboo basket containing sweets is weighed and priced along with the sweets." If we fall in with lowly company, our intellect is fouled. We start to weigh ourselves with those people's measures and spend most of our time looking for their praise. Thus, losing our real virtues and values, we become neglected by others, as well as by ourselves.

Both good and lowly thoughts keep arising in our minds. It is totally up to us to choose one course of action or the other. If we make a right decision, we definitely will obtain the *Aghor* state. We will be able to grasp the Divine element and stand in the category of high souls. We will be one of the great *upasaka,* worshippers of the Divine, and obtain a seat near It.

Although the *Aghor* state is always available to us, it eludes our grasp because of our weaknesses. We keep roaming in a world of dreams. Our dependence on our sensory organs gives birth to all weaknesses.

On this auspicious day of Sankranti, we are entering a new season. This day is dedicated to all holy spirits who have come on this earth. We bow to those souls and ask for their blessings to cultivate the seeds of knowledge that we have received from them. May we be able to grow trees from those seeds and harvest sweet fruits. Now the farmers among us have moved their attention from the fields to the barn. Fear of rain and storm is over. We have already lived so much of our lives. Now all we need is to bring those grains home from the barn. But for those who do not maintain a home—our true nature—all efforts are wasted. Ultimately, living such a life is of no use.

Finally, on this occasion I pray to God for the well-being of all on this planet. May God provide food, clothing and shelter for all. May forbearance replace our arrogance, which subjects us to troubles. On this auspicious evening, I expect you to dwell among people of good vibrations so you may fulfill your search. Please keep away from lowly company, no matter how dear these people are to you. Because of their vibrations, your heart-mind and senses will be constantly polluted.

Your tongue and erratic behavior are like the matchbox in your pocket. A fragile wall separates the igniting powder of the matches from the box. No one knows how, when and by whom friction could be caused, resulting in a terrible fire. If you keep company with the wicked, you inevitably will get burned. If you rear a rabid dog, it certainly will bite you someday. I hope you ponder the words you have just heard. With these words I bow to the "great unknown" residing within you all and take leave from you.

A DISCIPLINED LIFE IS A LIFE WORTH LIVING

Dear mothers and brothers, let me tell you what I know about the workings of your mind. You attach different meanings to one simple thing and then try to act according to them all. You become confused following these unsystematic thought patterns and later become angry with yourself.

Your nature allows you to know and understand *tantra* and mantra. You engage in them and practice them more often than I do. The omnipresent Lord Sada Shiva, that ever-happy *Aghor* Bhairava, keeps passing in front of you all the time. You keep getting indications of this presence all day long through the people you come in contact with—your children, family and friends. But you never find time to pay attention. Instead of keeping yourself empty and receptive, you gather so much mental trash that your mind gets clouded with its dust and you fail to recognize that presence.

Staying totally relaxed and centered, if you glance into the void in the sky, the Divine spirit you call God or the spirits of saints become visible to you. They are not very far from you. Once you are able to establish contact with these great souls, your life becomes a successful life. Your life will be for the well-being and happiness of all. You will be filled with unlimited peace. Only then will you be able to understand the importance of your life.

Respected mothers and brothers, a number of great souls have incarnated in this world and left their shadows behind. In the shade of these shadows, you are able to live a very happy and protected life. Just by remembering these great beings, or by invoking their memories, you find their guidance, inspiration and protection.

All this depends on your having a disciplined life. This is not merely a concept; it relates to all your daily activities. By living a systematic and disciplined life, by distancing yourself a bit from the usual mode of the ordinary world, even from the world of body-consciousness, you enter the world of *atma*, the soul, the spirit. In this state, you are able to establish contact with these Divine beings. As a result of this union, you will be able to know about happenings of the past, present and future. Simply by paying attention to subtle indications, such as those you might hear in the voices of your children, family and friends, you may have an inkling beforehand of what is about to happen. If your contemplation brings that experience and you start dwelling in that space, achieving that continuous state with complete devotion, you become a *sadhu*, a saintly person.

People like this are established in the realm of *atma*. They are not affected by praise nor blame. They must remain stable in that state or else their achievements lessen and eventually vanish. These people would be just like those who don't want to stay home and would rather spend all their time idly wandering, visiting one place and then another without any purpose in life. Those individuals lose the respect of friends. No one comes to visit them.

If you never sit with yourself, then who will come to sit with you? A *sadhu* who leaves home and wanders aimlessly is weighed and priced like a cheap vegetable. No one pays any respect. A diamond has its true value in the jeweler's shop, but if you place a diamond in a thrift shop, it automatically loses value. Not everyone buys diamonds. Very few people can recognize a real diamond, and even fewer can buy one.

By keeping the mind empty, the body loose and natural and the heart-mind centered in its nature and by sitting in a peaceful place for a minute or two contemplating that consciousness, we are able to nourish our lives in a satisfying manner. This is called discipline. By remaining disciplined, you can sit at your dwelling place, your hut, your ashram or anyplace else. Others, even stray travelers, can come and visit you and find peace. People who live afar can send letters to you when they know where you live. You shouldn't wander hither and thither aimlessly. Otherwise someone may think, "He is never home. He must have gone somewhere because his place is locked up. Let's break in and occupy it."

This happened in the same way to us. While we were too busy praying with folded hands to unknown deities, we became easy targets. Invaders cuffed our hands, and we had to remain under their rule for centuries. While we were too busy praying to deities made of stone, we ignored the real deities of our nation and society—human beings.

The same is happening today. By ignoring our rich cultural heritage, we are running toward the materialism of the modern world. The younger generation is being lured toward new values. Wherever this is practiced and encouraged, it becomes very easy for invaders to conquer.

Respected mothers and brothers, what you are seeking in the stone statues and symbols in places of worship is not there. It dwells away from all that in your centered *citta*, heart-mind. Whatever you were not able to find in the *shastras*, *puranas* and other religious texts, you will never find in statues and symbols. You can find it only in the centered *citta*.

Once your heart-mind is at peace, you will encounter the Divine. Once your life is disciplined, the Divinity will ascend within you. It will be for the well-being not only of yourself but also for all who come in contact with you. With the help of this Divinity, you will be able to be in the presence of good spirits.

You all will possess this *tantra*, but due to lack of correct vision and mutual cooperation, everything seems to appear contrary to your wish. You wish for one thing, but another thing happens. Then your *shakti* is wasted. It is a very awkward situation.

May God grant you all well-being. May we all live peacefully together. May all the inhabitants of the living world attain union and peace. With this I bow to the "great unknown" dwelling within you.

EXCESSIVE CLEVERNESS

Respected mothers and brothers, every week when I get a chance to talk with you, it makes me feel very good. But sometimes I wonder if I am becoming like those schoolteachers who spend their lives repeating the same things over and over. A few of you come here regularly, but I don't see any effect of my talks on you.

You are free to do whatever you wish, but sometimes freedom of this kind becomes dangerous and can lead you along the wrong path. Instead of practicing a few good lessons from your teacher, you jump around and start gathering all sorts of abstract thoughts from books. In this way, you certainly can get confused and waste precious time and your life, as well.

Excessive cleverness is the root of many of our agonies. Excessive cleverness produces poverty, trouble, hatred, envy and animosity. We become so clever that we practice the same kind of cleverness with our elders, deities, guru and even with ourselves. We imagine that no one is aware of our cunningness. As a result, we fall deeper and deeper into darkness.

We pray for something and expect God to fulfill our desires immediately. We do a good deed and expect to be rewarded and recognized as a good person. These actions are nothing but a type of cleverness. With this mental attitude we are never able to attain real virtues. We are deprived of them all. We are deprived of the bliss of our concentration and centeredness.

Such excessive cleverness expresses foolishness. Cleverness never has been able to bring stability nor success to anyone. It may appear to be successful for a moment, like lightening in the sky, but it is never stable. Excessive cleverness leads us toward failure, which produces anger. This in turn gives birth to destruction. When the mind becomes destructive, it leads us into infatuation and submerges us in grief. Thus, we become prone to attack by enemies. We should learn to understand this. The day we correct our attitude and do away with excessive cleverness, we will be able to live with the Divine. We will be able to experience unlimited joy and bliss within ourselves.

Pay attention to the gift that a blissful moment may bring you. If you are not aware of the possibility of a precious gift, you become your own enemy. You become like the jeweler who recognized a piece of diamond by the bathing pond. Other people, unaware of the value of this stone, used to scrub their feet on it. The jeweler thought, "How lucky I am, but before I take it home, why don't I scrub my feet on it, too?" As soon as he touched the diamond with his feet, it turned to coal. In the same way, once you know that a good thing has come to you, if you do not respect it, it will elude your grasp.

The simple teachings that your guru has imparted to you are no less than valuable gems. Practice one teaching instead of trying to practice many: *Ekai sadhe sab sadhai, sab sadhai sab jai*—"By practicing one, all is achieved; by trying to practice all, all is lost." If you try to run after them, you will achieve nothing. Running after them all is practicing cunningness with your guru. This kind of unawareness brings all kinds of hardship. People who become attentive to their guru become very careful; they never become slaves of *manas,* their surface mind.

Do not overlook Divine visions and inspirational thoughts that arise within you, because the grace of holy beings and their teachings come to you in that way. Neither should you cooperate with any wrongful activities of your loved ones nor try to hide them, because they can never be hidden. You should know the nature of the truth and the difference between the nature of the truth and the nature of a clever mind. If you do not know this and continue to be unaware, you are like the bull who keeps pulling the yoke tied to the cart, not realizing he continues to pull the whole load.

I pray to God that we may get relief from sorrow, be saved from being clever and succeed in convincing our surface mind that whatever it thinks, it is not the truth. The thing that does not even arise in the surface mind is real. The rest is nothing but an illusion. No one has attained happiness and peace because of it.

You don't even have to polish that diamond-soul of yours. It is shining all by itself. All you have to do is pay due respect to it. You have been neglecting it because of your excessive cleverness. Let go of this cleverness and surrender to that "great unknown."

I hope you will respect and not insult the diamond that has appeared in your hand. May that diamond become visible to you every day. With this wish and prayer, I bow to that "great unknown" dwelling within you all and take leave from you.

ABANDON WEAKNESSES

Dear mothers and brothers, you can make a statement of substance only when you are paying attention. If you are present and don't contemplate it or bring it into practice, it is of no value.

Before we proceed, let us calm ourselves. First, straighten your spine, empty your mind and relax your body. This will relieve tensions you are carrying. You will experience calmness as you do this, not just by listening to my words and wishing it to happen. Focusing your sight in the center of your eyebrows, stop your breath for a moment, then breathe normally. After a breath or two, inhale as much breath as possible, inflating your stomach and cheeks, gently pushing from within. When you can hold your breath no longer, exhale. This practice cleanses both psyche and body, bringing good health.

When your psyche is clear, your family and social life are calm and peaceful. When your psyche is disturbed, you are restless and subjected to all sorts of human weaknesses. Finding flaws even in good things, you run into difficulties everywhere. Divine beings are born out of human beings, not the other way around. We are very fortunate to have received this human body and a sacred place, earth, to live. It is unfortunate that because of our misunderstandings and weak psychological makeup, we keep harboring human weaknesses.

As we abandon these weaknesses, the Divinity within every human being appears. The share of Divinity is many times that of the weaknesses. Still, human weaknesses can erect such a wall that Divinity remains unseen. Even though we have virtues, keep good company, practice discrimination and are of service, we still can find ourselves helpless because of our human weaknesses. We must start using our strengths within to be considered well-endowed beings. In the "Yoga Vasistha," the sage Vasistha says to Rama, "O' Rama, the Divine is nothing but self-effort. Without self-effort, nothing is obtained. As far as human weakness is concerned, it will slowly lessen with effort."

I am not asking you to shun weaknesses all at one time. Even Divine beings had human weaknesses, even though by looking at the scriptures, it appears that only their Divine attributes were praised and their human weaknesses were never mentioned. But we know that we all have Divine attributes, as well as weaknesses. It is difficult to say why weaknesses overpower Divine attributes and not the other way around.

We have unlimited Divine *shakti* within us, together with various kinds of wealth: wealth of service, wealth of giving, wealth of faith, wealth of devotion, wealth of knowledge and wealth of discretion. We even have the capability of remaining absorbed in contemplating the consciousness of that "great unknown." Ignoring our *shakti* and wealth, we engage in useless discussions and meaningless affairs. This is the reason we are not ready to face the great consciousness. Before taking this human body, we made certain resolutions and knew we had a mission. Now, forgetting all that, we are involved in totally different things. As a result, liberation has become very difficult to obtain.

Those of us who have remembered and acted upon our resolutions live a joyous life. Material wealth makes no difference. Those who have forgotten their resolutions, although living in luxury, foster envy, animosity and selfishness. They keep returning to dust. Their life appears as a flash of lightning, disappearing very quickly.

To obtain *nirvana*, everlasting peace, we definitely have to abandon our human weaknesses. We have to find a little time for contemplation of the "great unknown" who keeps directing us to turn toward purity. Even if we spend only a minute like this out of a 24-hour day, we would be making a great stride forward. Yet we are unable to do this and keep burning in the fire of our attachments.

There are many who, weaving a web for themselves with their own saliva of greed like a spider, get entangled and make their lives chaotic. They are unable to recognize their own self, let alone the real self. They fail to recognize their own hands, feet, ears, mouth, tongue and eyes and have no control over any of these. All their actions remain undisciplined, and as a result, Divine virtues and joy elude their grasp. They roam about exclaiming that life is useless. What can be done in such a situation?

By sitting in the company of undisciplined people, symptoms of a lowly nature arise within us. Dwelling in good company, clean symptoms arise. It is said, "By dwelling in the company of sages and saints, we come nearer to God." We attain great knowledge by sitting in their company, listening, discussing and serving with devotion. We begin to understand more than what is found in holy books.

If you are able to comprehend only this much, your life takes a turn toward the Divine virtues. Giving up various weaknesses, you become conscious and able to grasp reality. With this understanding, great changes will take place in your life. Although you might not be able to experience them right away, others will see the difference. You will experience a sensation of joy deep within, and simplicity will begin to arise. In such a state, you will not give importance to the insubstantial talk of others. It will have little meaning for you.

I have seen many good people in the world who are very restless, worried and tense, not for the sake of God but due to their wandering minds. They are unable to have restful sleep. It is hard to imagine what is going on in their minds. As a result, they grasp nothing. Losing their spirit and strength, they feel empty inside. Life seems very dull, and hopelessness takes over. Hopelessness is a kind of suicide of the spirit within. This is the result of not maintaining a healthy psyche.

Contrary to this situation, those who entertain a steady consciousness and seek out the company of holy beings obtain peace by their grace. Such persons experience happiness in all different situations and remain fulfilled. Truly holy persons do not expound lofty theories. Just sitting in their presence and imbibing the vibrations emitting from their being is enough to give a new course to one's life. Progress will be slow, but steady. The storm caused by various habits and weaknesses will subside slowly.

By sitting in seclusion with a silent mind we observe ourselves. The entire unnecessary load is shed from our mind. New inspirations and directions arise within. We begin to hear the chirping of the birds. We feel the gentleness of the breeze and oneness with the clouds and rays of the sun. As this state continues, we begin to feel oneness with the universe. At times we might feel as if we belong to some other galaxy and are here to accomplish a certain thing, after which we will return to our original place.

Dear friends, to return to our true place, we definitely will have to make an effort. I hope you will practice moving toward the Divine attributes by using the priceless qualities of service, devotion and knowledge. This practice will help you abandon the weaknesses and adopt the Divine qualities.

We must strive to accomplish the goal of human life. Making an effort is something we can practice. Householders have tremendous strength and can do it very well. We reap the benefit according to our actions. By planting fruit trees, we harvest fruit, and by planting thorny bushes, we hurt ourselves. Today's action will be tomorrow's benefit. Using all our strength, we must quiet our restless minds.

As we begin to abandon weaknesses, envy, hatred, animosity and ego will surface. Speech will be compelled to praise the self and criticize others. Eyes will be tempted to see the faults of others. Ears will be eager to hear others' criticism. Aware of all this, the day we decide to work on ourselves, our speech will begin to express pleasing and compassionate words. Our eyes will begin to see Divine attributes in others, and our ears will begin to hear Divine wisdom everywhere. Our sensory faculties will be completely cleansed. In such a state, what remains is the feeling and knowledge that "I do not know anything, and that is all I know." Once this situation arises, all the separatism and disagreements disappear by themselves.

One who lives such a life is called a noble being, a sage or a saint. Vibrations emitted from the body of such a being cleanse us of our darkness. Virtues of service, devotion, true knowledge and compassion toward all beings arise within us. We find ourselves without enemies. Why is our modern world infested with so many wars? Where is the weakness of the human mind? These are topics to contemplate.

Friends! I urge you again to abandon your weaknesses so that the Divinity within you can arise. Living a peaceful life and accomplishing your goals on this planet, you may return to the place you came from. Otherwise, living like a ghost, you will keep wandering unfulfilled.

Finally, whatever I have shared with you today, you definitely would have grasped if you were here with your full attention. Otherwise, if your mind was somewhere else, plotting and reacting unconsciously, it would be very difficult for you to comprehend it. Not being able to comprehend it, life remains as usual. With these words, I bow to the "great unknown" residing within you and take leave from you to tend to other duties that are waiting for me.

PRECIOUS MOMENTS

Dear mothers and brothers, we engage in all types of practice, worship and contemplation on various occasions. The most important thing about these occasions is that we gather together. When we come together, we familiarize ourselves with each other's thoughts and behaviors and move toward each other. This familiarization is one of the most important activities in our lives.

The life of a human being is full of ups and downs. We are all human, so we all have ups and downs. But we forget this sometimes. We fail to remember it or just do not understand it. If we do understand it, it is only for a moment. A difficult situation arises, and we forget all about the insight we had. The situation becomes similar to that of the dust particle in the eye. Just one dust particle causes the vast scenery reflected in the eye to disappear, and the seen becomes unseen. Once we are able to remove that particle from our eye, the whole scenery becomes visible again. Being steady and calm in such situations is very helpful.

Not practicing steadiness in our daily life, we remain deprived of various means of contentment. We run to various Gods, Goddesses and saints looking for something. We run in a craze to get close to them, to become like them in a hurry. Losing our stability, we keep fostering our own discontent. If we felt that we did not lack anything in life, if we were content instead of running after something or someone all the time, we would have the inclination to be of service to others.

If by accident you came across a God, Goddess or true saint in human form, these holy beings would never advise you to shun your responsibilities and engage in seclusion, lengthy rituals, singing or other time-consuming practices. They would advise you to participate in the sorrow of others, to be of service to people, particularly those in pain. Many people invite these troubles due to ignorance or excessive worries. If you can be of any service to such people by removing their ignorance, you should do it. Help whomever you can. In my opinion, troubles like these are a bottomless pit.

Today, a gentleman came to see me. He was miserable and seemed to be alienated from his wife, children and home. I said, "Tell me, if you leave your family and go somewhere else, won't it be a big blunder? They depend on you. They must be waiting for you. What will happen to them in your absence? Because of your state of mind, you endanger their lives."

Friends, when we practice moderation in seeking sensual pleasure, conserve our semen, which is symbolic of *shakti*, and remain with one partner, it is our greatest austerity. Practicing this is much more valuable than engaging in all kinds of worship and running around to gurus and other holy beings. Women also should curb their excessive desires and cravings and help their mates resist too much indulgence, as it drains his vitality. He falls prey to weaknesses and sicknesses. For the welfare of the entire family it is most important to be attentive to the physical and mental well-being of each member. Weakness and sickness turn the whole family and society topsy-turvy.

Moderation is also a part of worship. When you engage in the worship of *shakti*, you cannot compare yourself with others or copy them. If you truly want to engage in the worship of *shakti*, you will have to seek the backing of *shakti*. You will have to conserve the seed, the semen in the form of *shakti*, within you.

If you do not preserve the *shakti* within you, you fall prey to all kinds of trouble. You shortchange yourself of the blessing of your worship. It will flourish only when you save yourself from all kinds of useless and erratic thoughts and behavior born out of the surface mind. Although the blessing is showering on you continuously, being busy with satisfying the hunger of your senses, you fail to recognize it. You fail to receive it.

Who is the remover of our obstacles and poverty? We will have to contemplate this. Not only contemplate it, but practice it. Whatever we earn, we save. If we are not conservative with our earnings and squander them carelessly, our own family and well-wishers do not have any respect for us. They avoid our company. On the contrary, when we save our earnings, practice moderation and use constructive endeavors, the same people love and respect us.

The *shakti* we worship is not on the outside. It lies within us. Not understanding the true nature of *shakti* and the modes of its worship, we engage in external rituals with things like flowers, incense and lamps. *Shakti* is not a "being" to appease with these commodities. Until we harbor good thoughts, feelings and behavior, we remain void of the purity and its quality. Although that purity keeps looking and waiting to embrace us, are we ready to embrace it?

Why do we miss out on this opportunity? We spend so much time praying. Are we going to spend a good part of our life, which already is so short, just praying? We neither go upward nor downward. We are just stuck in a situation. We do not even feel stationary because of our wavering mind.

I find it very difficult to believe that our prayers and rituals should be so time-consuming. Even a moment of contemplation or prayer in 24 hours is sufficient if done with a true heart and mind. If not, we can spend the whole 24 hours in prayer to no avail. The surface mind will run loose somewhere else. It never becomes absorbed in the self. In such a situation, how can we embrace purity, the *shakti*? We are running in the morning, in the day, in the evening, in the night, in sleep and in sitting. How can we come to grasp anything of substance when we are never still for a moment? This is the reason for all our delusions and troubles.

In such a situation, we waste our whole lives. Although we voice many grand principles, listen to many philosophical discussions and read many insightful books, it all turns out to be like trying to catch a shadow. Chasing our shadow, sometimes we fall in a ditch. As we move ahead to catch our shadow, it also moves ahead. A guru teaches you to just turn around. The whole world in the form of the shadow will turn behind you. But we find it so difficult to turn around. We do not want to turn around. What is the reason behind it? We want to catch the shadow. The more we run to catch it, it runs with the same speed and always is ahead of us.

The worship of our deity bears fruit when it is done with our total self. Even momentary contemplation brings about happiness in our lives and puts us in touch with good people. In the company of such supportive people nothing seems impossible. Things that seemed out of reach begin to come within our grasp.

By repeating the mantra, by meditation and contemplation, the vibrations coming out of your body change and your voice gets charged with the *shakti* that unfolds many things in your life. But, due to harboring doubts, you fail to recognize the value of your mantra that the guru made available to you.

Divinity is very close to us; we don't even have to reach out to it. All we have to do is stabilize ourselves and look straight ahead. Ignoring this simplicity, we roam about neglecting others in distress. As a result, we just keep going without paying attention to the path under our feet and the people on the path. Do we ever bother to look around and ask, "Who are these people? What is their suffering? What kind of pain do they have? What kind of trouble are they in? Can I be of help to them? Can I be the support, the cane, for the blind one?"

The more civilized or upper crust in a society we consider ourselves, the more possibilities to display arrogance. We never consider our dwelling as a hut or a humble place. We always try to exaggerate the reality and impress others. This behavior only shows underlying false pride and insecurity. This kind of mental attitude jostles us from our calmness and stability. It deprives us of that joy that comes out of simplicity. This is the reason for the enmity and jealousy in the world.

To save ourselves from this kind of life, we can sit in seclusion and meditate and contemplate that purity. Being still, without entertaining any thoughts, we begin to drink the nectar of the Divine bliss within us. Using the mantra and *mala* as a *rehat*, which lifts water from a well with a string of buckets, we become one with that purity within us. Divine attributes and characteristics arise in us every day when we engage in this kind of practice. If we do not pay attention to them nor embrace them, they appear and disappear. Our life remains in chaos.

Dear friends, the time that you spend in worship, contemplation and *puja* is very valuable. It is this time that gives you a chance to be close to the Divine. These moments are very precious and deserve your complete reverence and attention. These moments are not replaceable. I hope by paying attention to these precious moments you attain fulfillment and contentment. With these words I bow to the Divinity residing within you and take leave from you.

STATE OF COMPLETE ABSORPTION ENCOMPASSES ALL PATHS

During the occasion of worship and contemplation of the "great unknown," all the vices of our lives are removed. Various paths exist, but because there are so many, it is not possible to walk on all of them at the same time, let alone each of them one by one. We would never reach the end of any one path.

Seekers with a clear mind who perceive the nature of the Supreme within see the Divine in its true form. Such seekers, with all paths understandable to them, are able to measure each according to their own standards. Contrary to this, those individuals who have no inner vision face confusion. Their path becomes very long.

Letting go of restlessness, the mind is able to perceive not only the present but the past and the future. During periods of spiritual austerity such as Navaratri, the darkness of the nine nights is a kind of light in itself. Instead of fear, there is fearlessness; instead of sleep, there is consciousness; and instead of weakness, there is strength and determination. A life like this is worth living. It takes a seeker to new heights.

Speedy arrival at some place may be a good thing, but it is difficult when you are in a hurry to obtain something of substance. Although not arriving on time, if you move consciously and with stability at a much slower place, you are much more likely to obtain something of substance. Many yogis and seekers have reached various heights, but they are unable to obtain anything of substance because of their instability. If stability is not there, arriving someplace does not have much meaning and goes to waste.

If you want to acquaint yourself with the attributes of *shakti*, devotion, simplicity or whatever, you will have to patiently string your nature with those attributes like beads on a necklace. As we worship, contemplate or meditate on the nature of the Supreme Mother, in the same fashion, the Supreme Mother is also showing devotion and contemplating us, waiting patiently for the moment we become permeated with her attributes and are ready to face her.

It is our misfortune that, involving ourselves in lowly acts, we continue to live in darkness. This is the reason that, so far in this life, we have ignored the present to contemplate and worship the past. If we neglect the present, the future seems so dark. The day we begin to see ourselves in the present, we begin to see the Supreme Mother. We begin to see her nature and are able to dwell in her company. This is the greatest worship of all. It is not just *manas puja*, mental worship. Simply stated, it is wholesome worship. Otherwise, our life is passing by unfulfilled. Our life is short and narrow. We will have to abandon our narrowness by increasing our compassion for ourselves and others. With this practice, we are able to obtain everything. We become the knowers of worship, devotion, meditation and contemplation in their true form.

It is hard to direct the mind inward. In an introspective state of mind, everything is possible. This state is obtained only in the human body. In this state, all spiritual paths rally around you. There will be no need for you to walk on or with them. You become as still as a landmark, and all the paths and roads will pass through you. This is the attribute of *shakti,* and in reality this is *shakti*. All the different aspects of *shakti* that are worshipped here or in other lands under different names have the same path. It is the same *shakti* that permeates all Divine beings of different traditions. Those endowed with this *shakti* are worthy of respect and praise, worthy of being contemplated and talked about. Otherwise, influenced by different ideologies and ways of looking at things, we keep finding dissimilarities. As long as we keep fostering differences, we are unable to grasp the true meaning of mantra, worship, meditation, contemplation and practice as a whole. We are unable to comprehend our accomplishments and our true nature of simplicity.

We learn and accomplish all these things by dwelling in the company of sages and saints, by seeing ourselves in their nature of simplicity. That which we call God, Goddess or Divine is directly related to our attitude. It is said, *Bhave vidyate devah*—"Divinity resides in our attitude." Where there is a devotional attitude, there is Divinity. Where there is a lack of devotional attitude, there is a spiritual void. In this state of deprivation, a person keeps fostering uselessness, and such a life is without meaning.

What is the preoccupation of an ordinary human being today? He or she consumes to live and works to provide. During this preoccupation, moments spent meditating and contemplating that "great unknown," trying to find harmony between our nature and the nature of the Supreme, are meaningful moments. In reality, this is our true duty and Supreme virtue. This is the mode of worship in modern times.

Humans have a tendency to hoard, and this is one reason for their unhappiness. Because of this, during Navaratri, while repeating your mantra, offer all to the Divine. Have the mental attitude of offering all the merits you gain by this action to the Divine. Whatever merits you gain by even this action, you also offer to the Divine. This kind of practice verifies the saying *Tin guna, tin siddhi trina sam tyagi, so janahu vaha param viragi*—"The one who renounces the three qualities and the three accomplishments like pieces of straw is the real renunciate."

The Divine has much more faith in us than we have in the Divine. Whatever faith we have in the Divinity and the guru is because of the faith they have in us. It is faith that is Sarasvati, the Goddess of learning. It is another aspect of the Goddess. You are unable to have faith all the time. Often you find yourself faithless. These are the moments when Divinity has removed itself from your being. Thus, when faith overwhelms you, you should consider that Divinity has descended upon you. When devotion arises within, you should consider yourself in union with the Divine. At such a moment, all acts of worship are not done to something other than yourself. All acts of worship should be viewed as if you were doing them to satisfy yourself. When delusion, greed and anger descend upon you, faith and devotion disappear right away.

Dear mothers and brothers, the faith and devotion you have are none but attributes of the Divine Mother. If you could foster this continuously for 24 hours, you would be able to see the presence of the Divine Mother within you. Your heart would express it, and your mind would accept it. Just as by thinking of sour fruit your mouth starts secreting saliva, by remembering the Divine, boundless joy arises within you.

Whatever I have shared with you today, you can grasp only if your psyche is clean. Without a good psyche, nothing can be realized. When your psyche is clean and clear, you can create many things. You are able to accomplish both *svartha*, necessities for the self, and *paramartha*, the highest good. With these words, I bow to the Divine Mother residing within you in the form of faith and devotion.

YOU ARE THE GURU

You are the guru, you are the baba, you are the ashram, you are the country and you are everything. I am not in the picture except as an instrument. If you encourage me, I am encouraged, that is all. Whatever you see in me is seen with your eyes, according to your understanding and your faith.

Without an appropriate place to put your faith, the dream you are dreaming will remain only a dream. Achieving happiness, peace and dignity will be impossible because for the fettered, no happiness exists even in dreams.

The fact is, we are all slaves, fettered by our environment, our way of looking at things, our senses or the prevalent administrative processes. It is very difficult for those enslaved to feel happiness. Our friends and colleagues are not achieving it, nor are our children or the generation to come. Our educational system and the environment tightly chain the current generation. In this prison, even our renowned teachers, great souls for whom we had great expectations, have also been chained and relegated to mundane activities. They have taken their ideas and thoughts from books, heard them from various teachers or borrowed them wherever possible. They do not have any real experience of their own, even though they are in high places of learning, in the abodes of Sarasvati. If they had had that experience, our universities and colleges would have instilled that character. Instead of character, they produce fighting, quarreling and acrimony.

To liberate ourselves from this prison, those whom we call our venerated teachers tell us about many paths. All paths reach the same goal, I have heard. Yet on the road taken by the crowds, where caravans go by regularly, there is danger of being trampled. We can choose to walk by way of the narrow streets instead. When we need to cross rivers or streams, we can step into the boat of a person who knows the easy path, who knows the intricacies of the landing dock and the currents in the middle of the river. If that person does not know the intricacies of the dock and the deep, then the boat might capsize.

There are many ways to capsize on this ocean of life. Those who have risen very high in the world, such as revered scholars, wise people, leaders, kings, emperors and industrialists, may find the path going up easy, but the path back down very difficult.

Once a man wanted to climb to the top of a particular coconut tree. With effort he managed to get to the top and pluck some fruit. But he could find no way to come down with them. So he prayed to that "great unknown" saying, "Oh God, please help me down. I will offer so many sweets in your name."

His attention and willpower brought him down halfway, and physical effort brought him the rest of the way. When he reached the ground, he said, "I am never going to climb a coconut tree again, nor am I going to make an offering."

This kind of cleverness keeps us in darkness. It crushes our soul underfoot. When our *atma* is crushed we feel remorse and bang our heads. We start blaming ourselves and say that God did this to us because of our bad actions. God has done nothing of the sort. In the "Ramayana," Ravana's own misguided deeds killed him, not Rama. Nobody kills anybody. The sorrows, troubles and pain that come to us are the result of our own misguided thoughts.

"Time, the Lord of Death, never hurts anyone with a stick. It snatches away vigor, strength, ideas and intellect." In other words, time does not take a stick to you. When you are clever in a misguided way, time takes away those qualities you need to reach your goal.

We all know how to progress on this path. It is not as if we do not know how to walk on it. Yet when we see a train coming, we jump in front of it and get crushed. The proper way to use a train is to get on it from the side, not stand in front of it, and then we can reach the desired station easily. If we stand in front of it, in opposition, we will be cut to pieces and killed.

We all want to be worthwhile, beyond comparison. We want to be beyond evaluation. By doing inappropriate things, we fall to such a low level that every passerby evaluates us as just so many potatoes and tomatoes. We become absolutely worthless. We want to be unlimited. How can we become limitless? What is the way?

Travelers on the *Aghor* path remain on their trodden path. They do not like to speak about it too much, so if you learn about it from them, it will have to be in a proper way, with a proper understanding.

Only our own faith, belief and devotion can guide us in life. In addition, our parents and ancestors leave their protective shadows on us. The shadow of our teacher, our guru, is not that of a human body, my friends. It is a *pitha*, a place of devotion and faith. That faith is your own. You may put that faith in a wild animal, an undertaker, a butcher, anyone or anything, establishing a guru *pitha* of your *shraddha*. Wherever you put that faith and devotion, you derive guidance from it. Bhagwan Dattatreya had 24 gurus. Even an eagle was a guru.

The way you should walk on the path is like a person walking in a funeral procession—very quietly and calmly. Then you can experience something. The way ants walk in a procession, not even an elephant dares to step on them. A bird has only two feet and no hands, yet it makes such a beautiful nest. The bird did not learn how to do that in any university, school or college. Though it faces cold in winter and heat in summer, it lives happily. That is because of its *viveka*, its deep perception.

Friends, we are born with similar faculties, but ignoring them we keep acting inappropriately and devaluing ourselves. Only when we have character do we have dignity. Only then are we absolutely invaluable. We should learn how to be invaluable so that no one can set limits on us. If we are not able to do this, if we keep producing an oppressive environment and trouble for ourselves, then what can God, guru or anyone else do? Not even the Rishis and Maharishis who once sat in absolute solitude for us and the whole human race can help us.

What is required is our determination, our will. A weak person has desires. But the person who is strong has *samkalpa,* the will to accomplish things. One should not just depend on God. Only the lazy cry for God, clinging to their temple, mosque or church with a fossilized faith. You should start behaving in an ideal way, not paying attention to the low standards of the ignorant. Weigh yourself by the standards of good people, good souls of our times. When you weigh yourself by their standards, you will definitely be invaluable.

Fools rule the world, and the wise are the beggars. You who carry a load of books in your brain are like beggars. The Brahmins carry loads of books in their minds, while the Vaishyas, the tradespeople and shopkeepers, do not. They use their intelligence to do only things that will profit them. They are happy with their livelihood, while you, with all those books overloading your intellect, roam from one door to another as beggars.

Both excesses of cleverness and book learning are not good for the human race. Don't weigh yourself by these standards. Be steadfast on your own path. This is your *dharma*. This is your only *dharma*. Each person has his or her own *dharma,* and you should not try to escape learning this.

We did not achieve human life for such cowardice. Cowards were not born to live on this earth, which is a region for God-realized souls. This is a place where souls used to descend, and upon their entering, someone would make the unknown known and the known unknown. We should think about God in our hearts again and again, seeking guidance. Even the great *shaktis* like the Goddesses Sita and Parvati had to think of God again and again. On this path we have to become very conscious of how the voice within guides us. If we feel we are being forced to do something against the advice of that voice, friends, we will have to find a way to refuse that poison. We will have to leave it, even if it is dear to us.

Friends, there is a lot to achieve within the finite parameters of our lives, but we remain unaware of what drives us to misdeeds. That is why we must sit in front of our ancestors and investigate this life of ours. Our hearing faculty should not accept suggestive ideas. Our nose should not accept bad smells. Our senses should be able to navigate the ocean of suffering with discrimination.

You will understand things depending on how you see and think about them. For example, it is not my voice expressing these thoughts, it is yours. You may think it is I saying all this, but it is not. Why should I bother to say all this to you? You, inspiring me, are making me say it, and I keep saying it.

I do not have a book in my hand, but I keep saying it. If you ask me later, as Arjuna asked Krishna, "What did you say to me in the 'Bhagavad Gita'?" I would reply like Krishna, "That is past. I cannot tell you anything of that time. I can tell you better things than what is in the past and things worse, too. What I said to you earlier is past. I am not ready to say it to you again and again. Where was your attention when you were listening to me? If your attention had been there, if you heard correctly, if you understood correctly, then you would remember."

There are no gems bigger than this in the world. There are other gems you can buy or obtain in books. That is not our real property. I never pay attention to those things.

Our real wealth is that spark that keeps glowing like a little candle at night that sees us through the long dark passage of time from sunset to sunrise. When dawn comes, we say, ah, one more night is gone, the night in which our Motherly aspect, our active energy, gave light for ourselves and others. Therefore, no one wants to put out this light. Who wants to live in darkness?

By hearing these thoughts, which are your thoughts, by sitting quietly in unity, you can achieve your goal, wherever you are. You will be like the ants walking in procession that even an elephant avoids. By being quiet within, attentive and mentally poised, you can find a lost needle in a haystack. If you are not stable, you will not be able to find an elephant, even when it is right in front of you. If you are quiet and stable within, the most difficult tasks will be easy. This will make not only you happy but also that soul of mine sitting within you.

THE DIVINE MOTHER

On this occasion of Navaratri, we are involved in prayers, worship and some thought-provoking talks. You have been curious as to how to find Bhagwati, the Divine Mother. You have asked, "What is her actual form?"

Friends, you have to approach Bhagwati through your sentiments, your feelings. You will see her by your emotions. You absolutely will not find her if your feelings and emotions are lacking. She is hungry for your feelings. It has been said that Divinity resides in pure sentiments. Through your feelings, the essence of whatever fruits, flowers or water you offer reaches her. The medium of smell, the medium of air and the medium of fire carry your feelings.

The emptiness that lies between you and me, between the earth and sky, is the source of the Divine Mother. Some scriptures have described this emptiness as the creative belly of the Divine Mother. It is in this emptiness between earth and sky that uncountable souls take birth and into which they disappear. This belly of the Divine Mother is where you and I and all other creatures take birth, develop and grow. It is in this emptiness that great creative power lies. In this same emptiness we walk and roam around, we breathe in and breathe out. If this emptiness should end before us, our ability to live would end. Life itself would end.

All activities of life are due to this emptiness. In this emptiness, we have houses, homes, mansions, palaces, villages, towns, cities, plants and shrubs, mountain peaks and rivers. It is the source from which everyone derives warmth and energy. Everything appears and disappears here. If we did not have this limitless emptiness, if it were curtailed or limited, no creature would be able to find a place to live. Yet this emptiness does have a boundary on all sides and is hollow in the middle. Because it is empty, we can sit here and do everything we need to do in it.

You will have to know other things about the Divine Mother, about her food and way of living and that she never accepts even an iota of whatever substances are brought before her. She does not take these substances, she does not enjoy them. It is our feelings and emotions that enjoy them, our thoughts that accept them, our desires and objectives that use them. The Divine Mother is like the empty space between earth and sky in which all living beings are enjoying their gift of life.

The Divine Mother is the absolute whole, she is supremely whole. She is absolute peace, she is supremely peaceful. She is like fire, the sun and its rays. She is the embodiment of light. She is Divine.

Sometimes it is necessary to sacrifice a lot to find the Divine Mother. When we have been accepted into the company of a spiritually realized guru or teacher, we do not need to sacrifice anything. Until we have achieved the company of such a Master, we are invariably tied to the bonds of duality—virtue and vice, heaven and hell, action and inaction, enjoyment and pain—

all these opposites. As long as our perception of the world is in terms of these dualities, our mind remains unclear. If the mind remains unclear, all kinds of faults keep arising in it. It has been said: "The mind and its causal action lead to bondage or liberation."

It is through the mind that causality, bondage and liberation are produced and perceived. This perception exists in all creatures. It is an elusive perception where "what is not" is perceived as "what is." Things do not necessarily happen, they appear to have happened. Nobody can catch the sky, but everybody sees and perceives the sky. Nobody can catch the wind, but everybody experiences the wind. A fragrance or aroma does not have any form or color, but we still perceive it. We experience a peculiar sensation on touching somebody's skin. This is just perception. It is not reality at all. It just appears to be so.

Similarly, if we say that we can see or understand the omnipresence of the Divine Mother, it is a mistake, as this omnipresence is boundless. How can anyone measure through speech something that is immeasurable? You should know the Divine Mother to be without measure. She is part of the limitless joy and ecstasy of the play and action of *Mahabhairava*, the Supreme Being. To hear, to know and to understand the Divine Mother requires stability. This knowledge eludes us because we are so unstable and superficial.

Dear friends, to understand the Divine Mother and her actions, you have to do numerous things. Many people have sacrificed themselves several times for this understanding and yet have not recognized her. It is like the villager whose house caught on fire. He felt the heat and cried, "I am burning, I am burning." He ran away. Down the street, he felt cooler, safe and said, "Mine is burning, mine is burning."

A neighbor asked, "What is burning?"

He answered, "My boxes and my wealth, my children and my grandchildren, my cows, my whole house, everything is burning." He ran back to try to save his riches. When he neared the burning house again, he felt the heat and again said, "I am burning, I am burning." So he ran where he felt cooler and safer and in that moment of peace, he again said, "Mine is burning, mine is burning." Sometimes he thought, "I am burning," and sometimes he thought, "Mine is burning." His mind was unclear.

In the fire of life, when somebody says, "I am burning," he may get out of the situation and become stable temporarily. But because his mind is unclear, he begins to say, "Mine is burning," and then goes back to the same merciless situation that burned him in the first place. So he burns and burns and burns and turns into the charred remains of himself.

In a similar manner, we have been unsuccessful through numerous lives in finding the Divine Mother. What is the reason for this? Friends, the reason is that we have not accepted the Divine Mother in the right way. When she comes before us, we hide. The results are that we remain poor of all her virtues. We begin to revert to all our old ways, our minds get polluted and unclear and our own heart begins to hate us. The heart says, "Alas, I never moved toward that Supreme Power. I never moved toward finding my real self. I never tried to realize that I am not bound to anything, that in reality I am faultless and do not have confining egotism." The heart says, "I never vowed to myself that I would not do anything that would make me unhappy."

Since you have been born, you never made this promise to yourself. If you did, you broke your promise. When you break your promise to yourself, how can anyone else trust it? How can the Mother trust your mantra, your meditations and your prayers? You may have broken a promise you made to someone else. Thinking it would not matter so much, you might say, "Yes, I made a promise to you, but you did not keep your part of it, so I broke my promise." But the promise you made to yourself, which you should never break, is this: "Oh my self, I promise to honor you. I will never deceive you. I will never let you fall." One who makes a sincere promise like this actually makes a promise to the Divine Mother. That promise then has great value and becomes precious. On hearing such words, God arrives promptly to help.

Friends, you know that through mantra you can counter the effects of a poisonous snakebite or scorpion sting. What is the mantra for that situation? That mantra is actually a promise, as if you were saying, "Oh, God of snakes! Oh, bearer of poison! I will not harm you, your family or your relatives in any way. So help me. Please take away the poison that is killing the person you have bitten."

Thus, through our words, our speech, we receive everything. Through our words we make the Divine powers happy. If we say the wrong thing, we can be chastised, but on saying something good, we can receive sweets. It is the power of this word that results in millions of dollars of business undertaken every day. Some people do not even require a written record. People who are well respected for keeping their word just pick up the phone and ask this or that company to send them goods. If this faith in someone can move millions of dollars in our everyday practical lives, consider how important sincerity is in the world of the Divine Mother, in the world of that Supreme Being.

I do not ask you to make a promise to the Divine Mother. I ask you to make a promise to yourself. I ask that you will not break this promise to yourself. This is what is known as guru's initiation, guru's mantra. If you keep your promise to yourself, this mantra begins to grow, develop and give you the sweetest fruits. But we keep thinking the mantra is something else, that our word is something different, that the Divine Mother is something different, that the Supreme Power is something different. We think the Divine Mother has a superhuman form, endowed with four arms, riding a tiger or an elephant or a horse. This is not so, friends. Poster makers and picture makers have depicted the Divine Mother in those forms, but that is more like a cartoon than reality. But you keep meditating on those forms in those cartoons, you pray to them, you worship them. By doing this you cannot know the mysteries of the Divine Mother.

If you really want to know her, you have to make a promise to yourself. You will have to know that this empty space between the earth and the sky is the place where the whole world exists, where we exist and where the solar system exists. Above the sky is more sky, above that is still more sky and above that, even more sky. When you know that, you will know the Divine Mother, who is easily knowable through pure sentiments and emotions.

To know her in this way, we need to control ourselves and make ourselves stable. We keep thinking trivial thoughts and exuding them through our mouths like unending effervescence. We do not need to speak that much. In fact, we seem to have a disease of speaking. The more we stabilize our minds, the deeper we will become. When you become deep, you will become very stable. Then you will know how to be with the Divine Mother.

For example, when you go to a high-ranking officer, you immediately become attentive. You may be laughing or joking with your friends before that, but as soon as you are with the officer you pay attention to how much you should speak, what to say, how and where to stand. You do not stand with your back to that officer. If you did, you would be removed from the premises.

Similarly, we stand with our backs to the very Divine power that we worship. We never face the one we worship. If we face that power, we face it as if we are facing an oncoming train that will ram into us, breaking us into a million pieces. We don't stop to think that we can actually move to the side, to the left or right, get on the train in any car and go where we want to go. We face that Divine power head-on in the same way. The result can only be that we will be destroyed or, at least, we will not get to know that power.

So friends, be attentive, be stable, do not break that promise you made to yourself and you will know the Divine Mother. With this, I take leave from you.

FOCUS ON THE TRUTH

The different forms of the Supreme Power are like the bubbles within water. The bubble, the wave, the ocean, the water are all the same water. I feel hesitant to try to describe it to you, but those who are really curious will understand.

We do not realize that some things we usually think of as small or trivial that are found in every home, in every nation, are important aspects of the Divine Mother. Instruments of cleanliness, like the broom, dustpan and mop, and all our cooking utensils, like pots and pans, are like little Goddesses living with us even if we pay them no attention. We neglect them and do not understand that they merit attention and respect.

Every home has instruments for cleaning. With them, we can make this earth clean and beautiful. If we neglect them, garbage accumulates and causes disease and trouble of all kinds. Every home also contains utensils for preparing the food that satisfies our hunger. Without them, a house does not become a home, and a householder does not become a housemaster. Daily existence without these simple things would be like the life of the birds in the sky whose food lies on the earth. They may fly far, but in the end they have to come to earth for their food and water. They cannot find their sustenance in the sky. Whether spiritually realized beings, creatures with great wings or elementals that fly only in the void, everything and everyone has to take ultimate recourse to earth.

All these instruments and utensils are forms of the Divine Mother, but we do not pay attention to this fact and so remain ignorant of the deep value of everyday life. We are not able to evaluate life in its wholeness. We then feel our lives are unsatisfied and unfulfilled.

We clearly see that death extracts a heavy toll from human beings every day. Loved ones and unloved ones all leave us at one time or another. We ourselves will go like that, too. When is that moment going to arrive? When will you understand how to worship Divine power, how to make that power favorable to you, thus preserving yourself from unnecessary difficulties?

Friends, we have watched many leaders, politicians, businesspeople, yogis and scholars come and go. In their own time they have influenced world situations and conditions. Eventually those conditions reverse themselves. This is an ever-present, everlasting motion of Divine power, which is difficult even to think about, for she stays away from futile thoughts.

How, then, do we bring her into our awareness? It is by being mindful of everything in daily life. Therefore, a duster, a broom, the utensils with which we eat, all are very important. That is because there is a great fire inside us— the fire of hunger—and no one is satisfied except by providing oblations to this fire. Food oblations are what we put into our bodies for sustenance. Everyone is concerned with this, whether an ant or an elephant, a great man or a simple man. This act of offering, this *ahuti*, is symbolic of our remembrance of the Divine Mother with many names and metaphors.

To try to tie the Divine Mother within the confines of a few words is a mistake. How can we say anything about that which is beyond thought? How can we describe what she is like, what she is not like? Wise people seem to have a unanimous opinion of her. Their views, expressed in different religions and sects, point in the same direction. They have tried to point out various ways that may be taken and their pitfalls, but humans fail to understand and go on living in delusion until they die, without leaving anything behind of value.

In contrast to them, there are great souls who leave us with a few stories that can inspire us and wake us up. Sometimes what the Rishis have told us in these stories of ages gone by are not in keeping with the situation to-day. Their teachings, their real teachings, we have not understood. We keep reciting their stories, but we misunderstand what they have to say. We do not pay attention to the truth they have expounded. We go forward toward ephemeral things, transient thoughts, time-bound scriptures and imaginary events. Because of this we are not able to understand the truth about Divine creativity, the *shakti*.

Depending on what we have heard, we may understand that she is in threefold form or 10 great wisdoms or 64 yoginis or that she is the God of the village, the city and the home. She can exist to us also as time and action. Much of what we believe is a lot of hearsay that we have taken to be our religious duty. I hope you realize that some of those things were said in a different time and age and are strange for today. What is to happen will happen. We cannot stop it and we cannot do what is not to happen. That can be done only by the one who makes happen what has not yet happened, about whom it is said, "Fills the empty, drains the full, and, at will, refills again."

When we examine whether we understand these things, whether we are doing things rightly or wrongly according to our practices, do we know the reason for being unsuccessful? When we experience difficulties in fulfilling our goals, in sending oblations to the Divine, in attracting the people we want to attract, it is because of our own behavior, not the Divine Mother or the Supreme Nature. We do not understand how to harmonize all this, how to join the links that make things move by themselves. If this happens suddenly, as if by accident, then it depends on the internal vibration that rises differently and in mysterious ways in each person.

The sleep of illusion the Divine Mother creates overwhelms everyone, but even so, the Mother's heart is a sea of nourishing love. All animals, birds, human beings or other creatures harbor in their hearts what the Rishis and scriptures have described as Brahm. But, by naming it, calling it Brahm, they made the intellect Brahm oriented. All such efforts go to waste.

If all sorts of things keep arising in your mind, and you change your mind again and again, when are you going to be stable? You may have noticed often that you can see your face in still water, but if you throw a pebble or small stick into it or even a grain of mustard that causes ripples, then you cannot see your face in the water. So also, if such a disturbance occurs in a calm mind, you will not be able to see yourself in it. It becomes very difficult. Again, you have to calm yourself. Then in a sky without blemish, a blue pond or water in a plate without the slightest movement, you can see your true form as it is.

One's true form is also the form of that Supreme Power for which you pine, about whom you are curious. It is no different. It is that, and it happens in this way. Then you have to resolve within yourself, "Yes, this is how it is." Then you have to study carefully the truth that if such-and-such happens, its result is such-and-such. If you follow such-and-such an action, it leads to such-and-such an outcome. You think of such-and-such, and it happens that way! You will say to yourself, "If by thinking this way, a given result has come about, then this must be the right way of understanding that has arisen in me by itself." All this depends on that Supreme Power, whether you think of it as a trinity or a tenfold or any other form. You will know the mystery of knowledge and all the secrets behind it. Otherwise, whatever exists is a delusion and hearsay, not the real stories the Rishis of the past left for our inspiration.

Every human being is here because of the Divine Mother's creativity. This creativity is expressed through the *yantra*, the reproductive organs. There is no human being on this earth who does not feel an attraction for the *yantra*. This *yantra* represents the Supreme Power, the Divine Mother. It is not only a representation, it is That itself. By having a right view and reverence toward this *yantra*, the instability and restlessness of the mind are stilled.

The act of procreation is worship, but we do not always remember the sacredness of it. Other creatures in nature know instinctively the sacredness and seasonality of it. But human beings have lost such knowledge and are no longer attuned to the rhythms of nature. Forgetting the sacredness and overindulging in sensory pursuits result in feelings of emptiness and loss of purpose in life.

I hope that slowly you will understand this, that you will understand the true meaning of *yantra*. When you engage in such activities with the proper understanding, your intellect will not be a hindrance.

May the Divine Mother keep your intellect pure, may you experience that Supreme Power with your intellect, may you see the Divine Mother in each of your actions. May she be favorable to us all. I bow to the Divine Mother sitting within you, and take leave from you.

THE GOAL OF LIFE

Friends, there are moments we ask ourselves, "What should be the goal of my life? How should I live? What are my ideals?" These questions arise naturally in a person who has taken a few moments to reflect on the self and who is not being washed away by the mighty currents of time.

The ultimate goal of our life should be to know ourselves, to be in the presence of God or our highest ideal. We should be permeated with the qualities of our adored. Always striving to embody these ideals is called *upasana,* or worship.

There are many successful examples of *upasana* in all spiritual traditions. In Indian mythology, you always find Sita right next to Rama; Hanuman is also found sitting next to Rama. The complete devotion and unshakable dedication of Hanuman is considered an ideal. Hanuman was able to secure that position by completely immersing himself in his adored Rama. He also received the blessing of being immortal, timeless. Although Rama had to follow the call of time, Hanuman is considered still living. Hanuman's way of devotion or worship was total mental submersion in Rama. This attunement is called *manasic upasana.*

In true devotion, there is no need for ritualistic objects. There was a holy man who had a helper to plow his fields. This man would work all day in the fields and in the evening join others in listening to discourses given by the holy man. One day he heard about *manasic upasana* and liked the idea, since he could never find time or objects to perform the rituals the holy texts prescribed. He began to apply himself to this practice while plowing the fields.

One day, when the man was absorbed in his practice while plowing the fields, the holy man abruptly interrupted him. At that moment, a handful of yogurt spilled over the plow shaft. The holy man was surprised to see this, since no yogurt container was in sight. The helper explained that he was engaged in the practice he had learned from the holy man himself. He was absorbed in the *manasic upasana* of entertaining the deities whom he adored.

He was visualizing the act of serving food to his holy guests, whom he had invited to his house. He was interrupted at the point where he was serving yogurt to his company.

Further, he explained to the holy man, it is your teaching that I am following, *Kar se karm karo vidhi nana, hridaye rahe jahan kripa nidhana*—"May you be engaged in many worldly activities on the outside, but keep your heart-mind near God." It is the emotion, thought or action that emanates from deep concentration that is fruitful in finding the closeness of God or in bringing about healing and harmony in our lives. It is not polished talks or lavish ceremonies. It is the cleanliness and beauty of our heart that brings us closer to our adored. The holy man fell to the feet of his helper and begged to be taken as a disciple.

Dear friends, the purpose of all our devotional ceremonies or activities is to be able to cultivate love in our heart. Love is the way to bring the Divine closer to us. Without love, the Divine remains unattainable. Mira was able to find Krishna face-to-face by cultivating love and longing in her heart. Love is a Divine attribute. There is no rule, regulation or need of any worldly object in it. Repetition of your mantra, *manasic upasana* and love are greatly needed in everyone's life. These complement each other and are almost synonymous with each other. You cannot cultivate love without the relationship of the server and the served. A great need exists for mutual love between the two. As love grows, there is no separation between the server and the served.

As an *Aghor* saint says: "They both sit on the same seat. At that moment, the separation between Master and servant disappears." From outside they may appear to be different, yet both are the same. Divine love is something practical that can be cultivated by *manasic upasana*.

We say the prayer, *Sarveshwari tvam pahimam saranagatam*—"O' Mother, I bow to you and come under your protection." If we experience suffering and fear and end up doing lowly acts after surrendering ourselves to the Divine, it is because of our halfhearted proclamation. We just say it with our tongue, not with our deep self, and end up behaving differently with our heart and actions. When we totally surrender—together with our heart, action and voice—even the impossible becomes possible. If we left it all to Sarveshwari, there would never be any suffering.

The Divine Mother, Shakti or Sarveshwari, is nothing but the embodiment of our right actions. The demons mentioned in our texts are nothing but our own undisciplined minds. An undisciplined mind overpowers the senses, which have been weakened by their greedy nature. The Divinity within us cries out for help. By keeping good company, wisdom emerges. The wisdom, the *shakti*, empowered by the forgotten strength of the Divinity within, subjugates the demon, the undisciplined mind.

The deception of an undisciplined mind is great. Various kinds of wishes and desires lay hidden in this kind of mind. Once you completely surrender to the Divine, the *shakti*, Sarveshwari, delivers us from undesirable times. Without this surrender, the undisciplined mind keeps deceiving itself and never becomes centered. It is necessary to impede the flights of fancy of your mind. Repeating your mantra is the best tool for curbing restlessness of the mind. With a little meditation and repetition of your mantra, your mind begins to rest, and that momentary stillness becomes the sprouting ground for Divine attributes and characteristics within you. What seemed impenetrable begins to reveal itself, and many doors fly open to you.

The true meaning of meditation is not to shut your eyes and keep yourself in the dark. Meditation is paying attention with deep-rooted stillness in the mind. A mind that is not agitated like the seashore, but is calm and deep, is like the middle of the ocean. It is aware of its depth and richness. It does not clash with the world; it is self-contained with its riches and depth.

O' friend, remain absorbed in the sound of the mantra within. What else do you need? The mantra of the Divine Mother that you have is like the mythical stone that turns iron into gold. With the touch of this stone, iron becomes gold, not copper or aluminum. Once you repeat your mantra, absorbed in its vibration, the attributes of the Divine Mother begin to find their place in your inner being. You become Divine. The goal of our life is not to move closer to *aishwrya*, material wealth, but toward *Ishwara*, God.

Passion is bondage.
   Only in a mind free of desires
will God emerge.

Chapter 16 Baba Speaks to His Monks

WHO IS AN *AGHOR* ASCETIC?

One day Sudharma appeared before me and with due respect began to prepare to ask a question. Before he could speak, understanding what was on his mind, I addressed him with the following words:

> Sudharma, if you have any suspicion, I would not be able to relieve you of it, but if you have a query, I will definitely resolve it for you. Have you not heard that people with suspicion never succeed in achieving their goal? *Sanshayatma vinashyati*—"The skeptic destroys himself." There may be a time for inquisitiveness, but you must have heard the saying that there is no gain without a firm belief.
>
> *Aghor* ascetics stay very far from doubt. If one is newly initiated, naturally, that person has inquisitiveness at that stage. But *Aghor* ascetics do not dwell in the body-mind. They dwell in the consciousness of self and with resolve reach very substantial states. After they reach these states, they become so polite that their voices have nothing but sweetness. Their vocabulary has no place for defiling provocative words or those that spread enmity. Such words don't even arise.
>
> Whenever you come across such people, take them to be blessed by the *Kapaleshwar*, the "great unknown" who dwells in the cosmos, the spirit of *Aghoreshwar*. With unbreakable faith and reverence, they are moved by human sufferings.
>
> *Aghor* ascetics are cultivated people. They do not like to see anyone spreading disharmony. Their way is one of friendliness, compassion for one another and seeing love within each other.
>
> *Aghor* ascetics do not have any special appearance. They do not have any sign of class, caste or religion. They do not even worry about feeding themselves. Whatever comes their way they accept.
>
> Their life is the life of actionless action. That is, they do nothing, and nothing is left undone. Following this principle of actionless action, they remain blameless and firm in their austerity and respect everything. Others may cheat them, but they never cheat. Remaining prideless, they show respect to others.

They may use discarded pieces of cloth as their clothing, whether that cloth has holes in it or not, whether discarded in the trash or even having been used as a shroud for the dead. They want to use only such things that are of no more use to any other person.

Aghor ascetics renounce alcohol, sex, lies and deceit. They keep reminding themselves and others that by harboring these things, there is a constant fear of attack from the armies of lust, anger and passion. Therefore they avoid these things. Instead, *Aghor* ascetics are continuously engaged in manifesting something for the well-being of others. They also turn away from mundane differences in people such as race, color or religion.

The *Aghor* tradition is no different from the *Aghor* state of consciousness. This state is naturally attained by the noble person who keeps longing to offer respect and acquire faith through the grace of the teachings and initiation from the guru. Just as the ill-bred person practicing evil thoughts is possessed by evil, the well-bred ascetic contemplating Brahma becomes an icon of great peace and calmness. Those who speak pleasing words become disciplined. Noble healing words keep emanating from their speech.

Aghor ascetics who serve their egos by taking pride in the name of *Aghoreshwar* have strayed from the path and are deformed. They would do anything for the sake of meager gains. They are not role models. For these reasons, discerning people do not favor them. According to the view of many, these ascetics are never liberated.

The need for liberation arises for the one who is body conscious, not for the one who is soul conscious. There is no need of such distinction for the one who is Brahma conscious. That person remains totally absorbed in the quest of the truth, content in the self and living in good company. Have you not heard the saying, "Dwell among the renunciates for at least 12 years, then you will learn a dialect?" The word "dialect" refers to that very soothing speech of the accomplished ones. With the vibrations of that very speech, luster, glow and currents like electricity are experienced without the necessity for any rituals, worship or *pranayama*. In the very flow of contemplation, you obtain everything that is of the nature of consciousness.

Popular belief has it that *Aghor* ascetics do not abstain from liquor and meat, but that is not so. They do not encourage anyone to partake of these, including themselves. It is a different matter if they prescribe something of the sort for a person suffering from a cold or in ill health. But any medication is taken in moderation. Meat is never eaten like a full plate of rice, and liquor is not drunk like a full jug of water. You must have heard of the left-handed practice: Left is the side of the beloved or favorite. All the great beings of the past like Dattatreya, Abhinavagupta, Aghor Bhairavacharya, Kalu Ram and Maharaj Sri Kinaram attained realization by walking on the straight path. Once you walk on the crooked path, you may fall down and break your limbs.

Deformities may arise. Once you fall on the path, other vehicles may run over you. There is a great possibility of it.

To see a true *Aghor* ascetic is like getting a glimpse of Shiva himself. *Aghor* ascetics not only are impartial, they are unbiased, as well. In their greatness, they accept social relationships with everyone. They are not judgmental, just as the sun, moon, earth and fire are not judgmental. *Bhedo na bhasate; abhedo bhasate sarvatram*— "Discrimination does not arise; nondiscrimination permeates everything." Just as the sun, moon, earth, fire and wind are not here for any particular religion, class, caste or nation, the *Aghor* ascetic who has attained the stage of impartiality acts for the well-being of everyone.

Aghor ascetics are not the slaves of a lazy mind. Their virtues and modesty are for the well-being of all. These qualities help restrain one's mental modifications, causing foul thoughts and tendencies to subside.

DEVOTION

Darshi! Let me tell you about Shambhav, a true seeker and fully developed disciple of mine, who met me recently after a long interval.

He asked, "What is our worship, and who is it we worship?"

I told him, "The God within each of us, the 'great unknown,' or *atmaram*, the very life force that permeates us all, is the object of our worship. Acknowledging and revering our own higher self is our worship."

Shambhav was not satisfied and asked me again. He was a dear disciple and curious to know things. Of course, he was as I was at one time, eager to do something, but he had no direction and was therefore helpless and could do little. So I told him:

The desire to find the "great unknown," God within oneself, should always be burning. The true seeker must feed this fire. All our actions are offerings to that fire, offerings of love, gentleness and modesty to that "great unknown" within us. Making an offering of these attributes in the fire is worship to that "unknown." One feels a hunger to feed this fire, and if you ignore this hunger, you become sick. You develop a dislike for the things that can truly satisfy you, and soon you cannot even digest such food. The people around you notice this and call you a sick person. They say you have developed a dislike for the real food of courtesy, politeness and affection that would bring you in touch with good company—the kind of company that could help you find the "great unknown" within yourself.

We feel so much pain and intolerable suffering when the fire is left to burn out and the "great unknown" within remains a mystery. Only one who has kept the fire burning, one who has contained the life force from wasting away, knows the mystery of eternal life. Such a person has come face-to-face with real life. This person sees and knows the inner and outer reality of human life, as well as of the universe. One who knows these things gives meaning to the proverb "Wealth and earth are similar; they are the same inside or out."

After listening to my thoughts, Shambhav appeared to be very far from his own self. Although he wanted to come close to his own self, he did not know how to do so. His meeting with me could not act as a fast-moving chariot that would enable him to embrace immediately the great God within himself. So I went on to tell him:

As long as you live for yourself, your life is useless. The day you realize that you are living for others, your life will become meaningful. Encircled by great successes, you will automatically have a clear understanding of the great truth that lies within you. Then you will feel that my words have taken root in you.

I hope that you will be able to realize this mystery easily. The worship of the "great unknown" within you is not difficult. If you maintain the attachments to things of this world, you will be unacquainted with real life. These attachments, posing to be good things, turn the innermost self into a storehouse of refuse.

One must abide by certain practices. A man cannot perform the movements of the hands, feet and eyebrows of a woman in a natural way. However, with practice a man can attain proficiency in this art and then perform these movements in a natural way. Continuing your practices will lead you to perfection.

Darshi! Shambhav took this great secret as something that is accessible and became eager to engage in the search for the "great unknown" within himself. He related the following event to me, saying, "A few days ago, the guru of one of my friends died. His disciples placed the body in a box and lowered it into the water."

I asked, "Did your friend and his co-disciples worship the body or the life force of their guru?"

Shambhav replied, "There are many shortcomings in the worship of those disciples. That is why my friend could not comprehend. He kept worshipping his guru's body. Had he worshipped the very life force, the real life of his guru, he would not feel depressed and deprived."

I told Shambhav:

> The guru of your friend is the life force, for lack of which his body was offered to the water. It is not the existence of the body that denotes life for the guru, since the guru lives independently of the body. The guru in the form of life force is always easily accessible to the seeker with practice. By the guru who lives independently of the body, many hard-to-obtain accomplishments are made easily accessible.

Darshi! I went on to explain to Shambhav that through the grace of the guru in physical form, the disciple could develop his ability to become like his guru.

> Pay attention to the guru and remember his posture while he performs those deeds in which you wish to succeed. Pay homage to him with your life. If you wish to succeed in agricultural activities, you should meditate on his state, posture and efforts while he is engaged in agricultural activities or gardening. If you wish to gain an effective power of explaining things, meditate on the look of his face, his state and the effort he uses while he preaches. If you wish to give in charity, meditate on the look on your guru's face, his state at the time of giving. If you wish to serve the poor and the suffering like your guru, meditate on his state at the time he is serving the suffering. The guru will grant you strength and arm you with the necessary requirements for service. O' friends, the guru of your friend has not gone anywhere. The guru is always present with you as long as you are breathing. Your guru always dwells within you.
>
> It is unfortunate that many people are unable to be certain about the good results of practicing and following these activities. When doubts cease to exist and people become established in their faith, they will be able to recall the various postures, movements and expressions on the face of the guru in different activities in the guru's life. It is said, the guru comes in various forms and colors and is always with us. Remember the *Aghor Gayatri* mantra. It will help you find the "great unknown" within you. The journey will come to an end by walking on your own feet and not on the feet of any other person.

I asked Shambhav to come and sit with me in *Aghor* practice soon and strengthen his previous practices. Now go and perform your duties, the time and occasion of which are known to you. I am also going to perform my daily routine for which time and occasion are waiting.

PRANA

Darshi! Very early this morning, that inquisitive Shambhav met me and said, "Gurudev, my mind is disturbed and misinformed. Please give direction and stability to my mind."

I told him this: "For all causality, bondage and liberation, the mind is the instrument. O' Shambhav, doubts have afflicted you. You justify the proverb 'A half-empty vessel makes much noise.' Water in a vessel that is full to the brim does not stir."

I said that because of some misunderstanding he was in such a state, and there was a reason for it:

> You gather only tatters, yet you want a lovely cloak stitched from them. The patches will be visible everywhere from the outside, and the inside will let in the cold. By wearing a cloak stitched from tatters, you experience little warmth inside. All the scriptures are mere patches sewn together. They are not whole cloth. If you see clearly, you can see patches everywhere. The cloak sewn from such patches will yield to pressure. Hence, you see many seekers struggling in vain as their ideas yield to pressure.

Shambhav understood my words. He said, "You are very mysterious, Dada, your style is unique."

I went on with what I wanted to tell him, "Why are you groping around trying to understand a hundred theories? Understand one and be absolutely certain about it."

Shambhav said, "Dada, this certainly is what I am not able to achieve. Had I been able to understand, would I have tried to hide from respected *Aghor* ascetics?"

I replied, "O' Shambhav, I do not want the mere shell of your body, empty of you. Your presence is the presence of the Divine Mother. When you are present, you take right action. Right action is known as creativity; it is the fountainhead of *prana*, life energy.

"The superconsciousness, the *chaitanya* manifesting in a conscious body, is known as character. You don't need a personified God; you need the attributes and character of God. The presence of God's attributes and characteristics is the presence of God. It is God or *atmaram*—that is, *prana*—that permeates all beings and under various names we celebrate in all the poetry, literature and historical and religious texts."

Shambhav understood the value of my compassion, Darshi. He said, "I had heard that the nature of *Aghor* ascetics is very kind."

I answered him that they neither seek action nor inaction. Between being doer and non-doer, *Aghor* ascetics keep making offerings to their *prana*, to *vaishvanara*, the cosmic creative principle. That is why they are skilled in containing hundreds of vital life energies, *dhananjaya prana*, like yours in their own *kapal-khappar*, or field of consciousness.

Eternity, which is ever new, never becomes past and never becomes future. It is always in the present moment. *Prana* vibrates only in the present.

Darshi, you know that morning is the best time for *Aghor* ascetics to embrace their *prana*. At that very time, Shambhav comes strolling by with his curiosity. Explain to him for me that when the sun begins to set, the seeker, free from all duties, becomes reflective and thinks about all the things that have been told to him by the guru *Aghoreshwar*.

One should be like the *chataka*, a bird that takes a drop of water at the beginning of the season and is satisfied by that drop through the entire season. This is known as the ability to see things through, the ability to discern correctly. Darshi, explain this to Shambhav.

Now go and finish those things for which time and occasion are known to you. I too am getting ready for the routines for which time and occasion are waiting.

UNMANI CONDITION: KNOWLEDGE OF PRANA

Darshi! That homeless Shambhav met me again last evening. As he sat facing the west, the setting sun added even more beauty to that austere *sadhaka's* radiant face. It seemed as if the setting sun had left its own image behind. I heard Shambhav speaking in a serious voice, so I said with a smile, "Young ascetic, you are late today!"

Shambhav gave this reason, "Dada, since this morning many insincere people brought their troubles to me with folded hands. I wanted to suggest some easy ways to relieve them of their sorrows so that they may be happy, but it seemed they were happier in carefully protecting their sorrows and troubles. Perhaps they did not want to have their troubles removed because then they would think they would have no more reasons to visit saints and great souls and speak of their condition in front of them. This is just an excuse for trying to be close to saints and great souls."

I also have met with some artificial people, either disciples or visitors. These artificial people are two-faced. They act as if there is no better *sadhaka* or devotee than they are. Therefore, I was not surprised on hearing what that young ascetic had to say on the subject. O' brother, everybody knows that any untruth is impure and must be given up.

Shambhav then asked, "Dada, is *abhava*, the scarcity or nonexistence of something, the hidden element that activates *prana* in a person's life?"

I laughed loudly and replied, "Oh, no, Shambhav. Where *bhava*, the sincere attitude, has not even arisen, you won't see even a residue of *abhava*, the lack of *bhava*. The lack of *abhava* is actually *purnabhava*, complete sincerity. It's the same as the residue of day is not day, and the residue of night is not night. Rather, the cessation of day is night, and the cessation of night is day."

Darshi! The rays of the setting sun reflected on Shambhav's face, making him look so Divine. This whole world is slowly edging toward the pyre of death. Many of those who have come before, having neglected their *prana*, have edged into the pyre and been burnt and washed away. You can see it. Worship *prana*. If somebody chases you with a stone or brick, if somebody addresses you with vindictiveness, you become eager to retaliate because of your unfathomable affection for your *prana*. If *prana* is not moving in your body, you have no reaction or excitement when somebody abuses you with words or hits you with a stone or brick.

Darshi! You should know that getting free of the desire for either sleep or wakefulness, practicing to keep *prana* still within you awakens something new in the body that is true and evident. In that mental state no attack from anywhere feels hurtful and no excitement or anxiousness arises. The scriptures call this condition *unmani*. When you experience this, you are neither asleep nor awake, neither conscious nor unconscious, neither accepting nor relinquishing. You have no experience of either being or nonbeing. At that time, one with your *prana*, you are in ecstasy.

Darshi! You know that the absence of virtue is sin, and the absence of sin is virtue. When both sin and virtue are absent, that condition is called the illusion-free *citta*, a state in which wholesome consciousness manifests. It is also known as *pranamaya bodha*, the awareness of oneness with *prana*. Know this, and it will be with you forever. Be very alert to time. *Para prakriti*, the Divine nature, is not easily understood, but it is natural.

ADVERSE CIRCUMSTANCES

Shambhav! I generally see that people blame adverse circumstances for their misfortunes. The question is, How do such circumstances arise? Because of our weakness, we ignore our good instincts and perform lowly deeds that themselves create adverse circumstances. We bring them upon ourselves. Miseries and death can be the only results of these lowly deeds. Good and ideal behavior never causes inadequacy or misery. It is improper conduct, ideas and behavior that make us weak.

Shambhav! There is a popular saying that man himself invites misery and death. He does not do so because of unknown situations but, rather, because of known ones. You may ask how a person fully aware of the negative results of gambling still may adopt the gambling habit. Because of such misconduct, he loses not only money but also health. To make up the loss of money, he takes recourse to borrowing, and when people stop lending him money, he takes to deceiving others. When this door also closes, he is compelled to take to begging. Such a man becomes argumentative and tries to escape the world by indulging in uncontrolled sexual habits. He often is in trouble with the law. Then because of ill health, the man falls in the clutches of the twin miseries old age and death. What can all this be called but an invitation to adverse circumstances, misery and death?

There is another popular saying that the element of strength in the body, the semen, is the source of a healthy body and long life. When it is wasted and neglected, the body becomes weak and diseased. This waste and neglect leads to misery. If someone pleads ignorance, saying that none of this is his fault because he was unaware of what he was doing, even the patience to learn better habits abandons such a creature.

I do not say that we should attach importance to old ideas that the scriptures propound. I do not ask women or men to accept as ideal the conduct of those trapped by lust. I only say that they should be cautious and alert. They should not twist words around and give them absurd meanings. Neither should they adopt the false values created by cheap entertainment. They should be aware of the magical attraction of seductive temptations offered by these irresponsible amusements. I have seen children playing with dolls as a source of entertainment, and there is nothing wrong with that. They grow out of it. But Shambhav, how long will you continue to act like a child? Give it up!

Human life is not always available to all living creatures. I have heard yogis say that even Gods crave human bodies. Are you, too, afraid of adverse circumstances, Shambhav? Be fearless! Be calm so that no trace of fear is left. You don't own these circumstances. They exist on their own. They are unfamiliar, not yours. Whenever you have a familiar situation and still consider yourself to be helpless and unfamiliar, it is no less than deceiving yourself. You will have to understand that in this way. Then it will be not what is heard but what is seen.

Shambhav! Now go and perform the routines you know to be appropriate to time and occasion. I am also going to perform the routines for which time and occasion are waiting.

GREATNESS AND THE *AGHORESHWAR*

One day the young ascetic Shambhav asked me, "Dada, is the burning ground a holy place? Is the burning ground the altar of penance and worship?"

I laughed and said:

> Simple fellow! No other place can be holier than the burning ground. No one knows how many lifeless bodies of creatures have been given as offerings to the fire in the burning ground over the centuries. No one can say how many bodies of great warriors, kings, emperors, merchants, saints, gentlemen, thieves, fools, proud leaders and learned men have been given in the past, are being given in the present and will

be given in the future to the God of death appearing in the form of the fire burning in the burning ground.

The fire of many houses and cities has burned and vanished, but the fire in the burning ground has always been burning and fed with offerings of lifeless bodies. The people, frightened by delusion, appear to be burning in the pyre of anxiety as they neglect the "great unknown" within themselves. There is not much difference between the so-called living and the so-called dead. Lack of judgment will certainly draw one to the pyre of anxiety. There are no two opinions about it; it is inevitable. Just as the clean and pure hearts of *Aghoreshwars* and their Divine forms known as *Kapaleshwars* are the refuge of the lives of many people, the burning ground gives refuge to lifeless bodies.

No one can run away in fear. There is no place on this earth or in the sky or in the nether world where one can hide. The proximity of one's guru, one's life holder, is the only refuge that can enable us to face these pains, troubles and miseries. From infancy to adolescence, from adolescence to youth and from youth to old age, every moment the body undergoes changes and shall continue to do so. You can avoid these miseries only with the grace of the guru.

When you know this, you will not be afraid of seeing the offerings of lifeless creatures to the burning ground. Those creatures who are attached to their homes, families and relations are seen burning in the fire of anxiety even while there is life in them. Do you not see that the pyre is burning the dead while anxiety is burning the living? From ant to elephant, from man to God, from seers to sages, no one is able to escape it. Renounce all attachments and delusions. Renounce even the renunciation. When there is nothing you can call your own or that can live as one's own self, you will be free from your fears and delusions.

Young ascetic! This youth also is burning and undergoing change. This you must understand because it is the truth. I do not say that you should become stagnant after understanding only this much. This is not complete understanding. Move ahead of it. There is something beyond it, and there also is something beyond that that you have to know. To come to know the real self, you must get rid of attachments.

Young ascetic! Whatever you have said, heard or seen so far is only a small fraction of all the elements worth knowing. It is not the whole, so do not consider it to be the whole. It would be a mistake on your part to consider it whole. When a person goes to sleep reading a book, when he awakens he starts reading from where he left off. Until the last moment of your life, be engaged in the worship of life because only this mortal body will be destroyed. The living life will always be in the universe. So, too, will the memory of our practices, activities and remembrances always be in the universe. Whenever you like, you can enter a body, and remembering your previous awareness, you can perform every deed you need to perform. Young ascetic! It is not impossible nor is it surprising. It is in this way that I, the *Aghoreshwar,* move in the universe.

Many Divine beings move about the universe in this way. They call me whenever they wish, and they come to visit me, too. They are capable of making every impossible achievement possible and do so when required. These Divine beings, whose life is the Divine life, are known as *Kapaleshwars*. Although still in human form, *Aghoreshwars* are also not restricted by their bodies. They move from one place to another. Absence of the physical body does not stand in the way of this kind of movement, nor in availing oneself of their help.

Turn yourself into water, air, earth, sky, light or fire as required. Whenever and wherever you find an object needed by the living, present yourself in the form of that object. By turning yourself into articles of food, you can sustain the life of creatures. In the form of water, you can quench their thirst. In the form of air, you can provide coolness or heat, as required. You can give them refuge in the form of earth and free movement in the form of sky. Young ascetic! *Aghoreshwars* always perform such deeds mysteriously. There is nothing surprising in that. Now you, too, will have to do it.

Remember, attachments and anxiety burn men as surely as lust dwells in their hearts. In one endowed with tolerance and evenness in life, virtue and religious seeds reside. The one whose life is crooked and uneven is an abode of condemnation, vanity and scarcity. Those who are generous by nature are endowed with glory and greatness and are easily pleased. They show kindness without rhyme or reason. One who keeps such company attains joy and becomes joy for others.

Do this by detaching yourself and others from bad deeds. Deliver yourself and others from death. When cutting the attachment to bad deeds, you might weep and cry aloud. If cries of attachment move you, you will not grow strong. They will make you tie your feet with your own hands. It is because of attachments that your life looks sickly, tattered and worm eaten.

We see animals who, overcome by passion, run after each other. Real devotion does not mean that we remain a slave to passion. Rather, the meaning of devotion is doing away with passion. The day we are free from attachment to passion, we will be free from sexual desire. When we come to understand it, our life becomes free from sexuality, and then we are delivered from the bondage of birth and death.

Therefore, if you see young people doing wrong, go and do whatever you think is proper according to your opinion and capacity. Do not borrow someone else's opinion. You will have to understand for yourself. The scriptures alone will not cause you to embrace the life hidden within you. When a person is self-directed, this awareness awakens. Specialize in creating a mind firmly rooted in meditation. What can be better than this?

Through firm determination and practice, you can know the unknown. The knowledge given in the scriptures can neither be understood nor practiced. The knowledge given in the scriptures can only be a refuge for hypocrisy and discussion. Knowledge from holy books and scriptures cannot be literally understood nor directly practiced. You will have to understand and interpret books and scriptures according to the age in which you are living, not the one in which they were written. Devotee, you are practiced now to a great extent. Your practice is perfect. It will lead you toward perfection. It will inspire you not toward desires but toward selfless actions. It will enable you to see the otherworldliness and not this worldliness. I believe that the distance between "I and mine" and "thou and thine" must now be quite reduced in you.

The devotee, Darshi, and the seeker, Shambhav, bowed in gladness. Then they went away to perform their routines, the time and occasion of which were known to them. I, *Aghoreshwar,* also got ready for the routines for which the time and occasion were waiting.

PUBLIC CONDUCT AND ITS IDEALS

Darshi! Copying what others do justifies the proverb "One who imitates others has no substance and harbors weakness." So it is in the case of the enjoyment of the objects of the senses. Imitating others in this respect not only shatters the body, it also invites diseases.

Darshi! One who expects good results by deceiving himself and others is considered a person who wants to taste fruits that are not in season through verbal and visual description.

A person who is cunning by nature does not talk face-to-face with anyone after committing a crime. He looks down while talking, scratches his back with his fingers and the earth with his big toe. These are symptoms of a person involved in a lowly act or crime. Such a person is escaping the reality of a lowly act.

One who is innocent in mind, words and deeds always holds his head high and is not nervous alone or in a crowd. His eyelids do not fall down again and again. He does not scratch his head or back. He leads a fearless, innocent life and has proper vision.

Darshi! It's worth keeping the company of such a person. Nothing is unattainable for him in whose mind the good of others resides.

One who hides the truth becomes the abode of thousands of lies and only adds to perversity. You know the sages and seers told of the corrupt acts of those who took undue advantage of their situations with the wives of the sages and thereby earned infamy. The sages could have kept such horrible acts secret, but they feared doing so would adversely affect society. So the scriptures mentioned these crimes. Affixing their seal of approval on these books, the sages and seers showed that these incidents were real.

The reason for making such acts public is to forgive the corrupt deeds of the past and prevent the corrupt deeds of the future. Concealing these offenses would not only let their foul smell affect the wrongdoers, but it also would have been unbearable to the entire society.

Darshi! You can hide what has happened, what is happening and what is to happen from those who can neither help nor honor you. But you cannot keep it secret from the Lord of nature, the "great unknown" within you. You can hide it from others, but you can't hide it from yourself.

Robbers who, ignoring society, think they have fully satisfied themselves with the looted wealth of others, cannot relish the taste of even the best preparations of cream, dried fruits or sweets. Without experiencing true contentment, they just put something in their stomachs so they may live for more time. Darshi! It is strange and surprising.

Such people, devoid of understanding, are like moths. The moth knows that its death is certain if it goes near the light. Even then, it flies around the light and loses its life. In the same way, people of passion and unrestrained desire know that the misuse of their tongues and procreative organs takes them toward certain death, yet they give free reign to them and sacrifice themselves. Only persons of corrupt intellect keep company with such persons. No good person seeks their company. Darshi! It is necessary to root out such ideas and emotions, to control them and not let them come near. If you practice again and again, it is certain you will succeed in this effort.

The more readily you overcome these weaknesses by constant practice, the more capable you grow in obtaining natural happiness, peace, prosperity and success. You cannot obtain and recognize these great and ultimate aims of life by trying to escape, sitting in the loneliness of a cave. What is attainable a person of corrupt intellect can never attain. Who does not know this? Darshi! These days ignorant people want easy public recognition and support of their petty ideas and deeds. They move through society like the very personification of sacrifice and penance. Even when people recognize them, they pay little heed to the needs of the masses. The mockery of the situation is that these very people have been declaring that their only aim is the service and protection of the interests of society. They have forgotten the true worship, the service that can do good for society and be beneficial in fulfilling everyone's dream.

Darshi! Service to society and fulfillment of the needs of the masses is the greatest worship. No penance, knowledge or renunciation can excel this worship. One who is devoted heartily to this worship does not care for or run after public recognition. Only one who always is engaged in fulfilling the needs of the masses and does one's best to achieve it should be considered a saint. A real sage is the person with proper vision and knowledge.

Darshi! However much you might be insulted, do not give up your good ideas and conduct. Do not give up the good of others. In such activities, the beginning is assured, the middle is auspicious, and the impact is certain. This is real fame.

After one sheds one's body, this real fame remains. Darshi! Do not compel your conscience to permit you to do things that it does not condone; otherwise it will become heavy and unbearable. If you compel your mind to act improperly, the mind will be adversely affected and become inactive.

WHAT IS NEEDED TODAY

Darshi! Malang, the visiting Sufi ascetic from Afghanistan, searched for me today for a long time and at last found me. After bowing, he expressed his anxiety by saying, "You are a mysterious *Avadhut*. Before giving me your audience, you made me wander from place to place. *Aghoreshwar!* Why is my curiosity compelling me to run after you like a discontented soul?" I answered him in the following words:

> O' Malang! Listen to me. Hindus, Mohammedans, Christians and Buddhists are followers of their respective religions because of their birth, not through their actions or behavior. They have been diverted from the real path. This must be known for certain. It is only then that you will be able to know the truth about various religions. Curiosity is born of one's own ignorance. Although being so near to yourself, your seeking takes you far from yourself, Malang! You can only become stable

when you realize that the truth is already inside you. It is the same as when you want to see Mother Earth; you look down, not up. Being so near to the religions, you are unable to find yourself. In such a situation, you are bound to go astray.

The reason for this is neither imbalance nor the absence of imbalance. As a matter of fact, this curiosity arises only in a balanced mind, and having the inner vision itself may be the cause. *Prana*, the life force, is the substance of glory. Unawareness of it makes one roam far and wide like a perplexed traveler. When awareness becomes a natural constituent of one's nature, the race, the search and the curiosity cease. By constant pursuance of the source of life force, awareness arises. It is the body through which life force manifests. Being absorbed in the life within oneself is the attainment of great glory. After attaining this state, one does not know if it is morning or evening, or what the date is. The attainment of this state bestows ecstasy.

Malang! If you search only on the surface, you will never find it, as there is nothing on the surface. In reality, only that which is not, is. That is what you are looking for. Out of this awareness comes understanding.

How can the statement of the scriptures, "Not this, not this" be made meaningful? The company of fools makes one a fool. It is in one's own interest to remain unacquainted with them. Anything that comes from time-honored authority or a so-called expert is only a half-truth. That which you consider lost in thick darkness is actually present before you. You wander about in exile from your home. It is due to enmity that we have become our own enemy. Otherwise there is no other reason for being displaced from our own home.

For those who are fixed on the truth within them, kundalini— the energy hidden in the human body that is in the shape of a coiled serpent—holds its tail in its mouth. Such persons can clearly see the present and the future with their own eyes. In this state, the sight of something beautiful does not cause a distraction. Other people, however, create complications in their lives. The sight of beauty stirs them, which gives birth to complications. In such a state, they become victims of the weakness born of the loss of energy. They become like a mountain that gradually and continuously erodes. Beauty stirs the body in a flash. That is why sages have said, "Do not look at external beauty, don't indulge in its essence." Only the unenjoyed essence may prove helpful in knowing life, *prana*.

When keeping oneself unstirred, a person untouched by the sensory attractions toward another person becomes *turiyatita*. This stability transcends itself and becomes eternal bliss. True bliss is not found in the external entertainment of the sensory organs. It is not possible for this kind of entertainment to bear fruit of any substance. External enjoyments are incomplete truth.

Indulging definitely leaves a bad taste in the mouth. For this reason sages and saints of the past have advocated abstinence. But the day you come to understand that there is a great need to convert that foul taste into fragrance, this tendency of escapism will cease to exist. A true seeker, while living a family life, practices moderation and shuns escapism. The acceptance of "no" and "moderate" is wholesome and simple. Religions and historical viewpoints are something different, difficult to measure by the standards of time and situation. Malang! Are you listening to the lion like the roar of change? Everywhere what has happened in the past cannot happen in new times.

When *prana* departs, the body returns to the five elements. *Prana*, the life force or the soul itself, should be considered the symbol, the beholder of knowledge. No one will be able to know the world or its creator without becoming familiar with one's *prana*. It is through the soul contained in the body that one realizes the world and the creator of the world.

Darshi! Encourage Malang by telling him about these basic facts. If Malang still holds his old opinion, we can infer that his inner self has not come in contact with true knowledge and he has not yet understood.

One cannot measure the strength and power of the soul, for it is infinite. We give the name soul to the infinite, which has neither beginning nor end. Without knowing the "great unknown" one cannot know the arbitrator of the world. This knowledge and realization can come only through one's guru. So if Malang asks how he will learn the truth about it, tell him to go to the country where there are saints.

There have always been saints in this country, and there will continue to be. If a society does not ascribe appropriate respect to saints, the effects of undue perversity, acrimony and unfriendliness will be very evident. Where great souls and their virtues become absent, homes, villages, cities and countries give birth to lustful, oppressive and indecent people. Devotee Darshi! Only in the absence of friendship and compassion do nations give birth to characterless people, without dynamism. Revering the life force and the soul and acknowledging their dignity are the worship of a knowable God.

Lack of knowledge makes one see the leaves and not the roots. The popularly accepted mythological forms have been given the name *Mahapurusha*, saints. It is said that when a *Mahapurusha's* inner being touches you, you experience a vibration. If you come to know about the transient nature of this body, you are capable of knowing everything.

Darshi! There was a time when great men, indifferent to the world, had given two views about what a person must do and must not do for society. It may have been to protect their country from having outside influences become established there. They paid no attention to the production and procurement of all the consumable necessities, from grain to water.

In our present situation, the entire world is family. Each one of us is a member of this family and part of the great fire of life. It has become our duty to stop misuse of things required for sustaining the life of all living beings. We can do so only by ideal conduct and behavior. It has become essential to make efforts for maximum production and to inspire one another to do so, so that no citizen of any nation may suffer from scarcity. If everyone together offers life's essentials to the *pranamayi*, Divinity in the form of life force that resides in the body-altar of all people, our whole society could live a life of peace and prosperity. Because of siding with half-truths, we find ourselves far from this possible reality.

Devotee Darshi! This is what we need today. This is the worship of the "great unknown." It also is the duty of the great people and saints who by their conduct should be an example for the common people. There can be no other worship or duty greater than this. Let it be reflected in your own conduct to inspire others. Speaking of it without accepting it will merely be oral preaching, which will not only keep you ignorant but also keep others ignorant.

Living for others is the real worship.

The *Satsangs* of Aghoreshwar Bhagwan Ramji

Satsang literally means in the company of truth. This company can take many forms, including being in the presence of the guru imparting knowledge or wisdom, listening to the teachings of noble beings or reading inspirational books. All are *satsang*.

The relationship between guru and devotee develops in the environment of truth, often just by sitting together quietly or in an exchange of questions and answers.

Desires meet
    only with illusion.

Chapter 17

Questions & Answers

Gurudeva! I bow to thee with all my limbs. Please tell me what is the means of liberation—knowledge or action?

Purification of the mind takes place through action. Action and knowledge complement each other. Without one, the other remains incomplete. They are like the wings of a bird in the sky. It is with the help of both wings that the bird flies. When action purifies the mind, knowledge arises and liberation is attained. After realization, the life force becomes easy to comprehend. Perform your assigned ashram duties with undivided attention, and the vision of knowledge will blossom from there. Knowledge cannot be attained in inaction, and knowledge alone does not bring liberation. You can soar in the sky of liberation only with the support of both wings—the wing of knowledge and the wing of action.

Baba, please tell me something about prana.

Prana is the nameless name that dwells in the abodeless abode. *Prana* is the very life of each and every being who has come into existence. *Prana* is the "I" that is seated in all living beings. That is why living beings are called *pranis*. *Prana* is also known as the sound, the air. The Lord of Prana is the Supreme *atma*, which is unknowable, except when experienced in the stillness of the *pranic* force, your very life force.

Prana-shakti materializes in the form of all sentient beings and all creation. The origin, sustenance, dissolution and disappearance of the world are but a wave of the *pranic* ocean. Seated in all beings, *cidanand*, bliss absolute, vibrates as the air waves. The activities of the world, which have cast a spell on living beings, are nothing but the play of *prana*. No matter how pure beings may be, they do not see themselves in the waves of *pranic* breath unless they are calm within.

Even with knowledge, suffering will not cease. Living in seclusion will not destroy suffering. When you make knowledge and discernment your code of conduct, you will be free of the suffering of old age, death and the cycle of life and death.

Should we acknowledge or ignore the negative actions or words of others?

Near Sri Sarveshwari Samooh Ashram, some greedy people began to accumulate coal and its powder on their premises. When the eastern wind blew, the plants, trees, shrubs and residents of the ashram would become covered with coal dust. Black dirt would settle thickly every-where, including on the wounds of the lepers. The coal businessmen rejected our requests that they move away. They criticized us bitterly and abused me personally. The criticism and abuses did not remain with me, since I didn't invite them in. Therefore, they unavoidably returned to their senders.

We appealed to the authorities, and the coal people were brought to court. After the judge listened to their false accusations and foul words, he returned a verdict in our favor. In an appeal, the coal people kept shower-ing me with abuse and incivilities. The high court also decided that the coal people should stop fouling the ashram. Although the businessmen unwillingly complied with the law, they still showered us with undigni-fied words. With controlled mind, controlled thoughts and self-confi-dence, we gave no place to such incivilities. Because we had no room or interest in such abuse, it bounced back to them. As a result, that abuse continues to sit with them to this day.

Why do hundreds of people come to you, Baba, and what do they ask for?

They come to me to learn how to comfort themselves in this world so they may have stability in life and joy in their hearts. They want to learn how to lead their lives with spontaneity and truth. They don't come for philosophical discussions.

Can a householder experience God?

While providing for his family and engaging in good conduct, a householder can secure that Divine experience other men obtain only with austerities. A householder should constantly remember God with his entire heart, practice truthfulness, be devoid of pride and retain pure feelings for all women.

What can I do about being affected by the opinions, sentiments and words of others?

Those on the spiritual path should accept whatever comes their way, but they should allow abuses and negativities to be returned to their creators without acceptance.

Why should we perform actions, if whatever we create eventually gets destroyed?

But not doing so is also doing something, is it not?

So does it matter if I do anything or not?

Why wouldn't it matter? Life is flowing like a river, but if you try to obstruct the flow, it will matter.

One can sit by the river and just watch it flow?

But we ourselves are flowing steadily. One may sit or not sit, move or not move, but in this journey of life as day after day passes, you are the flow, as well as the observer of the flow.

What is the difference between the self and the mind?

The self is experienced through the mind. The mind is the reflection of the self. Just as there is no difference between the sun and its light, there is no difference between the self and the mind.

What is the function of the mind in regard to the self?

The mind feels worldly pleasure and pain, but they do not affect the self. The mind is restive, but the *atma,* the self, is quiescent. The mind, however, can be totally mastered so that the self is experienced.

How do I erase past karmas?

As you make an effort to look at yourself, all your past karmas and ideas imprisoned by your desires will dissolve and vanish. As long as you keep looking at others, you will find yourself helpless and apart from yourself.

What are the consequences of self-deception?

If you ingest poison and then say, "I didn't realize it was poison," to try to save your life, would you be saved? If you consciously jump from a mountain top with the idea that you can say later that you were not aware of what you were doing, would you live? If you consciously commit wicked deeds and later wish to escape the consequences by exclaiming that you did them unknowingly, would you be spared?

What causes animosity?

Mostly jealousy.

Is attachment ignorance or sin?

It is neither. It is an intoxication that can wear off.

What is it that the guru cannot do for me?

Cooperation between the guru and disciple is reciprocal. The guru's teachings will produce complete results only when the disciple assimilates them. The responsibility of the guru is to impart the real knowledge, but putting it into practice is the disciple's responsibility. You will have to consent to come out of the darkness yourself. The guru cannot do this for you.

What are the characteristics of hatred, forgiveness and love?

Lack of good sentiments is hatred, largesse of the heart is forgiveness, and seeing the self in everyone is love.

People flock to saints, but do a significant number of those who do really transform?

If we meet a saint, great being or sage but cannot remain steadfast, then such a meeting is purposeless, useless. Lack of motivation, forgiveness, modesty, idealism and good qualities, even after meeting with a great being, leave only disinterest. We then say to ourselves, "I'm not going to get anything here," and run away.

Why have I suffered so much in this world that I have lost the sunshine I once enjoyed?
Why are you afraid of sorrow? It is only a shadow. Wherever there is life, there is sorrow. Truly speaking, sorrow is a requisite of life. In the absence of sorrow, your own life will never become apparent to you. Keep smiling and continue to battle with sorrow. That is indeed true existence.

What is fear?
Out of fear, people eat, excrete, sleep, waken, dress and go to war. If there were no fear, we would become free and Godlike.

Is this fear based on the fear of death?
Death is inevitable, so it should not cause too much fear. As a matter of fact, fear is a kind of dream. We wander into this dream and move from one dream to another. Assuming a human identity, we live life in a dreamlike state. In reality, we forget we are the self.

Please tell us why at times your teachings bear fruit, while at other times they do not appear to work.
For my teachings to bear fruit, an aspirant must have faith and become close to the guru. Even if aspirants reside in the ashram, they also must have curiosity, listen with concentration, retain the teachings, contemplate the meaning of them, realize the essence and spirit of them and practice them accordingly.

Can we obtain true knowledge by diligent study?
There are three ways of obtaining knowledge: through the senses, the mind and the self. Knowledge gained via the senses is unreal. Knowledge obtained with the mind is closer to reality, but experiential knowledge of the self is the only perfect and real knowledge.

What are your riches, and for what price will you share them?
My self is my wealth. I see that my self pervades all. Complete surrender is the only way to attain the self.

If God is impartial, why does it appear as if those who love God more receive more?
Although God gives love equally, those who love God more are more receptive to that love and therefore absorb more of it.

Please tell us the difference between the saintly and the wicked.
To look upon all with equanimity is characteristic of a saint. To perceive all as bad is characteristic of the wicked. Creating union is one of the dispositions of a saint. Causing a rift is one of the dispositions of the wicked.

How do we avoid material difficulties?
Through diligent work with enthusiasm.

How can one instill hope in a despondent mind?
Patience.

What is the secret of a blissful existence?
To have no desires. As long as you keep feeding the fire of desire and passion, it will keep burning. Similarly, to rid yourself of attachment and aversion, all you need to do is stop feeding the passions. When the passions become free of heat, they become peaceful and cool.

I keep hoping for better circumstances so that I can meditate, but it doesn't seem like a possibility in the near future. Should I leave everything and become a monk?
Human beings are not slaves of their circumstances. Circumstances themselves are the slaves of human beings. They only test our capabilities. A capable person moves forward battling them. Confront life's circumstances with endurance. It is best to struggle with the trying situations of life. Just as exercising tones the body, profound issues tone the mind. Battling difficult circumstances produces spiritual strength.

I'm having tremendous difficulties with my teenaged son. He enjoys refuting
everything I say or do.

The intoxication of youth is like a blindfold for the eye and a plug for
the ear. They can cause a paralysis of discrimination if not handled correctly. Youth is like dust; it soils the clothes and gets into the eyes so that
the young can't discern which path will be propitious and which will be
disastrous. When one can't tell the difference between good and evil, one
doesn't feel remorse even after doing undesirable deeds. One begins to
believe licentious conduct is one's right.

I am aware that the company I keep is not of a higher kind, but I like it and find it
difficult to do without. Would Baba say something about that?

It is not possible to cross the river of life in the company of the lowly. If
you ride a light piece of wood to cross a river, you'll fall in and perhaps
sink. Similarly, with lightweight associations, you'll fall into the river of
life and perhaps sink and never be able to get across. Those who wish to
cross a river should select a heavy, strong and stable log and they will make
it across.

The scriptures say to seek refuge. How do I do that?

You should take refuge in yourself. If you do that and work hard and
support yourself, you become happy, attain knowledge and feel spiritually fulfilled. You live cheerfully, peacefully and without any desires. If
you neglect yourself, put yourself down or seek refuge in another, you
will suffer in ignorance. You are deprived of your own self. If you do not
find refuge in yourself, you will find it nowhere else on this earth and no
solace elsewhere, either. To become aware of and fulfill your duties is to
take refuge in yourself. To discard cowardice and dependence on others is
to take refuge in yourself. To stay absorbed in yourself, to stay satisfied in
yourself, to stay content in yourself is to take refuge in yourself.

I have practiced many different kinds of sadhana, *but it seems nothing works for me. What can be the reason?*

> If you take a very soiled cloth and dye it blue, yellow, red or green, the cloth remains soiled and will not reflect the pure hue of the dye. Similarly, if the mind is soiled, you may expect rough going in life. But if you take clean white material and dip it in any color dye, it will be evenly and purely tinted because the material was clean. Similarly, if the mind is taintless, you may expect smooth sailing in life and in *sadhana*.

Would you be kind enough to tell us something about how to change prarabdha, *fixed destiny, and how to obtain liberation from the cycle of birth and rebirth?*

> You can avoid or influence whatever has to happen by doing good deeds. It has been written in all the scriptures, and many saints and sages have experienced it. By contemplating the Divine and through the strength of your good character you can avoid a fixed destiny. To do that you will have to be different from the norm. You have to become like a roasted seed that doesn't germinate again to get away from the cycle of birth and rebirth. Like a lamp without oil, you will have to relinquish all *ashakti,* all attachments. Not being affected by feelings of good or bad and the temptations of the sensory organs, you obtain the state of *nirvana*, liberation. Although it is not easy, many people in the past and some people today have engaged in this search.

> You can obtain the state of consciousness that helps us in *nirvana* by constant practice. Consider the example of two experienced bicycle riders who are conversing, laughing and looking around while pedaling. It appears as if they are not paying attention to their riding but as soon as any object comes in their way, they immediately gather themselves to their senses and act accordingly. A deeper part of them is always in tune with their steering. In the same fashion, you can obtain the state of consciousness that helps achieve *nirvana* by practice.

> There are nine steps in this practice. The first step is to find the company of saints and noble beings and then listen to and follow their teachings. The second step is to listen to the scriptures and practice contemplation. Once you reach the ninth step, you begin to realize the falsity

of this world—that whatever we perceive through our sensory organs is deceiving.

About the form of the Absolute, it has been written in the scriptures, "Neither am I male, female nor hermaphrodite." What is the form of the Absolute?

Cidakasha is an all-pervading continuum. Take the example of clay: It has no particular shape until a potter makes different items or statues by molding it according to whatever shape emerges in the potter's mind. Although in reality it is clay, the beginning is clay and the end is clay, in the middle it is given different names, forms and denominations. The name, form and denomination are not the clay, but they have appeared in the subconscious mind. In the same fashion, Shiva and Shakti are not separate and distinct, but it appears as if they are. This perception is the cause of our suffering. A spider weaves a web and dies entangled in it. Had the spider not woven the web, it would be free to roam. Similarly, instead of the *cidakasha*, all kinds of names, forms and denominations keep rising in our subconscious mind, and we keep labeling them. We label them as *dharma*, religion, and *karm*, rituals. By giving them names, we give them shape, form, duty and symbols. For these reasons we spend our lives in frustration. In reality, they are not what they seem. Our subconscious mind only makes them appear to be what they seem.

If a piece of straw falls in a calm pool of water, ripples begin to arise. Similarly, the *citta* is a calm pool of water; nothing arises in it; it is *cidakasha*. As soon as a piece of straw—a thought pattern—falls into it, ripples begin to arise and become name, form and denomination.

Do we automatically unite with that "great unknown" after death?

Death only appears as if it happens, just as birth appears to happen. In reality it is a kind of dream in which we have taken this body. Everything appears as it is, but it is not real. The real self is somewhere else. This body is the prototype of our state of consciousness and now the variations have begun. If you really ask me for the truth, nothing is what it appears to be. The day we come to understand that, truly, we will experience that neither were we ever born, nor will we ever die. The body is subjected to the process of birth and death. We are in the form of *atma*, in the form of *cidakasha*, the all-pervading continuum.

We come to experience this truth only after submerging ourselves in constant *satsang* and contemplation. It is only then we come to experience, see and understand the real nature of life. If everything happens at its appropriate time, things are in order. If things happen by accident or at an inappropriate time, suffering is experienced. Had something happened at its appropriate time, we would feel nothing.

Can anything be done to help people who are leading a life of ignorance?

You cannot say anything of substance by shouting. Whatever you say silently is heard. Whatever is said by shouting is not even heard by the person saying it. Life in the world is very complicated. You constantly have to work on making it smooth because our mind lacks discipline. We cannot understand it until we discipline our mind. It is the mind that has to convince itself. Mind is the cause of bondage or liberation. We certainly will have to locate ourselves in the jungle of the mind.

Keeping the all-pervasive continuum form of the Absolute in mind, will we have to reevaluate the image and form of Jesus or will we have to wait for another Divine incarnation?

Contemplate it. I tend to see Jesus as a great saint, or *mahatma,* of his time. He was a great being, but later, those who followed him were the teachers.

Is the reason for so much division in Christianity that these teachers did not present the real teachings of Jesus?

His teachings were few and condensed. Later they were manipulated in all kinds of ways. At the time of Jesus, pen and paper were not in use. There were no printing presses. Whatever was available was in the form of *shruti* and *smriti*, that which has been heard and retained by memory. Jesus came from a tradition of sages and saints, not from the tradition of popes, bishops and priests.

You should not have any doubt about the life and teachings of such a saint. Without any hesitation you should try to see him in all different places and circumstances all over the world. But with a narrow outlook, how can you see him? You are not able to see yourself, let alone see Jesus. One object has hundreds of names in a hundred different languages. Just look at this flower: If you look at it from four different angles, it will appear a bit different and have a hundred different names in a hundred different languages. Similarly, why do you confine that great man to one name and one lifetime? He is born and crucified in all different times and places.

We should not try to limit the omnipresence of a great man. Jesus was a great man. Trying to limit his omnipresence is the weakness of our intellect. If Jesus appears here in person, we are not ready to accept him. The form we depict him in today, is that his real form?

You worship Christ by going to church and participating in rituals. Ritual is not worship; it is merely formality. Whether you go to church or not, whether you go by yourself or someone drags you there, if you ignore that great truth, if you disregard his teachings, all actions are in vain. The very moment the feeling of worship arises deep within you, your worship has begun and ended.

Baba, would you tell me something about the third eye?

For you, that is the Christ. Try to see the Christ in the middle of your eyebrows. If you try to see him on the cross, you will see him on the cross. If you try to see him sitting on a rose, you will find him sitting on a rose. You perceive the image of God according to your mental attitude.

When talking about the third eye I am not telling you anything that is limited to any one language, country or religion. This has nothing to do with religion. It is found in all different languages of the world—even Jesus practiced it. By walking on this path, Jesus became Christ. Whoever walks on this path can obtain the category of that greatness.

There are five elements and each element has five temperaments or characteristics. These are the 25 *prakriti*, and they can be classified in the three *gunas*, qualities born of nature. To master the three *gunas*, we do practices. Having practiced the concentration of the third eye, the seeker reaches a state called *Mahapurusha*, that of a great being or saint. There comes a time when all three *gunas* are mastered. This state is above and beyond the conscious mind.

What is a happy life?
A life devoid of desires.

How do I respond to evil deeds?
By forgetting them. Remember then that there is nothing evil in the world. If respect is at the root of our responses, no one will be inclined to do evil. Living like this you won't even imagine evil.

What is the difference between happiness and sorrow?
Lack of sentiments in the deep self.

Kindly tell me what should be the purpose of life?
To live away from wickedness as a human and let others live likewise.

When does a person feel that life is hopeless?
When self-confidence leaves.

What is the foundation of life?
The great bliss.

What is the greatest and simplest virtue of life to practice?
Practice of the truth. There is no greater nor simpler virtue to practice.

Please tell me when does a person face defeat?
When hopelessness becomes your consort.

What is the difference between a saint and a wicked person?
Maintaining equanimity with all is the characteristic of a saint, and harboring viciousness toward another is the characteristic of a wicked person.

Please tell me what is auspicious and what is inauspicious?

The blissful state of the self is auspicious, and gloominess is inauspicious.

What are the characteristics of happiness and suffering?

A balanced state of the self even in adverse circumstances is happiness, and to slip into depression and irritation in any ordinary situation is suffering.

What is the difference between a rich person and a poor one?

Living a self-respecting and moral life with love in the heart is the characteristic of a rich person. One saturated with vanity and wickedness is poor.

What is the simplest way to obtain peace in the soul?

By meditating on the guru and walking on the path shown by the guru.

How do you unite the self with the Supreme Self?

By giving up worldly wishes and desires, the self automatically unites with the Supreme Self.

How do you obtain clarity in the self?

By religiously adhering to the teachings and principles shown by the guru in daily life.

Who is the greatest friend in life?

The guru.

Please tell me what is the means to obtain immortality?

The grace of the guru.

Glossary

ABHAVA   Absence or scarcity.

AGHOR   That which is nonterrific, nonterrible; ancient, mystical spiritual tradition of India tracing its roots to Lord Shiva.

AGHOR ASCETIC   Monk on the *Aghor* path.

AGHORESHWAR   Highest state in the *Aghor* tradition in which union with the self is attained; literally, Lord of *Aghor*.

AGHOR PADA   State of *Aghor* or enlightenment.

AGHOR SIDDHA   Accomplished *Aghor* ascetic.

AHUTI   Act of offering to a ceremonial fire.

AISHVARYA   Material wealth, prosperity.

AKASHA   Space, ether.

ANNAPURNA   Goddess of grain and food; another name for Shakti.

ARATI   Ritual waving of light before a revered saint or idol.

ARJUNA   Great archer and hero of the Hindu epic "Mahabharata" to whom Krishna preached the "Bhagavad Gita" on the battlefield.

ASANA   Place on which to sit and the manner in which one sits, erect and still; posture in the practice of yoga.

ASHAKTI   Attachments.

ASHRAM   Place where spiritual discipline is practiced; dwelling of a sage or holy person.

ASHRAMITE   Resident of an ashram.

ATMA   Spirit, soul, self.

ATMARAM   Divine presence in an individual soul.

AVADHUT   Ascetic who has risen above duality and conventional standards.

AVATAR   Incarnation of a deity in bodily form on earth.

BABA   Term of respect and affection for a saint or holy man.

BABUVA   Dear one.

BENARES   Place of pilgrimage in northern India, holy city where Shiva resides; also known as Kashi or Varanasi.

BHAGAVAD GITA   Part of the sacred scripture "Mahabharata" containing about 700 verses that comprises the conversation between Krishna and Arjuna on the battlefield before the start of the Kurukshetra War.

BHAGWAN   God; Divine, venerable, holy.

BHAGWATI   Divine Mother.

BHAIRAVA   Fierce manifestation of Shiva; male *Aghor sadhaka*.

BHAIRAVI   Female consort of Bhairava; female *Aghor sadhika*.

BHAJAN   Devotional song with origins in the hymns of the Vedas.

BHAKTA   Devotee; follower of the path of love; one who surrenders to God.

BHARATA   Younger brother of Rama in "Ramayana" epic.

BHAVA   Attitude, emotion, sentiment; inner disposition.

BRAHMA   God of creation; one of the Hindu trinity with Vishnu and Shiva.

BRAHMAN   Supreme God; absolute reality possessing attributes of consciousness, existence and bliss. Also Brahm.

BRAHMIN   Priestly caste, considered the highest social class.

CAITANYA   Transcendental consciousness.

CIDAKASHA   All-pervading continuum of pure awareness.

CITTA   Consciousness.

DARSHAN   To see with reverence and devotion; to be in the presence of a deity, saint, holy person or guru.

DHARMA   That which upholds or supports; natural law, natural order of things; righteousness; path of truth, duty.

DHOTI   Traditional formal Indian garment men wrap around the waist and legs and knot at the waist.

DHUNI   Fire tended by a *sadhu*.

DOMINS   Wives of the caretakers of cremation grounds.

GANGA, GANGES   Major river of India considered sacred and to possess a purifying force.

GAYATRI MANTRA   Revered mantra based on a verse from a hymn in the "Rigveda" sacred texts.

GHAT   Series of steps leading down to water, usually to a holy river.

GHEE   Clarified butter.

GUNA   Three qualities born of nature that carry out the process of creation, preservation and destruction, respectively: *tamas guna*, *rajas guna* and *sattva guna*.

GURU   Teacher, imparter of knowledge.

GURUDEVA   Respectful address to a guru.

GURU PURNIMA   Full-moon day dedicated to the guru, usually celebrated in July.

HAVAN   Fire ceremony.

ISHWARA   God.

JI	Suffix denoting respect.
JIVA	Spiritual essence present in each living being.
KAMANDALU	Water pot with a handle made from a coconut, gourd or wood.
KAPALESHWAR	Divine being also known as an *Aghoreshwar*.
KAPAL-KHAPPAR	Field of consciousness.
KARM	Rituals; physical, mental or verbal actions.
KARMA	Force or effect of accumulated past actions.
KATHAK	One of eight forms of Indian classical dance.
KINARAM	Enlightened *Aghor* saint known to have possessed innumerable supernatural powers.
KIRTI STAMBHA	Pillar of victory; tower of fame.
KRIM KUND	Baba Kinaram's ashram in Varanasi, India; seat of the *Aghor* lineage where Baba Kinaram charged an ancient pond with the seed mantra *Krim* for healing purposes.
KRISHNA	*Avatar* of Vishnu considered the Supreme Being; participant in the "Mahabharata" often described as a young boy playing a flute or a youthful prince giving guidance in the "Bhagavad Gita."
KUMBHA MELA	Gathering of saints, sages and seekers at 12-year intervals.
KUNDALINI	Energy that lies coiled at the base of the spine, envisioned as the Goddess Shakti or a sleeping serpent.
LAKSHMANA	Rama's brother.
LUNGHI	Indian garment men wear around the waist.
MAGHA	Eleventh month of the Hindu calendar, beginning in January and ending in February.

MAHABHAIRAVA   Supreme Being, Shiva.

MAHANT   Religious superior; chief priest of a temple, an abbot or head of an ashram.

MAHAPURUSHA   Great being or saint.

MAHARAJ   Great king.

MAHASAMADHI   Great and final *samadhi*, consciously leaving the mortal frame to merge with the Divine; Aghoreshwar Bhagwan Ramji took *Mahasamadhi* on November 28, 1992.

MAHATMA   Great soul.

MALA   String of beads, usually numbering 108, used for counting while repeating a mantra.

MANAS   Heart-mind, surface mind.

MANASIC PUJA   Mental worship through active imagination.

MANASIC UPASANA   Total mental submersion as a form of worship.

MANTRA   Spiritually charged words imparted by a guru to a disciple; name of God or a Divine sound.

MAYA   Power that manifests, perpetuates and governs the illusion and dream of duality in the universe.

MOGHUL   Muslim empire that dominated the Indian subcontinent from the mid-16th century to 1858, when it was officially supplanted by the British Raj. Also spelled Mughal.

NAVARATRI   Festival of worship of Shakti that takes place in fall and spring over nine (*nava*) nights (*ratri*).

NIRVANA   Everlasting peace, liberation.

PARAMARTHA   Highest good.

PARA PRAKRITI   Divine nature.

PITHA   Seat, sacred site of devotion and faith.

PIYUSHA   Nectar in the form of milk given by a mother.

PRAKRITI   Nature. Numbering 25, these represent the five elements, each with five temperaments or characteristics.

PRANA   Life force, life energy; vital force of the body and
cosmos.

PRANAMAYA BODHA   Awareness of oneness with *prana*.

PRANAMAYI   Divinity in the form of the life force that resides in
the body.

PRANAVA   Chanting of sacred mystical syllables.

PRANAYAMA   Breath control.

PRARABDHA KARMA   Fixed destiny.

PRASAD   Food or water offered to God and thus considered
holy and blessed.

PUJA   Religious ceremony, worship.

PURANA   Religious texts consisting of narratives of the
history of the universe from creation to destruction,
including genealogies of kings, heroes, sages and
demigods.

PURNABHAVA   Sentiment of complete fulfillment.

RAMA   Seventh *avatar* of Vishnu.

REHAT   Device consisting of a series of buckets for lifting
water from a well.

RENUNCIATION   Freeing oneself from all worldly duties and
responsibilities to pursue spiritual enlightenment.

RISHIS   Divinely inspired seers and sages who developed
Hindu beliefs and the Vedas.

RUDRAKSHA   Evergreen tree whose seeds traditionally are used for mala prayer beads.

SADA SHIVA   One of five forms of Shiva, representing his philosophical aspect.

SADHAKA   Spiritual seeker, aspirant, practitioner of spiritual discipline.

SADHANA   Personal spiritual practice; with *seva*, the cornerstones of *Aghor*.

SADHU   Monk, saintly person.

SAMADHI   Nondualistic state of experiencing union with the Divine.

SAMKALPA   Strong will; setting intention.

SAMSKARA   Sacraments, sacrifices and rituals that serve as rites of passage to mark various stages of human life.

SANKRANTI   Festival of the harvest.

SANNYASA   Vows of renunciation.

SANSKRIT   Indo-Aryan language; primary language of Hinduism.

SARASVATI   Goddess of learning and wisdom; one of the three main aspects of Shakti, along with Kali and Lakshmi.

SARBHANG RISHI   Lineage of monks whose philosophy aligns with that of *Aghor*.

SARKAR   Form of address to a person in authority.

SARVESHWARI   One of the names of the Divine Mother meaning Mother of all.

SATSANG   Company of saints and devotees; to sit in the presence of the guru.

SEVA   Selfless service in the world; with *sadhana*,
the cornerstones of *Aghor*.

SHAKTI   Dynamic aspect of the Divine that projects, sustains
and dissolves the universe; energy, strength.

SHAKTI PITHA   Holy place consecrated to the Goddess Shakti.

SHASTRA   Treatise, sacred text.

SHIVA   God in the Hindu trinity with Brahma and Vishnu;
auspicious one, destroyer, God of transformation.

SHRADDHA   Faith and devotion.

SHRUTI AND SMRITI   *Shruti* are sacred texts recording that which is heard
from the Divine; *smriti* are religious texts recording
that which emanates from memory.

SIDDHA   One with spiritual accomplishment.

SIDDHI   Highest form of attainment, perfection, final beatitude;
union with the Divine; supernatural powers.

SITA   Rama's wife.

SRI SARVESHWARI SAMOOH   Nonprofit organization Aghoreshwar Bhagwan Ramji
formed on September 21, 1961 whose name honors the
Divine Mother.

STHAL   A place; for example, Kinaram Sthal means the place
of Kinaram.

STHAPANA DIVAS   Day when Sri Sarveshwari Samooh was founded in
Varanasi.

SWAMI   Master, lord, prince; term of respectful address.

SVARTHA   Necessities for the self.

TANTRA   Esoteric spiritual discipline that evokes Shakti through
rituals, mantras and *yantras* to become one with the visible
world.

THAKUR   Feudal title; warrior class, a caste.

TURIYATITA   Transcendent state.

UNMANI   Condition in which one is neither sleeping nor awake, conscious nor unconscious, accepting nor relinquishing, being nor nonbeing; one with *prana*; in ecstasy.

UPASAKA   Worshipper.

UPASANA   Worship.

URDHVARETA   Movement of energy upward.

VAIDYA   A person practicing Ayurveda.

VAIKHARI   Voice of an enlightened Master.

VAISHNAVA   Follower of Vaishnavism, a tradition that worships Vishnu or his *avatars* such as Rama and Krishna.

VAISHVANARA   Cosmic creative principle; the ever-consuming fire, digestive fire.

VAISHYAS   Tradespeople, shopkeepers.

VEDAS   Sacred scriptures.

VINA   Stringed musical instrument.

VISHNU   Protector and preserver; one of the Hindu trinity with Shiva and Brahma.

VIVEKA   Deep perception; discernment.

YAGYA   Weeklong fire ceremony and ritual celebration.

YANTRA   Sacred geometric symbol; reproductive organs.

YOGA   State of oneness with the self, Divinity; spiritual practices leading to this state.

Index

Page numbers in italics represent illustrations.

cleverness
    excessive, 171–173
    keeping in darkness, 185
cloak sewn from patches, 206
company, keeping good, 167, 175, 213, 229
conceit, avoiding, 132
conduct
    code of, 224
    as example, 218
    friend or foe produced by, 54
    good, 82, 215
    improper, 209
    public, 213–215
    rules, honoring, 83
    undisciplined, problems caused by, 38
consciousness
    Aghor state of, 151, 202
    deepening of, 24
    field of, 207
    types of, 105, 209, 230
    "unknown" as, 157–158, 174
corrupt deeds, forgiving past and preventing future, 214
creativity, 195, 196, 206
cremation, 21, 24, 39
curiosity, 215–216

D

darkness, keeping self in, 150
darshan, benefits of, 26
Darshi, teachings for, 203–207, 208–209, 213–215, 217–218
Dattatreya, Bhagwan
    Baba Kinaram, appearances to, 75, 76, 77
    birthplace of, 61–62
    gurus of, 186
    haunts of, 54
    as incarnation of Shiva, 152
    parents of, 61
    peak of, 55
dead man brought back to life, 76–77
death
    bringing on self, 209, 214
    deliverance from, 212, 224
    fear of, 21, 227

Resources

SONOMA ASHRAM FOUNDATION
Sonoma, California

Sonoma Ashram, which Baba Harihar Ram established in 1991, is the only seat of the ancient mystical lineage of *Aghor* outside India. The ashram is a center for self-growth and spiritual retreat, as well as a community of residents who strive to live a meaningful life inspired by the practical wisdom of *Aghor*. The ashram welcomes people from all walks of life, regardless of religion or belief, and offers a sanctuary of peace and nurturing through day visits, personal retreats and long-term stays.

AGHOR FOUNDATION
Varanasi, India

The sacred fire that Baba Kinaram ignited in the 16th century still burns in the holy city of Varanasi as witness to the continuum of the *Aghor* tradition. Sonoma Ashram Foundation, through the Aghor Foundation, sponsors a family of social service initiatives in this ancient city. These include Bal Ashram, a safe home for abandoned and orphaned children; a working farm and environmental center; women's vocational training; free eye clinics; and Anjali School for street children.

MEMBERSHIP

Sonoma Ashram Foundation is a nonprofit organization sustained by the generosity of its members. Annual membership, which begins at $25, includes access to audio of Baba Harihar Ram's weekly *satsangs* and a subscription to *Aghor Times* newsletter. For more on our work, publications and membership, please visit sonomaashram.org.

Sonoma Ashram Foundation

Fullness
overflowing

P.O. Box 950 . Sonoma, CA 95476 . sonomaashram.org

Acknowledgments

Since the first publication of this book 16 years ago, awareness of the life and teachings of Aghoreshwar Bhagwan Ramji, a great saint who lived among us until 1992, has grown immensely in the West. Sages and saints do not belong to any particular country or religion; they belong to the whole of humanity. Those who carry out their teachings and work in the world are truly blessed.

The list of individuals who helped create this book during its first publication and this new version is long. When the need was felt to publish a second edition, Shivani and Richard Mendelson passionately took on the project and created a great team around it. Howard Morris dutifully reviewed and corrected the first draft. All the hard editorial work of Jeanette LoCurto with Stephanie Abbott at her side has brought cohesiveness to the presentation. Edoardo Beato contributed to expanding the Glossary. The look and feel of the book would not be the same without the contribution of Paul Chutkow and Brian Ruff. Jeanette's critical eye and Paulette Traverso's graphic design talents have brought the book into the 21st century.

I offer my love and heartfelt blessings for a healthy and happy life to all involved in *this noble project.*

BABA HARIHAR RAM

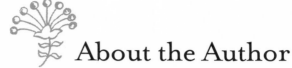

About the Author

While living in the company of Aghoreshwar Bhagwan Ramji, Baba Harihar Ram experienced the emergence of the Divine within. After receiving his guru's grace, he was asked to bring the teachings of *Aghor* to the West. He founded Sonoma Ashram in Northern California, the only ashram outside India dedicated to the principles and practice of *Aghor*. He also created The Aghor Foundation, which sponsors numerous social service initiatives in India.